Setting Up Your Business
In South Africa

Legal Dyna*mix*
™

Disclaimer

This book is intended as a helpful non-exhaustive guide to setting up a business in South Africa. It provides general information on various topics including business structures, taxes, employment law, regulations, marketing, and operations. However, the information supplied does not constitute legal, financial, accounting, tax, or other professional advice. We strongly recommend consulting with relevant qualified professionals, such as lawyers, accountants, tax advisors, and other specialists, depending on the specific needs of your business and for any specific questions or concerns you may have.

Please note that laws, regulations, taxes, and fees in South Africa can change periodically. While we have made every effort to ensure the information in this book is correct and up to date at the time of publication, we encourage you to stay informed by checking for official updates directly from relevant government websites or contacting us to join our mailing list for updates.

This book includes references to external websites that we believe offer valuable resources. However, please be aware that we cannot be held responsible for any issues you may encounter or losses you may suffer on these external sites, including broken links or malicious software. We recommend you always exercise caution when clicking on or using links, installing, and keeping updated security software, and follow best practices for information security. If you find any broken links, please let us know, and we will do our best to provide you with updated information.

The author utilised AI tools (Google Bard and ChatGPT4) to enhance the readability and clarity of this book, focusing on language refinement, flow, and structural improvements. While AI occasionally generated complete sections, the author reviewed all suggestions to ensure they reflected a unique voice and perspective. All information and expert opinions presented are based on the author's own research, experience, and verified sources.

The content contained in this book is subject to copyright and intellectual property rights of the publisher, Legal Dynamix (Pty) Ltd. You are welcome to use the information for your own non-commercial business purposes provided you purchased this book directly on the author's website or third-party platforms from which this book is sold by the author. However, this book may not be distributed, sold, shared, made available, copied, or transmitted to others without the prior written consent of the author.

While we have taken all reasonable steps to ensure the accuracy and completeness of the information in this book, we make no representations or warranties, express or implied, with respect to its accuracy, completeness, or usefulness. We also disclaim any liability for any damages or losses, direct or indirect, arising from the use of the information in this book.

We strive to keep the information in this book as up to date as possible. We plan to publish revised editions as needed and may also provide periodic updates. You can sign up for our mailing list to stay informed of any changes or updates.

This disclaimer is governed by and construed in accordance with the laws of South Africa.

You can contact us on **info@legaldynamix.co.za**

About the Author

The author of this book is a qualified advocate (non-practising) with extensive experience as an in-house regional general counsel for multinational companies. Proudly South African, he has a deep appreciation for the country's diverse people. Despite acknowledging the challenges faced by South Africa, he holds a strong belief in the potential of its people – their grit, grind, and resilience. The author's decision to leave the corporate world and establish his own consultancy business was motivated by a desire to break free from corporate constraints, take control of his own destiny, and immerse himself in the entrepreneurial world while leveraging his legal background. Achieving a better work-life balance, which he found difficult to reach at a senior corporate level, was another significant goal. While he is poorer for not having a regular income, he sees himself as richer for having a better work-life balance and for embarking on a new journey – not just a new chapter, but a whole new book, so to speak.

While setting up his own business, the author was surprised by the lack of a comprehensive resource on conducting business in South Africa for entrepreneurs, small businesses and start-ups. Although there are many great resources available on specific topics, there was a notable absence of a guide that consolidated general information applicable to all businesses. It was this realisation that prompted him to author this book, intending to provide a practical guide for those navigating or considering a similar entrepreneurial journey. This book also aims to help existing companies looking to transform their legal entity for various reasons and to offer valuable insights into the South African culture and business environment for international companies looking to set up a local subsidiary.

The aim of this book is to provide readers with a concise overview of the legal requirements and processes involved in various areas. Rather than going into the intricate details of each law, regulation, topic or registration procedure, the primary focus is to offer sufficient information for readers to obtain a basic understanding of what is needed and the necessary steps to be taken. It acknowledges that subjects such as taxes, employment, business plans, financial statements, marketing, operations, laws, and other topics are vast and complex, and an entire book could be written on each of these topics.

The author hopes that readers will find immense value exploring the wide range of topics covered in this book as they embark on their own adventure.

Contents

Who is this book for?

This book is meant for:
- **Entrepreneurs** wishing to set up a business.
- **Foreign companies** wishing to establish a local subsidiary company.
- **Existing businesses** wishing to consider options to convert to another legal form.
- **Advisors** wanting a general guide to understanding the business and legal landscape.

For the entrepreneur

Many people find contentment in stable employment. Stable employment provides certainty, security and reliable income, and coveted benefits like bonuses, medical aid, and retirement benefits. Yet, completely distinct reasons beckon some to entrepreneurship. They have their own aspirations, needs, and a daring mindset. This book will assist aspiring entrepreneurs on their journey to starting their own business, navigating a future filled with both opportunity and challenges.

As daunting as it may be, fear not. If you have the desire, strength, and an unwavering commitment to achieve your goals, this book is for you. It will help you understand how to start a company in South Africa and provide valuable advice to overcome challenges and make your business successful.

For an existing business transitioning to a private company

Are you currently a sole proprietor, part of a partnership, or a member of a close corporation? Or are you contemplating the evolution of your current business structure into a private company? Whether driven by a desire for enhanced governance, increased scalability, or strategic repositioning, we have tailored this book to equip you with the essential knowledge and guidance to smoothly navigate the process of transforming your existing business into a private company. From legal considerations to operational nuances, discover the comprehensive insights needed for a seamless transition.

For a foreign company embarking on a local venture

Are you representing a foreign company seeking to expand its footprint into the vibrant landscape of South Africa? The prospect of establishing a local subsidiary company brings forth a myriad of opportunities and challenges unique to this dynamic market. This book serves as your essential guide, providing in-depth knowledge of the local requirements necessary for the establishment and successful operation of a company in South Africa. This resource ensures that you embark on your local venture, well-informed and well-prepared.

The learning mindset

As Lao Tzu famously said centuries ago but which resonates for all great ventures and adventurers "A journey of a thousand miles begins with a single step".

This book serves as a practical guide – a series of many steps – for individuals interested in starting their own businesses or existing business owners looking to take their venture to the next level. While business owners are not expected to be experts in every topic discussed, having a basic understanding can empower them to use their knowledge for the growth, success, and sustainability of their ventures. It requires readers to embrace a mindset of openness to innovative ideas and explore areas beyond their expertise, gaining a basic understanding of the essential components that impact all businesses. Cultivating a mindset of continuous learning and growth becomes a valuable tool for entrepreneurs, allowing them to adapt, innovate and thrive in an ever-evolving business landscape. The same holds true for existing businesses, including foreign companies looking to establish a foothold in Africa.

What to expect from this book

We explore the fundamental aspects of starting, growing and managing a business in South Africa. This book covers a wide range of essential aspects for aspiring entrepreneurs, existing business owners seeking to transition to a private company, or foreign companies aiming to establish a local subsidiary. It begins by exploring the key attributes and motivations necessary for starting a business, specifically aimed at aspiring entrepreneurs. Additionally, it provides valuable insights into the legal requirements, regulatory landscape, and other critical factors that should be considered regardless of whether you are a budding entrepreneur, existing business or a foreign company looking to set up a local subsidiary. By offering comprehensive knowledge and practical tools, this book aims to equip readers with the necessary resources for embarking on a successful business venture. Whether it is understanding the prerequisites for starting a business, facilitating growth through transformation, or navigating the complexities of establishing a subsidiary, this book strives to guide the readers towards achieving their business goals.

Understanding the different forms for conducting your business

Legal forms of business

Navigating the legal landscape of South Africa and understanding the regulatory framework that governs businesses will help you to be familiar with the different company formations, operations, and compliance. A solid grasp of these legalities is essential to ensure your business operates within the bounds of the law.

The foundation of a successful business lies in its setup. The chapter on legal forms for conducting a business emphasises the significance of laying a solid groundwork, navigating through legal intricacies, and aligning with the unique regulatory framework of South Africa. A well-established business not only thrives but also contributes to the growth and stability of the national economy. Dive into the characteristics of sole proprietorships, partnerships, and companies of varying types.

Examine the advantages and drawbacks associated with each business structure. From the simplicity of a sole proprietorship to the complexity of a company, this analysis will guide you in choosing a structure that not only suits your current needs but also allows for future scalability.

Legal requirements and registration process

Embarking on the journey of establishing a business in South Africa requires a thorough understanding of the legal requirements and the step-by-step process of company registration. This book serves as your guide through the intricacies of ensuring your business is legally sound and compliant. From name reservation to obtaining a registration certificate, we will break down each step, offering practical tips and insights to streamline the process. Understanding the paperwork and timelines is key to a smooth registration experience.

Compliance with the Companies Act

The Companies Act of South Africa 2008 governs the formation and operation of companies. Delve into the key provisions of this Act, ensuring that your business aligns with legal requirements. Compliance not only ensures a strong legal foundation but also fosters trust with stakeholders.

Armed with this knowledge, you will be better equipped to make informed decisions as you progress through the business setup process and decide on the right type of business form to use for your venture.

Understanding taxes

One of the crucial factors in business structure selection is taxation. Explore the various types of taxation such as corporate and personal income tax, value-added tax and other relevant taxes. This section aims to help you understand each tax, when it is relevant, due, the tax periods and deadlines, among other issues.

Corporate income tax and personal income tax

Understand the principles and rates of corporate income tax applicable to businesses in South Africa. Explore how profits are taxed and the implications for your company's financial planning. We also discuss personal income tax for those owners who will derive a salary from their business.

Provisional tax

Understand how provisional taxpayers (companies and some individual taxpayers) pay their income taxes at designated periods during the tax year.

Value-added tax

Analyse the ins and outs of value-added tax, a key component of South Africa's indirect tax system. Learn about the registration requirements, rates, and implications for your business operations. Compliance with the regulations is pivotal to avoid penalties and ensure smooth financial management.

Employee taxes

Explore the tax obligations associated with employing staff in South Africa. From Pay-As-You-Earn to the Unemployment Insurance Fund, Skills Development Levy, and fringe benefit taxes, understanding these obligations is vital for both legal compliance and effective human resource management.

Tax incentives for small businesses

South Africa offers various tax incentives to assist small businesses. Discover the incentives applicable to small and micro businesses including Small Business Corporations and turnover taxes, exploring how these benefits can positively impact your bottom line.

Other taxes

Gain an understanding of other types of taxes and levies, and methods of tax collection, relevant to your business.

Navigating the taxation landscape is a critical aspect of setting up and running a business in South Africa, remaining compliant with the laws, and operating a sustainable business.

Financial statements, planning, and funding

As you embark on the journey of establishing and growing your business in South Africa, a robust financial plan and access to funding are critical elements. This chapter investigates the intricacies of financial planning, offering insights into creating a solid business plan and exploring various funding options.

Funding options for startups and existing businesses looking to grow

Whether you are a small startup or looking to expand an existing business, funding is a key consideration. Uncover the diverse funding options available in South Africa, from traditional bank loans to venture capital and government grants. Evaluate the pros and cons of each to determine the most suitable funding avenue for your business.

Creating a business plan

A well-crafted business plan is your roadmap to success particularly when seeking funding. Explore the essential components of a business plan, including your business goals, target market, competitive analysis, and financial projections. Learn how to articulate your vision in a way that attracts investors and enhances your business decisions. A business plan also helps you to focus on your goals, structure, and operational requirements.

Financial statements

Understand the importance of the public interest score and how it impacts whether your financial statements are subject to an audit, an independent review, or neither. Get to know the importance of understanding the financial statement requirements in South Africa. Financial literacy is an important part of any successful businessperson.

By the end of these chapters, you will have the tools and knowledge needed to create a robust financial foundation for your business.

Employment

Building a strong and motivated team is a cornerstone of business success. In this chapter, we will navigate through the intricacies of employment laws in South Africa, providing you with the knowledge needed to attract, manage, and retain top talent.

Employment contracts

Navigate the legal landscape of employment contracts in South Africa. Explore the key elements that you should include in employment contracts, ensuring clarity on roles, responsibilities, and terms of employment. Compliance with employment laws is fundamental for fostering positive employer-employee relationships.

Labour laws

Understand the labour law requirements to ensure you have a successful business. From requirements for leave to collective agreements, understanding and implementing employment laws creates a positive and productive work environment. As you progress through this section, you will gain a comprehensive understanding of the human resources landscape in South Africa.

Legal system and laws

We provide an explanation of the South African legal system, including the process of passing and administering laws. You will gain an understanding of how the court system functions, as well as the role of arbitration and alternative dispute resolution. In addition to the laws concerning companies, taxes, and employment (which we cover in other sections of this book), we also explore other important laws and regulations that businesses need to be aware of. It is important to note that the specific laws and regulations applicable to your business will depend on the industry you operate in, and therefore it is not possible to cover all of them in this book.

Operations and marketing

The chapters on operations and marketing provide valuable guidance on the essential aspects that contribute to building a sustainable business. They cover topics ranging from the significance of establishing a website to considerations regarding your business operations, from leasing vs purchasing premises to insurance considerations and supply chain. The aim of these chapters is not to provide a detailed analysis as this will be dependent on your specific industry, but rather, to give you some of the critical factors to consider.

South Africa Inc – rich and diverse

South Africa is a country rich and diverse in many aspects – its history and heritage, its melting pot of cultures, languages, people, and biodiversity. As we explore this multifaceted nation, it will become evident that South Africa is not just a land of varied landscapes, people, cultures, and history but also a land of diverse opportunities for those seeking to embark on the entrepreneurial journey.

South Africa stretches across 1.2 million square kilometres from the southern part of Namibia meandering down the Atlantic Ocean to the Cape of Good Hope (also known as the Cape of Storms) and upwards along the Indian Ocean to Mozambique. From the vast, semi-arid plains of the Karoo and the Kalahari Desert to majestic mountain ranges, pristine beaches and lush coastal wetlands, the country's landscape is rich and diverse. Its 3000-kilometre coastline boasts iconic features like the Cape Peninsula, Table Mountain, Cape Agulhas where the Atlantic and Indian Oceans meet but never mix, the scenic Garden Route and the rugged Wild Coast. The upper and eastern regions, including the Highveld, the Bushveld, the Drakensberg Mountains, and Midlands, is a land of contrasts with vast plains, rugged mountains, and forests, and hold iconic natural wonders like the Cradle of Humankind and nine other world heritage sites. These wide-ranging landscapes play a fundamental role in shaping South Africa's culture, economy, and biodiversity.

South Africa's iconic flag symbolises its history and diversity. Nicknamed the Rainbow Nation, South Africa is one of the most racially and ethnically diverse countries in Africa. It is a nation woven from the Khoi, San, Ndebele, Xhosa, Zulu, Pedi, Sotho, Tswana, Swazi, Venda, Tsonga, Afrikaners, English, Coloured, Indian, Malay, and various other Asian communities, each contributing its unique culture, language, cuisine, and identity. The influence of European cultures such as the French Huguenots, Portuguese, Greeks, and Germans has also shaped the nation's rich heritage. This collective amalgamation of these people is the quintessential defining feature of South Africa.

The official languages reflect the country's rich linguistic diversity. isiZulu, isiXhosa, Sephedi, SeSotho, Sestswana, siSwati, Tshivenda, Xitsonga, isiNdebele, South African Sign Language, Afrikaans, and English are the official languages of the country. Other languages spoken include Arabic, German, Greek, Portuguese, French, Hebrew, Gujarati, Hindi, Tamil, Telegu, Urdu, and the languages of the Khoi and San people with their distinctive clicking sounds. The South African national anthem, *Nkosi Sikelel' iAfrika* (God Bless Africa) consists of four stanzas making up five of its official languages – isiXhosa, isiZulu, seSotho, Afrikaans and English.

It is the birthplace of famous individuals like Shaka Zulu, Trevor Noah, Charlize Theron, Siya Kolisi, Tyla, Gary Player, Ernie Els, Wayde van Niekerk, Caster Semenya, Dricus de Plessis, Francois Pienaar, Desmond Tutu, FW de Klerk, Oliver Tambo, Albert Luthuli, Candice Swanepoel, Zozibini Tunzi, Princess Charlene of Monaco, Pretty Yende, Nadine Gordimer, William Kentridge, JM Coetzee, Irma

Stern, Christiaan Barnard, Black Coffee, Shekhinah, Miriam Makeba, Hugh Masekela and Johnny Clegg (and half of Roger Federer), to name a few.

And, of course, the most revered of them all – the great Nelson Mandela.

The country's musical landscape is as varied as its people, with groups like Ladysmith Black Mambazo, Die Antwoord, and Freshly Ground, and genres ranging from Kwaito, Gumboot Dancing (*isicathulo* in Zulu), gospel, traditional African, contemporary Afrikaans and the rhythmic *Amapiano*. Songs like 'Water' by Tyla, 'Jerusalema' by Master KG and Nomcebo Zikode, and '*Asimbonanga*', a tribute to Nelson Mandela by Johnny Clegg and Ladysmith Black Mambazo, resonate deeply with the nation's spirit.

In sports, the Springboks, the Blitz Boks, Bafana Bafana, Banyana Banyana, The Proteas, Olympic athletes, golfers, netball and hockey teams, and other sporting codes, embody the country's competitive and passionate nature.

Christianity is the dominant religion, with approximately 80% of South Africans adhering to various denominations. However, traditional African religions, Islam, Hinduism, and Judaism also have significant followings, highlighting the country's religious diversity.

The foods of South Africa are a celebration of the rich melting pot of the varied cultures. Potjiekos, bobotie, biltong, braai, bunny chow, chakalaka, malva pudding, koeksisters, milk tart, peppermint tart, vetkoek, pap and vleis, to name but a few.

The story of South Africa is inseparable from the legacy of apartheid, which cast a shadow over much of its 20th-Century history and continues to have a disproportionate impact on many of its people. Apartheid was characterised by racial segregation and the oppression of the majority black population by the minority white population, resulting in crimes against humanity, economic disparities, and disenfranchisement, to name but a few critical consequences. The dismantling of apartheid in the 1990s, culminating in the historic democratic elections of 1994, the inauguration of Nelson Mandela as the first African president, and the adoption of the Constitution, marked the birth of modern South Africa.

While considerable progress has been made in addressing the racial disparities stemming from the apartheid era, the legacy of apartheid, along with other social, economic, and political challenges such as unemployment, income inequality, racial tension, crime (and particularly violent crime), poor governance, slow economic growth, the ongoing power crisis, and failure to maintain critical basic infrastructure, continue to shape the country's trajectory and stymie its growth. Nevertheless, the people of South Africa are recognised for their vibrant character, resilience, determination, and collective strength, united by a shared history and cultural richness.

The South African coat of arms features the motto !ke e: /xarra //ke, written in the Khoisan language of the /Xam people. Translated, it means 'diverse people unite'. This motto highlights the importance of combining individual efforts to achieve unity between thought and action. On a broader scale, it calls for the nation to come together in a shared sense of belonging and national pride, emphasising the concept of unity in diversity.

The complex dynamics of South Africa offer abundant opportunities for those wishing to set up or grow a business. This book aims to guide budding entrepreneurs and existing business owners through the considerations and challenges of setting up a business venture in South Africa.

Understanding the market - challenges and opportunities

This section offers an introduction to SA Inc. It caters to foreigners seeking an overview of South Africa, as well as local businesses and aspiring entrepreneurs looking for a general understanding of the country.

Setting up a business in South Africa involves more than just dealing with paperwork and legal matters. It requires navigating a dynamic business landscape and understanding the distinctive array of opportunities, challenges, and cultural intricacies that shape the country's business ecosystem. In the earlier chapter, we provided an overview of the richness and diversity that defines the South African identity, as well as a general understanding of both historical and present challenges. In this chapter, we delve deeper into the South African market to provide you with an understanding of the specific challenges and opportunities that await you from a business perspective.

The economy

The South African economy is a sophisticated and mixed economy comprising of industries such as mining and natural resources, agriculture (such as wine and fresh fruit), banking and finance, technology (like cybersecurity and data centres), tourism, retail, education, media and telecommunication, construction and engineering, legal, manufacturing (such as textiles, automotive, steel and food processing), healthcare, energy, and many other sectors. Understanding the economic landscape is of paramount importance for any aspiring business owner, as it provides insight into market trends, consumer behaviour and potential opportunities.

Some key statistics and facts

- GDP (PPP – Purchasing Power Parity): USD865.8 billion (2023E), World Bank, IMF Data Mapper
- GDP (nominal): USD424.8 billion (2023E), World Bank, IMF Data Mapper
- GDP per capita (PPP): USD14,396 (2023E), World Bank
- Currency: South African Rand (ZAR)
- Major industries: Mining, banking and finance, manufacturing, agriculture
- Big Mac Index: 25.57 (October 2023), The Economist
- Population: 60.14 million (July 2023), Statistics South Africa
- Life expectancy: 65.3 years (2022), World Bank, IMF Data Mapper
- Literacy rate: 95.3% (2022), UNESCO Institute of Statistics
- Birth rate: 17.2 births per 1000 population (2021), World Bank
- Mortality rate: 9.4 deaths per 1000 population (2021), World Bank
- HIV/AIDS prevalence: 12.6% (2020), UNAIDS

- Access to improved sanitation: 80.5% (2020), WHO, UNICEF
- Political system: Constitutional democracy
- Head of State: President
- Capital cities: Pretoria (administrative), Cape Town (legislative), Bloemfontein (judicial)
- Time zone: UTC+2. CAT (Central African Time)
- Corruption Perception Index: 41 (2023), Transparency International. Lower scores show higher perceived levels of public sector corruption.
- Human Development Index (HDI): 0.705 (2022E), UN Human Development Program. This places South Africa in the high human development category. This figure, however, is skewed due to the high inequality rate.
- Global Competitiveness Index (GCI): 62 (2022), World Economic Forum. A higher score shows greater competitiveness. South Africa ranks 64th out of 140 countries.
- Doing Business Index: 84 (2023), World Bank. A higher score shows a more business-friendly environment. South Africa ranks 84th out of 190 countries.
- Unemployment – 33.3% (2022E), Statistics South Africa, with highest rates experienced among youth and the Black population.
- Major cities: Johannesburg, Ekurhuleni, Cape Town, Durban, Pretoria, Gqeberha, Bloemfontein
- Number of provinces: Nine

Gauteng province contributes over 30% of the country's GDP despite being the smallest province. It is also home to three of the country's eight metropolitan cities (Johannesburg, Ekurhuleni, and Pretoria) and accounts for 25% of the total population. The Johannesburg Stock Exchange (JSE), the largest in Africa, serves as a testament to its financial prowess, complemented by a world-class banking sector and vibrant industries. Sandton, in Johannesburg, is known as the 'Golden Mile' of Africa as it has the largest concentration of South Africa's biggest banks, companies and the JSE. KwaZulu-Natal is the second largest contributor to the country's GDP and home to one of Africa's largest ports. The Western Cape province is the third largest contributor to the country's GDP and with Cape Town as its main city, is home to some of the world's most beautiful scenery, pristine beaches, expensive homes with breathtaking views and famous winelands.

Special economic zones

South African has special economic zones (SEZs) distributed across the country. The eligibility criteria for operating in a SEZ is dependent on government approvals and include a) focus on priority sectors, b) minimum investment that companies must meet, c) focus on job creation within the SEZ, and d) technology transfer by encouraging the sharing of knowledge and expertise with local businesses. SEZs provide companies with many opportunities; it should form part of your business plan if this is the space in which you plan to operate your business.

The benefits for companies operating in SEZs include:
- Reduced corporate income tax, customs duties, and VAT exemptions.

- Simplified regulations including streamlined permitting and administrative procedures.
- Efficient infrastructure including high-quality roads, utilities, and logistics facilities.
- Financial incentives such as grants, subsidies, and access to specialised funding.

The current SEZs are:

- **Atlantis SEZ.** Established to promote green technology manufacturing, capitalising on Cape Town's renewable energy sector.
- **Nkomazi SEZ.** Strategically located on the Maputo Corridor between Swaziland and Mozambique, offering geographic advantage for logistics and manufacturing.
- **Coega SEZ.** South Africa's largest SEZ, attracting foreign and domestic investment in agro-processing, automotive, and other sectors, driving regional socio-economic development.
- **Richards Bay IDZ.** Purpose-built industrial estate linked to international seaport, focusing on mineral beneficiation and export-oriented manufacturing.
- **East London IDZ.** Directed at customised solutions for industries like automotive and agro-processing, offering growth-oriented companies a specialised manufacturing platform.
- **Saldanha Bay IDZ.** Aims to be Africa's premier oil, gas, and marine repair hub, serving upstream industry in Sub-Saharan Africa. Already attracted over R21 billion in investments.
- **Dube TradePort.** Combines international airport, cargo terminal, and various business sectors, serving as a gateway for global trade and a hub for value-added manufacturing like automotive and agriculture.
- **Maluti-A-Phofung SEZ.** Strategically located on the Durban-Johannesburg route, offering a logistics base for exporters and light/medium manufacturing with good access to agricultural produce.
- **OR Tambo SEZ.** Focuses on beneficiation of precious metals and minerals, attracting investment with its multi-site development and proximity to OR Tambo International Airport.
- **Tshwane Automotive SEZ.** Africa's first automotive city, attracting investment with world-class infrastructure, skilled workforce, and strong regional connectivity.

SEZs are governed by the Special Economic Zones Act of 2014. You can find more details on SEZs at the Department of Trade, Industry and Competition (DTIC), which oversees SEZs, at this link: *https://www.thedtic.gov.za/sectors-and-services-2/industrial-development/special-economic-zones/*

Central supplier database

For companies and individuals (sole proprietors and partnerships) that intend to do business with government entities, it is essential to register on the Central Supplier Database (CSD) which is a platform for government entities in South Africa to manage and register potential suppliers. It aims to streamline procurement, enhance transparency, and enable suppliers to participate in government tenders.

To register on CSD, go to the CSD portal: *https://secure.csd.gov.za/* and provide details about your business (contact details, banking details, tax status, BBBEE information and relevant documentation). Upon approval, you will receive a unique CSD number for identifying and verifying your business in future tenders.

The benefits of such registration particularly for small- and medium-sized entities is:
- **Increased opportunities.** Gain access to government procurement opportunities.
- **Transparency.** Promotes fairness and clarity in the procurement process.
- **Convenience.** Online registration simplifies the process.

South Africa's strengths

- **Abundant natural resources.** South Africa is rich in minerals like gold, platinum, diamonds, and coal, which contribute significantly to the economy.
- **Sophisticated industries** like banking and finance, tertiary education, technology, manufacturing, and industry.
- **Well-developed infrastructure.** The country boasts an advanced infrastructure network, including a sophisticated financial system, transportation network and telecommunications system.
- **Strong legal and regulatory framework.** South Africa has a sound legal and regulatory framework, which makes it attractive for foreign investment.
- **Growing middle class.** The middle class is expanding, which is creating a larger domestic market for goods and services.

Challenges facing the country

- **High unemployment rate.** South Africa has a high unemployment rate, particularly among the Black youth, which is a major challenge for the economy.
- **Income inequality.** The country has high levels of income inequality, which when taken together with the high unemployment rate, leads to social unrest and impeding economic growth.
- **Infrastructure maintenance.** Despite South Africa having advanced infrastructure, the maintenance of this infrastructure has been neglected by the State, which has led to significant challenges in areas such as electricity, sanitation, rail, road, and ports. Poor infrastructure maintenance acts as a barrier to economic growth and the upliftment of people from poverty. The ongoing electricity crisis resulting in blackouts (loadshedding) is a critical concern.
- **Over-dependence on commodities.** The economy is still heavily reliant on commodities, which makes it vulnerable to fluctuations in global commodity prices.
- **Crime and corruption** pose significant challenges in South Africa, impacting foreign investment and impeding economic growth. These issues create a

deterrent for potential investors who may be concerned about the safety of their investments and the integrity of the business environment.

- **Red tape.** The ease of doing business and regulatory red tape are significant challenges and constraints on economic development and job creation. The Government needs to focus on simplifying the legal and regulatory environment to attract investment and ensure sustainable economic growth particularly for small businesses.

Key organisation memberships

South Africa is a member of several international organisations, including the United Nations (UN) and its General Assembly, the World Trade Organisation, the BRICS group of emerging economies, the African Union, the G20, the International Criminal Court, the Commonwealth of Nations, the International Monetary Fund (IMF), the World Bank, the New Development Bank, the African Development Bank, and is a regional leader of the Southern African Development Community (SADC – promoting economic integration, political stability and sustainable development in the region) and the Southern African Customs Union (SACU – facilitating the free movement of goods, services and labour between member countries). It is a member of the Common Market for Eastern and Southern Africa (COMESA), another regional trading bloc. South Africa is also a major contributor to UN peacekeeping operations, particularly on the African continent.

South Africa as a launching pad and combatting unemployment

Many companies, domestic and foreign, use South Africa as their launching pad to invest not just in the country but into the rest of Africa. A recent McKinsey report *"Reimagining economic growth in Africa" dated June 2023*, highlights, among other things, several key factors about Africa and South Africa including:

- Trade between African countries represents only 10% of imports but South Africa has 53 African trading partners representing 32% of intercontinental trade (approximately US$35 billion) while Nigeria, in second place, has 51 African trading partners yielding US$7 billion in trade.
- In Africa, there are around 345 companies with annual revenues surpassing US$1 billion, cumulatively earning over US$1 trillion. Out of the total 345 companies mentioned, approximately 230 of them are considered homegrown. This means that they were started in an African country, typically by a local entrepreneur. These companies reflect the entrepreneurial spirit and innovation of individuals within the African continent, contributing to the growth and development of businesses within their own countries. Notably, South Africa stands out in this landscape, hosting approximately 40% of these companies, a figure that is significantly higher in proportion to its GDP. This highlights South Africa's dominant corporate presence on the continent, with 118 of the 147 large companies based here being homegrown. In contrast, other African nations, despite their sizeable economies, have fewer large companies. For example, Nigeria (23 large companies) and Egypt (33), with considerable GDPs, have significantly fewer large corporations compared to South Africa, underlining a potential for corporate expansion in these countries.

This scenario highlights the varied business landscape throughout Africa, emphasising the distinct role of South Africa as a pivotal business hub.

While South Africa's position as a significant player in Africa's corporate landscape is clear, with a substantial share of the continent's billion-dollar companies, it only illustrates part of a complex environment. It does not address the context of the high unemployment in the country. This situation presents a complicated challenge, but also an opportunity for growth and development.

High unemployment, particularly among the Black youth, is a pressing issue in South Africa. However, this also means there is a vast pool of potential talent and entrepreneurial spirit waiting to be tapped into. Addressing unemployment could involve a multi-faceted approach such as:

- **Encouraging entrepreneurship.** There is a significant opportunity to nurture entrepreneurship, especially among the youth. This can be achieved through educational programmes, support for startups and creating a more favourable business environment. By doing so, South Africa can transform its high unemployment rate into a catalyst for innovative business creation.
- **Skills development.** Focusing on skills development and training tailored to market needs can bridge the gap between unemployed individuals and the requirements of the modern job market. This includes not only technical skills but also digital literacy, given the growing importance of technology in all sectors. Skills development is a critical focus area under Broad Based Black Economic Empowerment (BBBEE), which we discuss in *Chapter 50*.
- **Public-Private partnerships (PPP).** Collaboration between the government and private sector can lead to the creation of job opportunities and training programmes. These partnerships can effectively address specific industry needs, aligning workforce skills with market demands. A typical example would be the independent power producers' renewable energy programme to address the electricity crisis.
- **Investment in high-growth sectors.** Targeted investment in sectors with high-growth potential, such as technology (like data centres and information security), renewable energy, and services, can create new job opportunities. This, coupled with South Africa's strong corporate presence, can catalyse economic growth and employment.
- **Support for Small and Medium Enterprises (SMEs).** SMEs are often key drivers of job creation. Providing support through funding, mentorship, and market access can empower these businesses to expand and employ more people. Various chapters of this book focus on the tax breaks and funding available to SMEs.
- **Ease of doing business.** To enhance the ease of doing business, South Africa can make improvements by streamlining its laws and regulations. Simplifying these complexities and reducing bureaucratic processes and delays would contribute to a more favourable environment for businesses operating in the country.

In conclusion, while South Africa faces challenges with high unemployment, its strong corporate sector and entrepreneurial potential provide a solid foundation for economic growth and job creation. With strategic initiatives and investment in human capital, South Africa can turn its challenges into opportunities for sustainable development.

Legal and political system

South Africa has a robust legal framework and an impartial and competent judiciary. South Africa's history is one of triumphs and tribulations. The oppressive apartheid system, which disenfranchised the majority population, was the low watermark that symbolised much of the country's history in the 20th Century, until in 1990, Nelson Mandela, one of modern history's most revered figures, was released after serving 27 years imprisonment for his fight against the oppressive regime. Mandela played a pivotal role in unifying a deeply divided nation. In 1994, South Africa held its first democratic elections, allowing all citizens to participate in shaping their nation's destiny.

South Africa is a constitutional democracy, with the Constitution being the supreme law of the land. The President is the head of the government (responsible for executing on laws passed by Parliament, proposing new or amendments to laws, and for setting and carrying out government policy), and is seated in Pretoria. Laws are passed by the bicameral parliamentary system consisting of the National Assembly and the National Council of Provinces (NCOP), which is seated in Cape Town. Unique among the world's nations, South Africa has an official third capital – Bloemfontein, which is the seat of the Supreme Court of Appeal, even though since the advent of the Constitution in 1996, the highest court in the country, the Constitutional Court, is based in Johannesburg.

Parliamentary elections in South Africa occur every five years at both national and provincial levels. Voters cast their ballots for their chosen political party, with the party garnering the most votes in the National Assembly forming the government and its leader becoming the President. Proportional representation ensures smaller parties also have a voice in the Assembly.

Beyond the National Assembly, the National Council of Provinces (NCOP) serves as the upper house of Parliament. Elected every five years through proportional representation, it differs from the National Assembly in that it represents provinces instead of political parties. Each province sends ten delegates to the NCOP. This structure is designed to ensure that all provinces have an equal say in the legislative process, particularly in matters affecting the provinces, and to balance the representation in the National Assembly, which is based on proportional representation.

Beyond the national arena, each of South Africa's nine provinces has its own provincial government and legislature. These entities are responsible for enacting legislation and policies on matters delegated to them by the Constitution. Some key areas of provincial responsibility include education, health, local government (overseeing the municipalities within the province), agriculture and economic development (within the province). It is important to note that while provincial governments exercise a degree of autonomy, they operate within the framework of the national Constitution and national legislation. The national government can intervene in specific provincial matters if necessary to uphold the Constitution or protect national interests.

South Africa is made up of 257 municipalities that are categorised into metropolitan, district, and local municipalities. Each municipality has its own elected council and executive that are responsible for providing local services, facilitating development, issuing local business permits, and administering local levies and rates. It is worth noting that local government elections are held every five years, although they do not coincide with national and provincial elections. This decentralised structure allows for local governance and decision-making, enabling municipalities to address the specific needs and priorities of their communities.

These three spheres of government – national, provincial, and local – work together within a framework of cooperative governance to meet the needs of all South Africans.

The President heads the government and forms a cabinet responsible for executing laws, formulating policy, proposing new legislation, and overseeing service delivery to the people.

The reality is a challenge and an opportunity

Recent opportunities that have gained attention are:
- International and local investments in the burgeoning data centre industry.
- The telescopic Square Kilometre Array (SKA) project and related industries.
- Renewable energy projects both in the public (solar and wind) and private sectors (primarily solar).
- Investments in maintenance and introduction of new power generation plants.
- New factories in the automotive industry.
- Investments in the mining, retail, and manufacturing industries.
- Cybersecurity.
- Infrastructure development in sanitation, road, rail, and ports.
- Development of new smart cities.
- Tourism.
- Further development of Special Economic Zones (SEZs).
- Continued expansion by South African businesses into the rest of Africa.
- The African Continental Free Trade Area (AfCFTA) is expected to provide new opportunities for South African businesses to export their products and services to other African countries. AfCFTA was established among the 54 African countries with the goal of creating a single market for goods and services on the continent.

This is not an exhaustive list and depending on your niche, passion or expertise, there are many opportunities beckoning. Doing your own research, building your business case, and maintaining a mindset open to learning will hold you in good stead.

Foundations for entrepreneurial success

"I choose to live by choice, not by chance,
To be motivated, not manipulated,
To be useful, not used,
To make changes, not excuses,
To excel, not compete,
I choose self-esteem, not self-pity,
I choose to listen to my inner voice, not to the random opinions of others.
I choose to do things that you won't so I can continue to do things you can't."
~ Unknown

We have written this section specifically for those contemplating an entrepreneurial journey, whether as a sole proprietor, part of a partnership or establishing an owner-managed company.

Deciding to embark on the entrepreneurial journey is a profound choice, one that requires more than mere motivation. As we explore the essential qualities every entrepreneur must have, it is critical to recognise that motivation, though a driving force, is just the beginning. This chapter will explore the attributes that form the bedrock of a successful business journey and the vital aspect of knowing into what business areas you want to venture.

Your motivations

Any person considering a life as an entrepreneur needs to consider what their driving force and motivations are for embarking on such an adventure. Take a moment and see how many of the following resonates with you:

- I crave control over my destiny.
- I have a brilliant business idea or invention and want to develop the opportunity.
- I dream of turning my passion or hobby into a thriving business opportunity.
- While employed, I wish to build additional income streams.
- Working under someone else's rule does not align with my spirit.
- The corporate environment feels confining, and I thirst for independence.
- Corporate ceilings have hemmed me in, and I long for my own growth.
- The boss does not suit my liking. (This may well be reciprocal!)
- Flexibility in managing my working hours is critical to managing my life.
- Risk and failure do not daunt me; they fuel my determination.
- Approaching retirement, I seek purpose beyond mandatory retirement ages.
- I prefer deciding my retirement timeline, not my employer or the State who foists an arbitrary age at which I must stop working.
- In the bloom of youth, the prospect of working for others lacks appeal.
- I am an unemployed youth looking to create my own opportunities.

- Sales and marketing are my forte, and I want to leverage them for my own venture.
- I aspire to start a business that contributes to a charitable cause.
- Necessity: I have been retrenched, and the job market seems elusive.

Whatever your motivation, embarking on your entrepreneurial journey presents a genuine opportunity to unleash your potential, cultivate a profitable venture, attain financial independence, generate employment opportunities for others, and contribute meaningfully to the economy. However, as with any grand undertaking, the path of entrepreneurship is not without its hurdles – from the inception and management of the business to financial stewardship, establishing a customer base and reliable suppliers, cash flow management, profitability, compliance with laws, regulatory filings, financial statements compilation, employee recruitment, and the complexities of legal, accounting, audit, and tax matters.

Building the pillars of success

Starting and sustaining a business is no small feat – it demands a unique set of attributes that lay the foundation for success. Whether you are navigating risks, making informed decisions, or adapting to challenges, certain qualities distinguish successful entrepreneurs. Let us look at the key attributes every entrepreneur should cultivate:

- **Positive mindset.** Having a positive outlook on life and its tribulations are an essential characteristic for any businessperson, and especially entrepreneurs.
- **Willingness to take on risk.** The ability to embrace risk is at the core of entrepreneurship. Understanding these risks and making informed decisions are essential components.
- **Resilience and perseverance.** The entrepreneurial journey is rife with setbacks. Resilience and perseverance are your allies in overcoming obstacles. 'Rolling with the punches' as the saying goes.
- **Learning from failure.** Failure is not an endpoint but a stepping stone. Successful entrepreneurs view failure as an opportunity to learn and grow. Do not fear failure – fear not trying.
- **Leadership** skills extend not only to guiding others but also to leading oneself through the challenges of entrepreneurship.
- **Patience.** Setbacks are inevitable in any business venture. Patience is the virtue that allows you to navigate challenges with composure.
- **Adaptability.** The ability to adapt to changing circumstances is essential in the dynamic business landscape. But adaptability is also about accepting that some of your ideas may fail and not be worth pursuing. Accepting that such failures come with the territory of being your own boss is par for the course.
- **Focus and determination.** Maintaining focus on your goals and the determination to see them through are paramount.
- **Financial literacy.** While you need not be an expert, understanding the basics of financial management is essential for the health of your business.

- **Learning mindset.** Having a constant learning mindset, being open to new and diverse ways of thinking and challenging yourself, pushing your boundaries into the unknown and even into scary spaces, is all part of the journey of any businessperson. Embrace it.
- **Management and organisation skills.** Juggling responsibilities – from clients and suppliers to finances to governance and managing employees – require effective management skills complemented with organisation abilities.
- **Effective communication skills.** The ability to communicate with clients, suppliers, and employees is vital for building and sustaining relationships.
- **Sales and marketing prowess.** The ability to sell and market your business is essential for growth and sustainability.

Even if you find yourself lacking in some of these attributes, the key is recognising your weaknesses and either developing those skills, or enlisting the support of others who excel in those areas. Success is a collaborative effort.

Exploring business ideas and considerations

Once you have internalised your motivations and considered the attributes to build a successful business, the next step is defining your business activities. Consider the following factors:

- **Areas of knowledge and expertise.** Use your existing knowledge and experience to give your venture a competitive edge and a head-start.
- **Strengths and weaknesses assessment.** Assess your risk tolerance, discipline, communication, and leadership skills to determine your readiness for entrepreneurship.
- **Legal form of your business.** Decide on the legal structure – sole proprietorship, partnership with others, or forming a legal entity.
- **Financial planning.** Consider the financing options – savings, personal loans, bank loans – and the associated security requirements.
- **Employment plans.** Consider whether you will be employing people and the implications of this decision.
- **Expert consultation.** Identify areas where you may need expert advice in legal, accounting, audit, tax, human resources, health and safety and other areas relevant to your specific business.
- **Operational considerations.** Determine the operational needs of your company – premises you will operate from, leasing or owning the premises, insurance requirements, systems to effectively run your business and other key considerations.

A comprehensive business plan will guide you through these considerations, helping you document your objectives, define your business, and set a clear path for success. We detail business plans in *Chapter 18*.

Pouring concrete, planting seeds, and embracing patience

As you flip through the pages of this book, you might feel a wave of inspiration and excitement, but also a tinge of overwhelm. That is perfectly normal. The sheer volume of information, the countless tasks, the intricate web of legal and operational requirements – it can all feel like a tidal wave. But take a deep breath – remember many have done this before and many are starting just like you. Daunting, yes – but undaunted! That is the key. Building a business is not like rushing through a field – it is more akin to constructing a solid structure with careful, steady progress.

Think of it like laying a foundation. Imagine the raw, unyielding concrete poured into a frame, setting the stage for a towering structure. It is not the most glamorous thing to see or do, but it is crucial. Just as buildings take months, sometimes years to rise, your business needs a sturdy base built with patience and perseverance.

There are companies that specialise in pouring concrete, just as there are experts to guide you through the intricate process of building your venture. But even the most skilled architect needs a blueprint, an understanding of the overall process.

Much like the majestic Baobab tree, a symbol of strength and resilience, every successful business starts from a small, unassuming seed. The journey of a Baobab, from a tiny seed into one of the largest and longest-living trees in the world, mirrors the path of building a business. It requires patience, nurturing, and time. In the arid landscapes where Baobabs thrive, they stand tall and robust, weathering harsh conditions and thriving against the odds. Similarly, in the dynamic and challenging business environment of South Africa, your venture will require the same resilience and determination to grow and flourish. Remember, the Baobab takes years, even decades, to reach its full stature and grandeur, teaching us that the most enduring successes are often those that are cultivated slowly and with great care. But do not worry – we are not suggesting it will take decades for your business to flourish! With the right strategies and a healthy dose of entrepreneurial spirit, you might just find your business growing faster than a Baobab in the rainy season.

This book is your blueprint, your roadmap to navigating the exciting yet sometimes daunting terrain of entrepreneurship.

Bite-sized steps

Remember, no great undertaking was ever achieved in a single day, and neither will your business. Like the concrete that slowly sets, or the seed of a Baobab that slowly germinates, your success will come in stages, each step leading you closer to your vision. Do not let the magnitude of the task paralyse you. Instead, embrace the power of progress, one brick at a time.

Here is how you can break down the overwhelming into manageable bites:

Step 1: Absorb the knowledge – start by immersing yourself in this book. Let the information seep in at your own pace, taking the time to understand each concept before moving on.

Step 2: Lay the groundwork – choose the business structure that best suits your venture. Whether it is a private company or a sole proprietorship, familiarise yourself with the legal requirements and take the necessary steps to set up your foundation.

Step 3: Register and comply, if this is your choice – register your business with the Companies and Intellectual Property Commission (CIPC) and obtain your tax registration number. Remember, compliance is key, so ensure you register for relevant company, tax and employment requirements and follow all legal guidelines outlined in this book.

Step 4: Build your roadmap – develop a comprehensive business plan, outlining your goals, strategies, and financial projections. This will be your guiding light, keeping you focused and on track.

Step 5: Assemble your team – consider your employment needs, whether it is hiring a team or simply managing yourself as a sole proprietor or sole business owner of the company. Alternatively, seek the help of experts such as accountants, tax practitioners, industry peers, legal advisors, etc. Ensure you understand and follow all employment regulations.

Step 6: Navigate the financial landscape – explore funding options, secure the resources you need and develop a sound financial management strategy. Gain a basic understanding of financial terms and how to read and understand financial statements.

Step 7: Know your rules – familiarise yourself with the laws and regulations that govern your industry, adhering to all applicable standards.

Step 8: Plan your operations – think about your operational needs, from equipment and supplies to workspace and technology.

Step 9: Craft your message – develop a compelling marketing strategy that resonates with your target audience and helps you stand out from the crowd.

Step 10: Maintain meticulous records of your business dealings, ensuring compliance and laying the groundwork for future success.

Step 11: Adapt and evolve – be prepared to adjust your plans as needed. The business landscape is ever-changing, so flexibility is key.

We know this seems simplistic, and the reality is far more difficult. But that is the path of all entrepreneurs. The journey of entrepreneurship is a marathon, not a sprint. Embrace the slow, steady progress, learn from failures and setbacks, celebrate the milestones along the way, and trust that with each step, you build a stronger, more resilient foundation for your dream. One step at a time, one brick at a time. It is daunting but be undaunted. And if you have read this far, you have already taken a few steps. Think of each section in each chapter as a step in your quest to gain information and lay the groundwork for your venture.

CONDUCTING A BUSINESS IN SOUTH AFRICA

"The greatest danger for most of us is not that our aim is too high, and we miss it, but that it is too low, and we reach it."
~ Michelangelo

In the next chapters, we will discuss:

- The different legal forms recognised under South African law for conducting your business – from sole proprietors and partnerships to the most common type of conducting private enterprise, private companies, and its many variations, to public listed and stated-owned companies.
- The process to register your company.
- Understanding some of the most important company documents all companies require.
- Governance of a company – understanding the corporate governance and management requirements from annual general meetings, resolutions, roles, and responsibilities of the board of directors and other officers of the company, board committees and management.

Chapter 1: Legal forms for conducting your business

South Africa has a sophisticated framework governing the diverse ways businesses can conduct their enterprises. While this system offers flexibility tailored to each business' unique requirements, it also comes with a complex web of legal intricacies and bureaucratic red tape – elements that can be both detailed and complex. This chapter aims to demystify the diverse legal structures available for conducting your business.

The different legal forms for your business can be summarised as follows:
- Sole Proprietor.
- Partnership.
- Close Corporation (CC).
- Non-Profit Company (NPC).
- Proprietary limited companies, more commonly referred to as Private Company.
- Personal Liability Company.
- Ring-Fenced Company.
- External Company.
- Public Company.
- State-Owned Company (SOC).

The Companies Act of 2008 serves as the primary legislation governing most legal entities. Close Corporations are an exception as it falls under the governance of the Close Corporations Act of 1984, along with provisions from the Companies Act. Sole proprietorships and partnerships, not being legal entities, find their governance in other laws, such as tax laws, and the general common law.

Legal entities are all governed by the companies' regulator, the Companies and Intellectual Property Commission (CIPC). All persons and legal entities are regulated from a tax perspective by the Income Tax Act of 1962, the Tax Administration Act of 2011 (and related regulations), and overseen by the revenue authority, the South African Revenue Service (SARS).

In the next chapters, we discuss the different business and company types.

Chapter 2: Sole proprietorship

Key attributes

- Meant for a sole owner.
- No need for legal registration as it is not a separate legal entity.
- No separation between personal and business assets and liabilities.
- Ideal for small businesses and certain professions.
- Not recommended for complex businesses or those with higher risk.
- Business terminates upon owner's death, sequestration, or decision to cease operations.

Sole proprietorship offers individuals with the simplest way of conducting their business venture. There is no need to legally register any entity as the business is conducted by the business owner in their sole capacity and for their own profit and loss. All reward and liability are attached to the business owner in their individual capacity, and this can be an advantage and a disadvantage.

Advantages

- Simple to set up and operate.
- No need for registration with the company's regulator, CIPC, and hence no company regulatory red tape.
- Owner receives all profits.
- Sole decision-making.
- Owner can easily decide to cease operations.
- Tax efficient depending on the tax bracket applicable to the sole proprietor.

Disadvantages

- Liabilities of the sole proprietor can put personal assets at risk and pose danger to the sole proprietor's private property and family assets.
- All business interests (profit or loss) must be declared by the sole proprietor in their personal tax filings with SARS.
- Owner accepts all liabilities.
- Business ends upon the owner's death, or if the estate is liquidated.
- Limited ability to raise capital.
- Customers and other parties may prefer to deal with a legal entity rather than a sole proprietor.

Considerations

Operating as a sole proprietor is streamlined, especially for small businesses with low expected risk and revenue. It offers simplicity, flexibility, and faster decision-making for the business owner. There may also be tax benefits to operating as a sole proprietor depending on your tax bracket. However, the lack of legal separation between personal and business assets poses significant risks. For higher-risk businesses, those with predicted growth and seeking loans, and those employing personnel, protecting personal assets from creditors, and presenting a professional image to corporate clients may warrant considering a legal form for conducting your business venture, primarily through a private company.

Chapter 3: Partnerships

Key attributes

- Meant for individuals combining interests for a common business purpose.
- No legal registration needed, not a separate legal entity.
- No separation between personal and business assets and liabilities of each partner.
- Shared risk for partners if other partners create liability.
- Ideal for small businesses; not recommended for higher-risk or complex ventures.
- Partnership terminates when any partner dies, is sequestrated, or withdraws.

A partnership, also known as an unincorporated joint venture, is a fusion of two or more individuals pooling their resources for a shared business interest. Partnerships lack the legal entity status, sparing them from the regulatory registration and tax filings required of incorporated entities. However, each partner is individually responsible for reporting their tax returns and declaring any profit or loss within the partnership.

Partnerships share similarities with sole proprietorships, but with a critical distinction – the risks and rewards are distributed among partners on an agreed-upon profit and loss sharing basis. To ensure clarity and prevent disputes, a comprehensive partnership agreement is essential, outlining each partner's contributions, rights, liabilities, and the process in case of partnership termination. In the unfortunate event of a partner's death or sequestration, the partnership automatically dissolves. The addition of new partners requires all partners to agree, and a new partnership agreement should be put in place.

Joint and several liability is a notable feature, meaning partners share the risk that any liability arising from one partner's actions can lead to claims against the others. Silent partners (who remain unknown to the public but share in profits) and *commanditarian* partners (limiting liability to financial contributions) are possible configurations.

Advantages

- Ease of establishment and administration.
- No separate tax filings for the partnership itself.
- Simplicity in tax responsibilities.
- Leveraging the strengths of individual partners.
- Shared financial and operational strength.
- Personal interest and involvement in the partnership.

Disadvantages

- Not a separate legal entity.
- Each partner declares income from the business in their own personal tax filings with SARS.
- Shared liability for risks arising in the business – each partner bears individual liability and liability for the other partners (joint and several liability).
- Potential delays and disputes in decision-making, especially with more partners.
- Partnership ceases when one partner leaves or dies, or when the estate is sequestrated.
- Limited to individuals – legal entities cannot enter partnerships.
- Limited growth potential and difficulty raising loans as each partner will need to either take their own loan or apply for a joint loan while standing as surety for the loan.
- Customers and other parties may not wish to deal with partnerships or require disclosure. Some customers know-your-client (KYC) requirements may require disclosure of all partners including silent partners as part of their onboarding and risk management policies. They may also deem partnerships as risky and choose not to do business with them.

Considerations

Partnerships thrive when built on trust, clear delineation of contributions, and the partners see the financial and operational contributions as complementary and proportionate to the profit/loss sharing arrangement. However, inherent challenges, such as shared liabilities and potential disputes, need careful consideration. Each partner should agree on key decisions, and the addition or departure of partners requires approval and renegotiation of the partnership agreement. While partnerships offer flexibility, the politics of the relationship is critical to ensure harmonious and successful collaboration. For (a) partnerships looking to protect their personal and business assets from the risk of running the business, (b) partnerships looking to scale-up and take loans to grow the business, and (c) those with employees and higher risk, an alternative legal structure, such as a private company, may need consideration.

Chapter 4: Companies – Common characteristics

Now that we have discussed sole proprietors and partnerships as two forms of conducting a business, we will move on to discussing forming a legal entity to conduct your business as a possible option. The next chapters deal with the diverse types of companies recognised under South African law. Regardless of the type, all companies share fundamental traits.

Key characteristics of all companies

- **Juristic entity.** The company is distinct from its owners, possessing rights and obligations independent of the shareholders or officers of the company.
- **Regulatory obligations.** The company being a separate legal entity must be registered with CIPC, and submit and pay income tax, and other taxes, to SARS. Other regulatory bodies also have authority over the company.
- **Perpetual succession.** Companies exist independently of their owners and continue to exist regardless of changes in shareholding. As such, they have perpetual succession until they are de-registered.
- **De-registration.** Companies cease to exist only through a complex process of de-registration or liquidation.
- **Constitutional document.** The Memorandum of Incorporation (MoI) sets out rights and duties of shareholders, directors, and others in relation to the company. The MoI is a public document.
- **Shareholder agreement.** Shareholders can enter into an agreement among themselves provided it does not contradict the MoI or deviate from mandatory provisions of the Companies Act.
- **Shares.** All companies must have at least one shareholder who is issued shares in the company.
- **Share capital.** All companies must have a share capital but there is no stipulation as to what amount of share capital is needed. The company can have a nominal share capital when it is set up and registered with CIPC. A close corporation, however, does not need to have share capital.
- **Ownership terminology.** Owners are known as shareholders, except in the case of a Close Corporation, where they are known as members.
- **Directors.** A board of directors (or members in the case of a Close Corporation) governs the company with management overseeing day-to-day affairs. A sole owner managed business will just have a single director to oversee the activities and obligations of the company. All private companies must have at least one director while public companies and NPCs must have at least three directors.
- **Governance and management.** The company must adhere to various laws and governance requirements and manage various stakeholders such as shareholders, employees, trade unions, customers, suppliers, regulatory bodies,

etc. The considerable demand on companies requires adequate management time and skills to ensure proper governance and compliance with laws.

- **Limited liability.** Shareholders, directors, and management are generally shielded from personal liability, and the company bears the risk and responsibility of its officers.
- **Personal liability.** Despite there being limited liability for shareholders, directors, or officers of the company, this will not be the case if there is reckless or fraudulent conduct on the part of such individuals.
- **Foreigner involvement.** Foreigners can be shareholders and directors, but if the sole director is foreign, the company must appoint a South African resident public officer for tax representation.
- **Asset protection.** The formation of a company mitigates the risk of the shareholders' personal assets being seized in case of business failure, safeguarding shareholders from legal liability.
- **Litigation in the company's name.** The company, being separate to its owners and having juristic personality, can sue and be sued in its own name.
- **Profit orientation.** Apart from Non-Profit Companies (NPCs), most companies operate for profit.
- **Record-keeping.** Sound record-keeping is essential for the governance of the company and to comply with legal requirements.
- **Financial reporting.** All companies must produce annual financial statements (or where permitted and appropriate, management accounts may also be acceptable), but only certain types of companies must have such statements audited or independently reviewed. Private companies do not have to make their financial statements publicly available. Public companies must disclose their financial statements to shareholders and the public in accordance with applicable laws and stock exchange listing requirements.
- **Income tax.** Companies are subject to a flat income tax rate of 27% on profits, with exceptions for certain small businesses.

The MoI and shareholder agreements

The MoI is the primary constitutional document of a company and a legal requirement under the Companies Act. It sets out the relationship, rights and duties of the shareholders and directors, and the company. The MoI is a public document that is filed with CIPC. It can be a standard one issued by CIPC on registration or can be customised to the requirements of the shareholders provided that certain provisions of the Companies Act are not amended. Any changes to a standard MoI must be registered with CIPC. Should you be seeking to amend the standard MoI, you should consult with an attorney to ensure the customised MoI is compliant with the law.

Shareholders are free, but not required, to enter into a shareholder agreement that governs the relationship between the shareholders. Matters covered under such agreements are, for example:

- Shareholder voting rights and procedures.
- Dividends and profit distributions.

- Transfer of shares (such as pre-emptive rights and consent requirements).
- Deadlock resolution mechanisms where the directors have a tied vote.
- Dispute resolution mechanisms such as referral to mediation, arbitration, or to court.
- Confidentiality, non-solicitation, or non-compete provisions.
- Board composition (including shareholder representation on the board) and board committees.
- Drag-along and tag-along rights.
- Share buy-back provisions, shareholder exit strategies (such as buy-outs, put-options, or other mechanisms), etc.

Drag-along rights allow a majority shareholder to force minority shareholders to sell their shares when the company is sold or acquired, while tag-along rights give minority shareholders the right to sell their shares when a majority shareholder is selling their shares. A share buy-back is when a company opts to repurchase shares from its shareholder. A put option grants a shareholder the right to sell their shares to the company at a predetermined price. A call option grants the company the right to purchase shares from a shareholder at a predetermined price.

A shareholder agreement, unlike the MoI, is not a public document and does not need to be filed with CIPC or disclosed to third parties unless the shareholders agree otherwise. Shareholder agreements must not contain any provisions that are contrary to the MoI, or in other words, they can make provisions that are not dealt with in the MoI but not override the MoI. Similarly, the shareholder agreement must comply with the Companies Act. Seek legal advice when drafting a shareholder agreement to ensure it complies with both the MoI and the Act.

Considerations

Establishing a company provides a robust framework for growth, funding, and profit generation. The various elements of companies offer both flexibility and complexity to businesses. While offering protection to shareholders and facilitating business dealings, careful adherence to legal, financial, and other managerial responsibilities is a necessity. Understanding the nuances of financial reporting, tax obligations and regulatory compliance is essential for steering your company towards a sustainable and profitable future. We will discuss these other crucial factors in later chapters.

In the following chapters. we will discuss the different types of companies recognised under South African law.

Chapter 5: Non-profit company

Key attributes

- Legal entity.
- Meant for public benefit purposes.
- Owners or founders have no right to assets, income, profits, etc, generated from the business of the non-profit company.
- Must register for legal and tax purposes.
- Stringent legal and tax regulation.

Understanding NPCs

A Non-Profit Company (NPC), recognised under the Companies Act, serves as a unique entity designed for the benefit of public causes, succeeding the Section 21 companies under the Companies Act of 1973.

NPCs have specific characteristics that are distinct from other types of companies:
- **Profit generation.** While NPCs can generate profits, these funds cannot be distributed to founders. Profits must exclusively serve the public benefit objectives of the organisation.
- **Purposeful initiatives.** NPCs find application in various domains such as humanitarian relief, education, healthcare, environmental causes, cultural and religious activities, and legal and constitutional/human rights protection.
- **Ownership restraints.** Founding members, directors and officers cannot claim income or assets, thereby ensuring there is focus on the organisation's mission. However, officers are entitled to remuneration.
- **Registration.** NPCs must register under the Companies Act, with their approved name ending with 'NPC' to signify their status as a registered NPC.

Legal requirements for NPCs

- **Incorporators.** A minimum of three incorporators, including juristic entities, serve as the founders of the organisation.
- On registration with CIPC, the NPC must have its name registered; it cannot register with its registration number.
- **MoI.** The constitutional document of the company, signed by the incorporators.
- **Directors.** Appointment of at least three directors who can also be incorporators.
- **Company secretary and audit committee.** While not mandatory, having a company secretary and audit committee is recommended for good governance. This will depend on the size and complexity of the governance requirements of the NPC.
- **Audit requirements.** An NPC is subject to audit or independent review of its annual financial statements as with any other company depending on its

public interest score – see *Chapter 19* regarding the public interest score and its implications on the requirements for financial statements.

- **Compliance.** Adherence to the legal requirements of the Companies Act for registration.
- **Tax exemptions.** Can apply to SARS for exemptions on donor contributions. SARS may also grant them further relief by exempting income and other taxes. NPCs who register with the Department of Social Development beforehand can actively pursue grant opportunities.

Public benefit organisation (PBO)

- **Tax exemptions.** PBO, a subset of NPC, registered with SARS is exempt from income tax, donation tax and estate duty tax on donations received.
- **Donor benefits.** Donors to a PBO can deduct the donation from their taxable income provided a Section 18A certificate is issued by the PBO.
- **Management.** PBOs must be non-profit, open to the public, managed responsibly, and be accountable. Annual financial statements may need auditing based on the public interest score.

Difference between NPC and PBO

Understanding the intricacies of NPCs and PBOs is essential for those seeking to champion public causes. Whether embarking on humanitarian endeavours or contributing to societal well-being, navigating the legal, regulatory and tax landscape ensures the effective functioning of these entities devoted to public benefit. The following table summarises the key differences between the two:

Characteristic	NPC	PBO
Legal entity	Yes	Yes, type of NPC
Primarily regulated by	Companies Act	Income Tax Act
SARS approval	No	Yes
Mandate is for public benefit, or charitable cause	Yes	Yes
Can make profits	Yes	No
Open to the public	Yes	Yes
Tax exemption	Yes, but only on application to SARS	Yes

CIPC will assign a unique registration number to an NPC comprising three digits, a hyphen followed by three more digits. For example, XYZ NPC 123-321. Upon registration, CIPC will assign a PBO an NPC number and SARS will issue a PBO number that starts with '9300' followed by five unique digits specific to the organisation.

Chapter 6: Close corporation

Key attributes

- Close Corporations (CC) are a legacy type of legal entity still recognised in South Africa.
- Perpetual succession.
- Independent of the owners.
- Governed by the Close Corporations Act of 1984 and the Companies Act.
- Owners, called members, must register the CC for legal and tax purposes.
- Regulated by an association agreement among the members.
- In terms of the Companies Act, CCs created prior to that Act can continue to exist but new CCs cannot be created.
- CCs can convert to a private company.
- Only individuals and trusts, not other companies, can be members of a close corporation.

Understanding CCs

CCs function similarly to private companies, regulated by the Close Corporations Act of 1984 and aspects of the Companies Act. A CC can have one to ten members, who own interests in the company (the members' interest). A CC does not need share capital and has perpetual existence, existing independently of its members. Registration for tax purposes (with SARS) and as a company (with CIPC) is mandatory.

Assets and liabilities of the CC are independent of its members. The association agreement governs members' interests, rights, and obligations. The members can be individuals or trusts. While a bookkeeper or accountant is required, a statutory audit is only required depending on the number of points scored under the public interest score – see *Chapter 19* for the public interest score and its relevance to financial statements.

Members, like private company directors, can be personally liable for reckless or fraudulent conduct.

CCs created before 2008 operate under the Companies Act, designated by CC in their names. CCs can convert to private companies, but the reverse is not possible. Since 1 May 2011, new CCs cannot be created. Conversion to a private company requires a 75% members' approval, a MoI, and the filing of relevant forms and payment of the necessary fees to CIPC.

Advantages

- Legal entity providing protection for members.
- Ease of incorporation with fewer legal requirements.
- Perpetual succession.
- Members' interests are easily transferable.
- Ideal for small to medium and family-owned businesses.
- Only individuals and trusts can be members of the CC – not companies.

Disadvantages

- Members carry personal liability for reckless or fraudulent conduct.
- Needs registration and tax filings like private companies.
- Suitable for a maximum of ten owners.
- New CCs cannot be created.
- A company cannot be a member of a CC.

Considerations

Although existing CCs continue to possess full legal personality, new registrations are not possible. Close corporations seeking to grow their business by having more than ten owners, or to have companies as members, and for other reasons, will see advantage in converting the CC to a private company. For instance, a foreign company looking to acquire a CC to grow its business in South Africa would not be able to directly acquire the CC. The CC members would need to convert the CC to a private company, and then the foreign company could acquire that company in whole or as a shareholder.

Chapter 7: Private company

Key attributes

- Legal entity separate from owners who are the shareholders of the company.
- Most common form of company for conducting private enterprise.
- Perpetual succession.
- Minimum of one director and one shareholder.
- Shareholder(s) can be another company.
- Registration as company (with CIPC) and for tax (with SARS) is mandatory.
- On registration with CIPC, the company can choose its registration number as its initial name and change it later.
- MoI restricts transfer of shares to the public.
- Private companies do not have to produce audited financial statements unless their MoI requires it, the public interest score is triggered (requiring either an audit or independent review) (see Chapter 19 on public interest score), or the company elects to have its financial statements audited.
- No requirement for independent auditors (except if above point applies).
- No requirement for audit committee unless MoI requires it.
- No requirement for a company secretary unless MoI requires it.
- Financial statements are not public.

A proprietary limited company, more commonly referred to as a private company, identified by the designation (Pty) Ltd in South Africa, represents the most common form of business entity in the country. It provides flexibility and a streamlined structure, emphasising simplicity in its operational framework. Governed by an MoI, private companies exhibit perpetual succession, paving the way for a sustained business operation that is independent of its shareholders or any changes in the shareholding. However, this legal structure places onerous legal obligations on directors and officers.

Functioning as a privately owned and operated entity, a private company operates within the regulatory framework set by the Companies Act. The (Pty) Ltd suffix signifies its proprietary limited nature. Shares in a private company are not publicly traded, and limited liability shields owners (and directors and other officers of the company) from extensive financial risks. While distinct from its owners, the company still requires vigilant adherence to the legal and tax obligations outlined in the Companies Act, as well as other legislation.

The registration number allocated by CIPC after registration of the private company will follow a designated format – the first four numbers being the year of registration, the next six numbers being unique to the company, and the last two digits will be '07'.

Advantages

- Limited liability for both owners and management.
- Perpetual succession ensures continuity despite changes in shareholding.
- Shares are easily transferable, promoting fluid ownership structures.
- Although shares are easily transferable, they cannot be sold to members of the public, maintaining a controlled ownership environment.
- No limitations on the number of shareholders, which will appeal to various business sizes.
- Companies and/or individuals can be shareholders.
- Flexibility to engage in any industry without restriction unless the MoI says otherwise.
- No limit on the number of shareholders and other companies can be shareholders.
- The MoI can be customised to suit the needs of shareholders.
- Unlike public companies, private companies are not obliged to file quarterly or annual reports, reducing administrative burdens.

Disadvantages

- Compliance requirements can be onerous, demanding significant attention, skills, expertise, and experience.
- Personal liability for shareholders or officers in case of reckless or fraudulent conduct.
- The company can only cease to exist if deregistered or liquidated. The liquidation process can be a complex, onerous, and time-consuming process.
- Registration of shareholders and directors with regulators is a prerequisite, as well as with other officers.
- The company does not have to disclose financial statements to the public.

The responsibility for managing the company lies with the board of directors (or in the case of a sole-owner managed business, by the sole director), which may delegate day-to-day operations to appointed managers. While adherence to the King Code on Corporate Governance is considered good practice, it is not mandatory for private companies. Read more about the King Code in the section on *Public Companies*.

Despite the considerable obligations placed on directors and officers, private companies in South Africa offer a myriad of advantages, making them an ideal choice for businesses of varying sizes. From limited liability to perpetual succession, their form and structure offers the ideal type of legal entity for growth and adaptability for private enterprises.

Financial statements of private companies

As with all companies, private companies must produce annual financial statements that accurately reflect the company's transactions. In *Chapters 19* and *20*, we discuss whether such statements need to be audited or independently reviewed.

Regardless of whether the financial statements are audited or independently reviewed, there is no legal requirement to publicly disclose a private company's financial statements. However, there are instances where third parties may require the disclosure of financial statements such as for opening a bank account, or when taking a loan from financial institutions and other lenders, or customers and suppliers who wish to assess the risk of doing business with the company.

In any case, if private companies need to produce the financial statements, they must ensure that there is a non-disclosure or confidentiality agreement in place to ensure the third party does not disclose it to others without their consent; or at the minimum, mark the financial statements as confidential.

All shareholders and parties with a beneficial interest in the company are entitled to a copy of the financial statements. Subject to certain conditions, creditors and trade unions may be similarly entitled to a copy of the financial statements, as is anyone exercising an enforceable right under the Promotion of Access to Information Act (PAIA) – see *Chapter 51* for more details on PAIA.

Chapter 8: Personal liability company

Key attributes
- Legal entity, which is a special type of private company.
- Minimum of one director and one shareholder.
- Used for certain professionals to provide certain limited liability but not complete immunity from personal liability for its directors.
- Must register for legal and tax purposes like any other company.
- Perpetual succession.
- Onerous legal obligations on directors and officers of the company.

A personal liability company is a type of private company in which the directors (including previous directors) carry personal liability for the debts and obligations of the company for the time such directors held office in the company. The reason for this is that the professional associations that govern such professions permit their members to have some form of legal liability protection while still ensuring personal liability by such professionals.

It is primarily associated with certain professions such as lawyers, medical practitioners, architects, stockbrokers, engineers, and accountants who conduct their business as an association of its directors. The directors carry joint and several liability (ie the obligations created by one director of the company can be binding on the others).

A personal liability company can be distinguished as its name will end with the words Inc. or Incorporated. The registration number allocated by CIPC after registration of the personal liability company will follow a designated format – the first four numbers being the year of registration, the next six numbers being unique to the company, and the last two digits will be '21'.

Advantages
- Provides most of the legal protections enjoyed by private companies.
- Permitted by certain professional associations for members to use.

Disadvantages
- Directors (including past directors) carry joint and several liability.
- Only used by certain professions.

Considerations
Personal liability companies only apply to specific professions, and you should consult your professional association body for any guidance. Registration of professional liability companies (incorporated entities) with CIPC is a manual process.

Chapter 9: Ring-fenced company

Key attributes

- Legal entity.
- MoI of company places certain restrictions on what the company cannot do unlike normal private companies.
- Minimum of one director and one shareholder.
- Must register for legal and tax purposes.
- Perpetual succession.
- Governed by MoI.
- Onerous legal obligations on directors and officers of the company.

A ring-fenced company is a type of company, public or private, where the MoI limits the business of the company to certain activities (including limitations on its purpose, objectives, powers, or other limitations). Such companies can be identified from their names which contain the 'RF'.

A ring-fenced company is particularly advantageous for companies whose financial losses in certain areas of business cannot be set off against income from other areas. This ring-fencing is particularly relevant in sectors where income is highly variable or where speculative or high-risk activities are involved. In South Africa, the concept is often applied in the context of certain investments or activities that are isolated for tax purposes to prevent the offsetting of losses against taxable income from other sources.

Ring-fencing in South African business is not just a matter of tax compliance, but also a strategic tool for financial management. For entrepreneurs, understanding how to utilise ring-fencing can help in effectively structuring business activities. For instance, if you venture into a business with multiple operations, some of which are high risk and others that are more stable and profitable, ring-fencing can help in managing financial risks. By isolating the losses from the high-risk operations, you protect the profitable segments from being affected by these losses. This approach ensures that your successful business areas continue to contribute positively to your overall financial health.

Moreover, ring-fencing can also be a vital factor in investment decisions and investor confidence. From an investor's perspective, a ring-fenced operation within a larger company can be seen as a safeguard, as it limits potential losses to the specific area of investment, without endangering the entire company's assets. This can make investment opportunities more attractive, as the risk is contained and managed more effectively. For entrepreneurs, presenting a business model that effectively uses ring-fencing can be a compelling aspect of business plans or pitches to potential investors.

In summary, while ring-fencing imposes certain limitations, it also offers significant benefits in terms of risk management and financial planning. As a business owner in South Africa, leveraging ring-fencing can lead to more strategic financial decisions, helping to navigate the complexities and uncertainties of the business landscape. Understanding and applying this concept can be a critical aspect of establishing and running a successful business in South Africa.

Chapter 10: External company

Key attributes

- Specifically applies to foreign companies who conduct business in South Africa by way of a branch office.
- Minimum of one director and one shareholder.
- Must register for legal and tax purposes.
- Perpetual succession.
- Governed by MoI.
- Onerous legal obligations on directors and officers of the company.

A foreign registered company may wish to conduct business, whether for profit or not for profit, in South Africa. In this case, and under certain circumstances, it must register a branch of itself in the form of an external company.

The requirement to register an external company with CIPC is triggered when the foreign company either enters employment contracts in South Africa or conducts activities in the country for a continuous period of six months, giving the reasonable belief that it intends to conduct its business in South Africa. Examples of such activities include holding meetings, maintaining financial accounts, establishing, or managing offices, acquiring debts or mortgages, managing debts due to the company, and acquiring interest in property.

If a foreign company wishes to establish an external company, it must register the external company with CIPC. This involves completing COR20.1 documentation, adopting a MoI, registering directors and public officers, appointing a registered auditor if necessary, and providing a registered address within South Africa.

It is important to note that while the external company is a branch of the foreign company, it does not have a separate legal status. However, the local assets of the external company are still subject to potential liability and claims. The regular requirements applicable to local companies and non-profit companies also apply to external companies. The registration number assigned by CIPC for the external company will end with the number 10.

Given the complexity involved in determining whether to register an external company, we recommend that foreign companies seek legal and tax advice to understand the requirements and assess whether registration is necessary. If the foreign company intends to conduct business beyond the specified activities, it may be more appropriate to register a local subsidiary company, which can be a private or public company listed on the stock exchange.

Chapter 11: Public company

Key attributes

- Legal entity.
- Minimum of three directors.
- Many shareholders as company's shares are publicly traded.
- Must register for legal and tax purposes.
- Perpetual succession.
- Governed by MoI and stock exchange listing requirements.
- Onerous legal obligations on directors and officers of the company.
- Significant board and management requirements due to listing requirements.
- Audited financial statements that are publicly available.
- Enhanced reporting obligations such as publication of quarterly financial performance and other reporting requirements.
- Independent auditors required.
- Audit committee and other board committees required.
- Company secretary required.

A public company, identified with the company name followed by Ltd, is a publicly traded company, or in other words its shares or at least some portion of its shares, are traded on a stock exchange such as the JSE, A2X Markets or the Cape Town Stock Exchange. Some public companies may also be dual-listed – they may have a primary or secondary listing locally and other listings on a foreign exchange.

A public company, as with any company regulated by the Companies Act, has the same stringent legal, tax, accounting, and governance requirements as a private company. However, given that it trades publicly, it has even more regulatory requirements with which to comply such as the need for (a) audited financial statements and independent auditors, (b) compliance with the relevant stock exchange listing requirements including quarterly and annual reports, (c) sustainability reporting, (d) rigorous fiduciary responsibilities placed on the board of directors and executive management, etc.

All shareholders have rights to share in the profits of the company, when declared by the board of directors and approved at an annual general meeting.

Unlike other companies that must provide annual financial statements within six months of their financial year-end, public companies are required by the JSE listing requirements to file their financial statements as soon as possible after their year-end and no later than four months.

King Code on Corporate Governance

In addition, public companies are required to comply and report on compliance with the King Code on Corporate Governance (currently King IV version, 2016), which is a set of guidelines setting out best practices for corporate governance.

The main objectives of the King Code for companies are:
- Promoting good governance and creation of an ethical corporate culture.
- Encouraging a sustainable business model.
- Improve stakeholder communication.
- Improve decision-making to meet strategic business objectives.
- Reduce risk.
- Promote transparency and accountability.
- Build a good reputation for companies as part of an ethical society.

The concepts central to the King Code are:
- Ethical leadership.
- The role of companies in society.
- Corporate citizenship.
- Sustainable development.
- Stakeholder inclusivity.
- Integrated thinking and reporting.

Details on the King Code are available on the Institute of Directors, South Africa website *https://www.iodsa.co.za/page/king-iv*

The registration number allocated by CIPC after registration of the public company will follow a designated format – the first four numbers being the year of registration, the next six numbers being unique to the company, and the last two digits will be '06'.

This book does not cover public companies, as this is unlikely to be relevant to the readers of this book.

Chapter 12: State-owned company

Key attributes

- Legal entity.
- Minimum of three directors.
- Government is the shareholder in the company.
- Must register for legal and tax purposes.
- Perpetual succession.
- Governed by MoI and public laws, eg the Public Finance Management Act.
- Onerous legal obligations on board of directors and senior officers of the company who are appointed by the government.
- Significant board and management requirements.
- Publication of financial performance and other reporting requirements.
- Independent auditors required.
- Auditor General can audit the state-owned company and has oversight over independent auditors.
- Audited financial statements required and disclosable to the public.
- Company secretary required.

As the name suggests, a state-owned company (SOC), is a type of company that is wholly or partially owned by the State to achieve the socio-economic goals of the government. Being a public body, it is heavily regulated including under the Companies Act and other legislation governing state bodies, primarily the Public Finance Management Act of 1999 (PFMA) as well as by independent auditors and/or the Auditor General of South Africa. Governance and management of SOCs is overseen by the government who appoints the board of directors and senior officers. The King Code on Corporate Governance also applies to SOCs. Such companies usually end with the words SOC Ltd, and examples are Airports Company of South Africa SOC Ltd (ACSA), Denel SOC Ltd, Development Bank of Southern Africa SOC Ltd, Eskom SOC Ltd, SASRIA SOC Ltd, South African Broadcasting Corporation SOC Ltd (SABC), Telkom SOC Ltd and Transnet SOC Ltd.

The registration number allocated by CIPC after registration of the SOC will follow a designated format – the first four numbers being the year of registration, the next six numbers being unique to the company, and the last two digits will be 30.

This book does not cover SOCs, as this is unlikely to be relevant to the readers of this book.

Chapter 13: Business and company types - Summary

As we reach the conclusion of this section on the different legal forms of conducting a business in South Africa, it is important to reflect on the diverse array of business structures we have explored. From sole proprietorships and partnerships to close corporations, private companies, ring-fenced companies, external companies, public companies, and state-owned companies, each has its unique features and implications. Your choice of business structure should align not just with your current needs but also with your long-term vision. Consider factors like the level of personal liability you are willing to accept, the amount of administrative work you can manage, your financing needs, and your growth ambitions. Remember, the structure you choose will have significant implications for tax, legal obligations, and your capacity to expand.

In making this essential decision, consider both the practical and legal aspects of each business type. For instance, while sole proprietorships and partnerships offer simplicity and direct control, they also involve personal liability. On the other hand, private companies provide limited liability but require more rigorous compliance and governance. Ring-fenced and external companies come with their specific conditions, particularly around financial management and international operations. Public and state-owned companies have the most rigorous governance and disclosure obligations. Keep in mind that setting up new close corporations is not possible but converting an existing close corporation into a private or other type of company is permissible.

The choice also affects your relationship with stakeholders, including investors, employees, and customers. It is essential to carefully weigh these considerations, possibly with the assistance of a legal or business advisor, to ensure that your chosen structure aligns with your business goals and personal risk tolerance.

Lastly, keep in mind that the business environment is dynamic, and what works today might need adjustment tomorrow. Stay informed about changes in South African business laws and market trends. Flexibility and a willingness to adapt are key in the business world. As you embark on your entrepreneurial journey, remember that choosing the right business structure is just the beginning. Continuous learning, resilience, and strategic planning will be your allies in navigating the complexities of the business landscape in South Africa.

Chapter 14: Registering a company

The registration of companies focuses on three key areas:
- Registration of the company with CIPC.
- Registration of the company for tax purposes with SARS.
- Registration of the company for VAT and other tax purposes with SARS or other regulatory bodies, where applicable.

In this chapter, we focus on the registration of companies with the South African companies' regulator, CIPC.

The CIPC portal and its associated platform, BizPortal, make the application for registration of a company simple and user-friendly. Note that you need to first register as a customer on the CIPC portal before you can proceed to register a company on the BizPortal.

Also only private companies and NPCs with standard MoIs can be registered on BizPortal currently – all other company types (and companies with customised MoIs) need to be registered manually – see this link: *https://www.cipc.co.za/?page_id=149*.

Before starting the formal registration process, consider some of the following:
- The registered name of your company.
- A for-profit company needs to provide at least one (and up to a maximum of four) proposed names; if CIPC does not approve the preferred names then it will use the company registration number for registration purposes. It is possible to use the company registration number as the company name. Once you have decided the company name, you will need to apply for the change via CIPC.
- We recommend registering with a company name and consider up to four names.
- The company name cannot be of a company that has already registered with the name. You can check the availability of your chosen company name on the CIPC website.
- Note that CIPC requires an NPC to have a name on registration – unlike for-profit companies, CIPC does not allow an NPC to use the registration number as a company name.
- A company can also have a trading name that is different to its registered name. However, the company must register the trading name with CIPC.
- You need to register at least one director when setting up a private company and three directors for a NPC, public company, or SOC.
- One director will be the incorporator of the company for registration purposes with CIPC.
- The directors need not be South African citizens. However, if the sole director is a foreigner, then the company needs to appoint a South African resident public officer as the tax representative of the company. The tax representative must submit tax filings timeously.

- The following information for the directors will be required for registering a company: (a) valid South Africa identity number, or in the case of a foreigner, then their passport number, (b) date of issue of the identity document, (c) address, (d) email, and (e) cell phone number (the email and cell phone number cannot be the same). Note that the director will need to provide, in addition to their own details, information on their spouse's name, identification number and date of marriage. The Department of Home Affairs needs this information for verification purposes.
- A director must (i) at least be 18 years of age, and (ii) not be disqualified from acting as a director under the Companies Act nor convicted of certain criminal offences (such as fraud).
- Decide on the type of company to be Incorporated, ie private company, NPC, external, public, etc. Remember a CC can no longer be created.
- Information on the shareholder(s) will need to be provided. The shareholder can be an individual, or a trust, or a company, including a foreign company.

Registering a company

Registering your company on CIPC follows this process:
- The CIPC home page is www.cipc.co.za
- To see the many services available through CIPC: *https://eservices.cipc.co.za/*
- First time users of CIPC will need to register as a customer *https://eservices.cipc.co.za/Customer_register_id.aspx*
- Once registered, you will be issued a customer code.
- To see information on name reservation *https://www.cipc.co.za/?page_id=10102*
- Once you have registered with CIPC and received your customer code, you can login to the BizPortal: *https://www.bizportal.gov.za* and click on Login at the top.

Note that you will need a South African ID number to register and login to CIPC and BizPortal. If you do not have a South African ID number then you can register to obtain a CIPC customer code *https://eservices.cipc.co.za/* and once you have successfully registered for the customer code login to *https://www.bizportal.gov.za/login.aspx*, select 'No' at the top where it says, 'Do you have a South African ID number?' and use your customer code to proceed.

Once you have logged in to the BizPortal, you can start to register your company by clicking on 'Register a New Company' and take note of the instructions and requirements:
- Review and agree to the terms for CIPC, Compensation Fund and UIF.
- Select the company type to register.
- Provide directors' info – ID numbers, date of issue, address, contact details, spouse's info, and date of marriage.
  - Directors' email and cell numbers must differ.
  - At least one director must be the incorporator; up to ten directors allowed.
  - Verification with Home Affairs is mandatory.

- Complete new company details – financial year-end, number of shares, physical address in South Africa.
- Insert company name and alternatives.
    - Options: name already approved, apply for a new name, or register without a name.
    - If applying for a new name, choose from available options or use the registration number if names are unavailable.
- Decide on Compensation and UIF registration if employing individuals for over 24 hours monthly. Further details in *Chapter 27*.
- Apply for a BBBEE certificate if eligible. There is no cost for turnover under R10m and the certificate is valid for one year. See *Chapter 50 for more details*.
    - Note that you can also apply for the certificate later.
- Opt for opening a business account to link with your chosen bank. See *Chapter 21* for more details on opening a business account.
    - Other bank documentation may be needed.
- Make payment using credit (if sufficient funds), electronic fund transfer, or credit card.
- Registration cost: R125 per company, R50 for name reservation.
- Registration timeline: a few days up to 15 business days, depending on information, verification, and payment.
- After payment and registration, CIPC sends relevant documentation to each registered director.
    - If you are looking for a comprehensive list of all types of CIPC documents and associated filing fees refer to this link: *https://www.cipc.co.za/?page_id=3804*

Company name recommendations

When registering your company, think of a name that is easy to remember, memorable and preferably describes the nature of your business. The same principles apply to the trading name. For a foreign company registering a local subsidiary company, we recommend adopting the parent company's name, so it is easily identifiable.

There are some useful company name generators online, which you can use:
- *https://www.shopify.com/tools/business-name-generator*
- *https://namelix.com/*
- *https://www.oberlo.com/tools/business-name-generator*

Chapter 15: Important company documents

In this chapter, we explain some of the most critical documents related to your company. This is not a complete list as there are many other types of documents depending on what is needed, or the industry in which your company operates.

Memorandum of Incorporation (MoI) (COR 15.1A document)

The MoI is the principal constitutional document of the company (replacing the Memorandum and Articles of Incorporation under the old Companies Act of 1973) setting out the rights, duties and responsibilities of shareholders and directors of the company as well as setting up the framework within which the company will operate. When you register your company, you must file an MoI. As most companies are owner managed and operated, a standard MoI will suffice and is automatically provided under law. If you wish to change the standard MoI or have a customised MoI whereby the shareholders agree to certain changes, waiver of requirements, etc then the MoI must be filed with the application to register the company (we recommend seeking legal assistance in drafting such changes as knowledge of the implications in terms of the Companies Act is necessary). If you make any changes to the MoI, you must also register the changes with CIPC. Note that the MoI is a public document and is available to anyone via CIPC.

Registration certificate (COR 14.3 document)

The registration certificate confirms that the company is registered with CIPC. It will confirm the company registration number, date of incorporation/registration, the income tax number issued, the registered and postal address, and directors' information.

Shares, share certificates and share register

All companies must have an authorised share capital, which refers to the maximum number of shares they can issue. The MoI will set out the first number of authorised shares, normally exceeding the number initially issued to the founders. For example, on initial registration of the company, the total number of authorised shares may be 1000 shares but only 100 shares are issued to the first shareholders. The remaining unissued shares can be issued to new shareholders by the directors later, according to the MoI and within the authorised limit. Companies are free to decide their first and authorised share capital within the framework of the Companies Act.

Under the Companies Act, all shares have no par value, meaning their price is not predetermined and can be set as agreed between the company and shareholders. Companies can also have different classes of shares with varying rights, such as voting rights or dividend entitlements.

Every company must have at least one shareholder. Public companies and SOCs have specific minimum shareholding requirements as per the Companies Act, other applicable laws, or listing requirements. A share certificate serves as proof of ownership, showing the shareholder's details and holdings. It is a signed document by the directors and company secretary (if applicable). Share numbers must be sequential, and once signed, the certificate becomes an original document.

The share register records every shareholder's holding and any changes in sequential order. This document keeps an historical record of ownership, and the company must continuously update it whenever shares change hands. The company must keep the share register at its registered office and be accessible for inspection by authorised persons.

Both share certificates and the share register must be correct, up-to-date, and compliant with the Companies Act and any relevant company resolutions.

The Companies Act does not require the filing of share certificates and registers with CIPC, making it a matter of internal governance for directors and the company secretary to manage.

Annual returns (COR 30.1 document)

An annual return (AR) is evidence that a company is still running. All companies must file their AR on an annual basis, within 30 business days of their date of incorporation; however, CCs must file their AR within the anniversary date of its incorporation up until the month thereafter.

For example, if a company (excluding a CC) was incorporated on 31 January 2022, then the company must file its 2023 AR with CIPC within 30 business days of 31 January 2023, and similarly for each year thereafter. An AR is a statutory filing and is a set form filed with CIPC via the eFiling website. The cost to lodge an AR is based on the annual turnover of the company, based on a sliding scale, ranging from R100 (for less than R100 million turnover) up to R3000 (for over R25 million turnover). Late or no filing of an AR risks the company being deregistered by CIPC. If you file your AR late, CIPC imposes a penalty. If your company does not file the AR and is deregistered then you need to file a reinstatement application form (COR 40.5) along with a fee of R200 together with filing and payment for all overdue ARs.

Note that even if a company is inactive in a particular year, it must still file and pay for the AR otherwise there is the risk of the company being deregistered. After 1 April 2024, a company or CC that fails to file its beneficial ownership declaration will not be permitted to submit its annual returns to CIPC – see the section on *Beneficial ownership disclosure requirements in Chapter 16.*

Any non-compliance with the Act or CIPC regulations will result in an investigation by CIPC.

Retention period for records

Under the Companies Act, there are various retention periods depending on the type of records. For the purposes of this chapter, the following should be noted in terms of the relevant retention periods:

- Notice of Incorporation/Registration certificate, MoI, share registers – indefinite.
- No retention period is specified for ARs and the various other company documents but the Companies Act requires a general retention for all company records (except where otherwise stated) to be at least seven years after it has been filed or the year-end of the company. We recommend that you seek legal advice for your specific queries related to your record-keeping and retention periods. See also *Chapter 59* on record-keeping and specifically the section on *Record retention periods*.

Chapter 16: Governance of a company

In this chapter, we discuss critical governance requirements of the company:
- Annual general meetings.
- Shareholder meetings.
- Resolutions.
- Board of directors.
- Director qualification requirements.
- Director's rights and responsibilities.
- Board committees.
- Auditor.
- Company secretary.
- Public officer.
- Data privacy / Information officer.
- Management.
- Beneficial ownership disclosure requirements.

Annual general meeting (AGM)

Private companies are not compelled to hold AGMs unless their MoI specifies it. If a private company is solely owned, an AGM is unnecessary. However, for companies with multiple shareholders, especially if some are not involved in daily operations, an MoI requirement for an AGM is recommended but not required.

The Companies Act mandates that all public companies hold an AGM within 18 months of incorporation and thereafter within six months after its financial year-end. All shareholders must receive prompt notice of the meeting's date, location, options for attending in person or electronically, and receive an agenda beforehand. The AGM must adhere to the Companies Act and the company's MoI. Meetings can be held electronically, and proxy votes are permissible. The quorum for a meeting must be 25% of eligible voters entitled to vote on at least one matter. The MoI may stipulate a higher percentage for a quorum but not less.

AGMs for public companies (or private companies as required by their MoI) are essential because they allow directors to present information to shareholders on:
- The company's operational and financial performance, including approval of audited annual financial statements.
- The voting of key resolutions, such as appointing, reappointing, or removing directors and auditors (where applicable).
- The approval of any dividends.
- The approval of any proposed changes to the company's MoI.
- Any other important matters.

Where applicable, the company must also invite the auditor to the AGM. Shareholders can question directors about business strategy and other matters, ensuring that company officials are held accountable. The company must keep proper records of shareholder attendance and minutes of the AGM.

Shareholders vote on matters at the meeting or by sending proxy votes beforehand. Proxy votes allow shareholders to authorise another person to represent them at the meeting.

Shareholder meetings

An AGM, as discussed earlier, is a mandatory shareholder meeting for public companies. However, both private and public companies can hold other shareholder meetings called for by the board or shareholders:

- **When required by law.** The Companies Act or the company's MoI may mandate shareholder approval for specific matters. These meetings are necessary to obtain shareholder consent for such decisions.
- **To fill board vacancies.** If a position on the board of directors becomes vacant, a shareholder meeting may be held to elect a new director.
- **At the request of shareholders.** Shareholders holding a minimum percentage of voting rights, as specified in the MoI, can request a shareholder meeting to pass specific resolutions or discuss matters. This allows shareholders to actively take part in company decisions.

Public companies must send notices for such shareholder meetings to all shareholders at least 15 days in advance; other types of companies have ten days. The notices must clearly outline the matters to be discussed at the meeting, along with the date, time, and location of the meeting. Like the AGM, electronic holding of meetings, proxy voting, minutes of the meeting and quorum requirements apply to such shareholder meetings.

Resolutions

The Companies Act sets out specific requirements for resolutions by the company:

- **Ordinary resolutions.** A simple majority vote (more than 50% of votes cast) for matters like approving annual reports, appointing directors, and declaring dividends.
- **Special resolutions.** A higher threshold of 75% of votes cast for important decisions like altering the disposing of major assets or approving mergers and acquisitions.
- **Alteration of MoI resolutions.** Like special resolutions, altering the company's MoI requires a 75% vote but may also need further approvals from specific shareholder groups depending on the MoI itself.

Other points to consider:

- **Quorum requirements.** A minimum number of shareholders or their proxies must be present for a meeting to be valid. This typically varies based on the type of resolution.
- **Notice requirements.** Companies must supply adequate notice to all shareholders about meetings and proposed resolutions.
- **Proxy voting.** Shareholders can appoint proxies to vote on their behalf in their absence.
- **Challenges.** Shareholders can challenge resolutions passed at meetings if they believe proper procedures were not followed.

Companies, and where applicable the company secretary in particular, must keep a proper record of all resolutions, which the chairperson of the meeting and the company secretary should date and sign.

Board of directors and criteria for directors' appointment

The Companies Act assigns the responsibility of managing the company to the board of directors. The board holds all necessary powers to fulfil its functions, limited only by the Companies Act or the company's MoI.

A private or personal liability company must have at least one director, while public companies need a minimum of three directors. The MoI may specify a higher number of directors.

Directors may receive remuneration for their services, subject to the MoI. If a director is also an employee of the company, they can receive both employee and director remuneration.

The Companies Act sets up eligibility criteria for directors – they must be natural persons (not legal entities), over 18 years old, and meet any other criteria set out in the MoI. Disqualifications from being a director include:

- Being declared delinquent by a court in certain prescribed circumstances.
- Being an unrehabilitated insolvent person.
- Ineligibility due to public regulations.
- Removal from a position of trust due to misconduct involving dishonesty.
- Conviction and imprisonment for crimes involving theft, fraud, forgery, lying under oath (perjury), misrepresentation, or dishonesty, or under other legislation.

The Companies Act outlines the standards of conduct, duties, powers, rights, and liabilities of directors. All directors should be familiar with and understand these requirements. We recommend that all new directors receive training on their fiduciary duties.

Director's rights and responsibilities

The primary rights and responsibilities of directors under South African law are outlined in the Companies Act. These rights and responsibilities are designed to ensure that directors act in the best interests of the company and its stakeholders. Unlike the Companies Act of 1973 (where the directors' primary obligation was to act in the interests of shareholders), the primary fiduciary duty of directors under the current Act requires that the directors act in the best interests of the company. This is because the company is a separate legal entity from its owners and therefore the directors must consider the interests of the company as paramount. This does not mean that the directors should not consider the interests of other stakeholders, like shareholders, employees, creditors, etc but rather that when there is a conflict or competing interests, then the directors must apply their minds to the issues and act for the benefit of the company.

The primary **rights of directors** can be summarised as follows:
- The right to access company information.
- The right to attend and take part in board meetings.
- The right to vote on board decisions.
- The right to seek legal or other expert advice when the situation requires it.
- The right to be indemnified by the company for losses incurred in the performance of their duties.

The primary **fiduciary duties of directors** can be summarised as follows:
- The duty to act in good faith and in the best interests of the company.
- The duty to exercise care and diligence in the performance of their duties. The duty of care requires directors to exercise the same degree of care and skill as a prudent person would in the circumstances. This means that directors must make informed decisions based on all available information, seek expert advice when necessary, and monitor the company's performance on an ongoing basis.
- The duty of loyalty to the company and to consider the best interests of the company and other stakeholders.
- The duty to avoid conflicts of interest, and where such conflicts cannot be avoided, to declare such interests to the rest of the board and excuse themselves from any decision-making involving the interest.
- The duty to keep proper records and accounts.
- The duty to report any illegal or unethical activities to the appropriate authorities.

In addition to these general rights and responsibilities, directors also have **specific duties** in relation to the following:
- **Financial reporting.** Directors are responsible for ensuring that the company's financial statements are accurate and prepared in accordance with all applicable accounting standards.
- **Corporate governance.** Directors are responsible for establishing and maintaining sound corporate governance practices within the company.

- **Risk management.** Directors are responsible for identifying, assessing, and managing the company's risks.
- **Compliance with laws and regulations.** Directors are responsible for ensuring that the company complies with all applicable laws and regulations.

Directors who fail to comply with their rights and responsibilities may be subject to legal action, which may include any of the following:
- Fines and penalties imposed by the relevant authorities such as CIPC and SARS.
- Civil proceedings by the authorities or stakeholders.
- Criminal proceedings in the case of egregious violations of applicable laws where any act or omission involves gross negligence or dishonesty (such as for fraud, embezzlement, insider-trading, etc).
- Application to court by any party recognised under the Companies Act to disqualify the director from being a director or to declare the director to be delinquent.
- Sanctions by professional bodies of which the director is a member, which could include being suspended, or being removed as a member.

It is important for directors to understand their rights and responsibilities as directors and seek expert advice when needed. Training of new directors is highly recommended, so they are familiar with their rights and responsibilities. For good governance, companies should also issue appointment letters to all directors.

Board committees

The board is empowered to establish board committees to aid it in managing the affairs of the company. Members of such committees do not necessarily need to consist of members of the board, but such members must still meet the criteria for qualification as directors (ie they cannot be disqualified as per the criteria set out above). Certain committees are prescribed board committees under the Companies Act such as the audit committee and social ethics committee, both of which we discuss below. The board may create other types of committees such as:
- Remuneration committee.
- Governance committee (sometimes combined with the audit committee).
- Health, safety, and environmental committee.
- BBBEE committee.
- Nomination committee (sometimes combined with remuneration committee).
- Sustainability committee.
- Risk management committee.
- Finance and investment committee.
- Technology committee
- Human resources committee.

Having such committees alleviates the pressure on the board having to deliberate on the myriad of issues facing a company, and the board committees report only the most critical issues and any key decisions that the board needs to make.

We recommend that the board put in place formal terms of reference or a committee charter for these board committees, setting out the mandate, duties, and rights of the committee along with membership and other administrative matters. These committees should also keep minutes of meetings recording attendance, the key issues discussed, and significant decisions made.

For small companies and owner-managed businesses having such committees may be unnecessary.

Audit committee

The Companies Act requires all public and SOCs to appoint an audit committee, which is a board committee. Private companies do not have to appoint an audit committee unless the MoI mandates it, in which case the requirements for audit committees under the Act shall apply.

Requirements of an audit committee:
- It shall include at least three non-executive directors of the board who have the requisite skills and knowledge to perform the duties of the committee.
- The members must not be:
  - Involved in the day-to-day management of the company.
  - A prescribed officer of the company nor an officer of the company within the preceding three years prior to their appointment.
  - A material customer or supplier to the company such that there may be a perception of a compromise to their independence.
  - Related to any person as set out above.

Roles and responsibilities of the audit committee:
- Nominate the appointment of the external auditors at the AGM after careful consideration of their qualifications, experience, and independence.
- Oversee the internal and external audit process of the company.
- Ensure the financial statements are prepared in accordance with auditing standards and applicable laws and regulations.
- Appoint and oversee the work of external auditors and communicate regularly and openly with the lead audit partner.
- Review the remuneration and external engagement of the external auditors.
- Approve any non-audit services that any external auditors provide.
- Ensure the external auditors have access to all records of the company and management such that the auditors can perform their duties in accordance with the auditing standards.
- Review and approve the qualifications and experience of the chief financial officer.
- Review the financial statements prior to submission to the board of directors.
- Provide a report for inclusion in the company's annual financial statements setting out how the committee carried out its functions, that the committee is satisfied with the auditors' independence, approval of the qualifications and experience of the chief financial officer, and any comments the committee

has on the company's financial statements, accounting practices, and internal financial controls.
- Make submissions to the board of directors on the company's accounting policies, financial controls, records, and reporting.
- Attend the AGM of the company to answer any questions by shareholders.

The company and the audit committee must also consider the best practices set out in the committee in terms of the King Code on Corporate Governance. They must also put in place formal terms of reference or charter for the committee setting out the mandate, duties, rights, membership, and other administrative matters (including keeping minutes of meetings).

As one can see, the duties of the audit committee are onerous and necessary to ensure accountability and transparency in the preparation of the company's financial statements. Independence of the audit committee members is critical to ensure the company complies with its legal obligations.

Social and ethics committee

A social and ethics committee is a board sub-committee overseeing a company's social and ethical performance. It ensures responsible and sustainable operations, considering all stakeholders – employees, customers, suppliers, the community, and the environment. The committee usually consists of three to five members of the board of directors or prescribed officers. It is advisable that the chairperson be a non-executive director, which is reasonable to achieve for public and SOCs; however, for private companies that do not ordinarily have any non-executive directors, this will not be practical to achieve.

The Companies Act specifies the following criteria for when such a committee is required:
- All SOCs.
- All listed public companies.
- Private companies that have a public interest score (PIS) of 500 or higher in the prior two years. See Chapter 19 for more information on how the public interest score is calculated.
- Companies that have been granted a licence to operate in a regulated industry, such as banking, insurance, or healthcare, may also be required to have a social and ethics committee as a condition of their licence.

The committee has the following primary duties:
- Developing and implementing a social and ethics policy for the company covering the following key areas:
  - Social and economic development by considering international standards such as the United Nations Global Compact Principles, labour practices, anti-bribery, and responsibility for the environment and to society.
  - Considering local issues such as compliance to the Employment Equity Act and the Broad-Based Black Economic Empowerment Act.

- Good corporate citizenship including the promotion of equality and prevention of unfair discrimination.
- Health and safety.
- Consumer relationships.
- Community development initiatives.
- Monitoring the company's compliance with its social and ethics policy.
- Identifying and assessing the company's social and ethical risks.
- Developing and implementing strategies to manage the company's social and ethical risks.
- Reporting to the board of directors on the company's social and ethical performance.
- Ensuring that the company is disclosing its social and ethical performance in a transparent and correct manner, usually contained in a sustainability report that forms part of the annual financial statement, or as a separate report filed along with the financial statements.

The committee plays a vital role in promoting corporate social responsibility in South Africa. It helps ensure that the company is operating in a responsible and sustainable manner, and that the company is considering the interests of all stakeholders. By doing so, the committee can help to improve the company's reputation, attract and retain employees, and build trust with customers, suppliers, and the community. The company should put in place formal terms of reference or charter for the committee setting out the mandate, duties, rights, membership, and other administrative matters (including keeping minutes of meetings).

Company secretary

The Companies Act does not require private companies to appoint a company secretary. However, it is recommended that a company secretary be appointed where the private company is a large and/or complex organisation as the company secretary will assist the board to comply with the fulfilment of statutory requirements and good corporate governance. Company secretaries need to comply with the same eligibility criteria as a director (ie they must not be delinquent, disqualified, and must comply with any other eligibility criteria set out in the MoI).

Public companies and SOCs must appoint a company secretary.

The key duties of a company secretary are to:
- Ensure compliance with applicable laws and regulations.
- Maintain the company's statutory registers including the minutes of meetings of the board, board committee and shareholders.
- Maintain the share register.
- Certify that the company's financial statements is compliant with the filing of annual returns.
- Convene and guide the process of board and shareholder meetings.

- Advise the board on corporate governance matters such as the King Code on Corporate Governance,
- Communicate with shareholders and other stakeholders.
- Work with advisors on governance issues.

The company secretary plays a critical role in ensuring the company is run in a compliant and ethical manner.

The company secretary is a prescribed officer of the company and once appointed, the company needs to register the appointment with CIPC. If a private company chooses to appoint a company secretary, they must also register the appointment with CIPC. The company must also notify CIPC of any changes in the company secretary (such as resignation or removal or becoming disqualified).

There is no prohibition from a director also being the company secretary, but this is rare. The key criteria are that the person must have the time and ability to be able to fulfil their functions.

The company must keep a record of its company secretaries including name and date of appointment and resignation or removal from office. A company secretary can be a legal entity that specialises in company secretarial services. A company secretary must be a permanent resident of South Africa and remain so for the duration of their appointment.

Public officer

The Tax Administration Act of 2011 requires all companies to appoint a public officer who acts as the tax representative of the company and is responsible for ensuring that tax filings are submitted timeously to SARS. Such tax filings include submission of annual tax returns and provisional tax returns, registration of the company as taxpayer and as employer, submission of employees' monthly tax declaration and annual returns, and notification of change of address and acceptance of notices by SARS on the company. The public officer acts as the primary spokesperson for all communications with SARS, and the company must timeously notify SARS of any changes to the public officer. The actions of the public officer are deemed to be the actions of the company.

A public officer must be a natural person who is resident in South Africa; a juristic person (ie a legal entity) cannot perform the duties of a public officer. The public officer must understand and comply with the obligations imposed by SARS, and must be a person with financial, tax or legal experience. SARS has issued a practice notice whereby it advises that registered tax practitioners cannot act as public officers of the company. In the case of a solely owned business, it would be the sole director who would be the public officer.

It is possible to outsource the public officer obligations to a third-party specialist accounting or company secretarial firm who will assign an individual with the necessary expertise to perform the necessary public officer obligations. It is important to perform proper due diligence on such third-party company and the nominated individual prior to formal appointment as the actions or inactions of the appointed public officer will have implications for the company.

The appointment and/or resignation of a public officer requires a letter of consent or letter of resignation, as may be the case, and a board resolution confirming the same. The company must file this on the SARS eFiling system. The company must update its records reflecting such changes as well.

Data privacy/information officer

All companies must appoint an information officer and register it with the Information Regulator. See *Chapter 51* for more details.

Auditor

A private company does not have to appoint an auditor except if the public interest score criteria is met as detailed in *Chapter 19,* or the MoI requires an auditor. A private company may also voluntarily elect to appoint an auditor in which case the other requirements mentioned below will apply.

Public companies and SOCs must appoint a registered auditor. The auditor must meet the same criteria as for directors (ie not be delinquent or disqualified), must be independent of the company, and avoid any conflicts of interest. The company's audit committee must satisfy itself that the auditor qualifies to fulfil such office as contemplated in terms of the Companies Act. A firm of auditors may also be appointed as the auditor but then an individual chosen by the firm to do the audit must meet the criteria mentioned above.

The auditor is responsible for conducting audits of the company's financial statements in accordance with auditing standards and has the following rights:
- Access to accounting records, books, and documents (note this is very wide and not just limited to financial documents).
- Information and explanations from directors and officers of the company necessary for the performance of the auditor's duties.
- Attend any general shareholder meetings and the AGM.
- Receive all notices and communications of such meetings.
- Be heard at any such meeting by shareholders related to the auditor's duties or functions.

An individual auditor cannot serve more than five consecutive financial years for the company and there must be a cooling-off period of at least two years between the next appointment of the individual.

The company must always act transparently and honestly in discussions with the auditor and provide truthful and accurate records.

Audit firm and auditor rotation

In many jurisdictions, auditing firms of large and listed entities are required to be rotated to ensure that there would be no perception that the independence of the auditor was compromised due to a prolonged relationship with the client and its management. This was also the case in South Africa with the Independent Regulatory Board for Auditors (IRBA, a statutory body created under the Auditing Professions Act of 2005 to regulate the activities of auditing firms) requiring audit firm rotation for public companies every ten years effective from 2023. However, the Supreme Court of Appeal ruled that IRBA had exceeded its powers in requiring such audit firm rotation. The case is cited as East Rand Member District of Chartered Accountants vs Independent Regulatory Board for Auditors. It is still possible that the legislature may adopt changes to legislation requiring such rotation for public companies in line with many other countries and considering the principles enshrined in the King Code on Corporate Governance.

Note that the Companies Act requires individual auditors (but not the auditing firm) to rotate after five consecutive financial years of service, with a mandatory cooling-off period of two years between re-engaging the same auditor. This rotation requirement will not be of any relevance though to private companies unless the auditor requirement is applicable.

In the interest of good governance, keep in mind that the auditor, where appointed, must play an independent role in evaluating the financial statements. This provides reasonable levels of assurance to shareholders and other stakeholders that the financial statements are fair and accurate.

Management

Depending on the size, type, complexity and/or whether the company is in a regulated industry, the company may need to appoint various officers to conduct the specific duties assigned to them and based on their individual skills, qualifications, and experience:

- **Chief executive officer/managing director/general manager**, the most senior officer of the company responsible for overseeing the day-to-day management of the company. This officer is normally a director of the company, appointed by the board and reports to it periodically.
- **Chief financial officer**, the senior officer responsible for the financial affairs of the company, adhering to relevant financial reporting standards, implementing risk management plans and controls for ensuring accurate financial reporting, and ensuring the audit of the company adheres to the relevant standards.
- **Chief operating officer**, sometimes known as the President of the company, responsible for overseeing the operational activities of the company including things like the manufacturing processes, factories, and facilities, and ensuring adherence to safety standards.
- **Chief legal officer** responsible for the legal affairs of the company including regulatory compliance, company secretarial, litigation, implementing contractual framework and overseeing external legal advisors.

- **Human resources manager** responsible for all labour and employment issues including employment contracts, hiring procedures, implementing, and advising on the disciplinary code, representing the company in labour disputes, trade union management, etc.
- **Health and safety officer** responsible for ensuring adherence to the Occupational Health and Safety Act, implementing health and safety policies and procedures, etc.
- **Tax manager** responsible for managing the tax affairs of the company, dealing with tax authorities, and working with human resources on payroll taxes.
- **Information management officer** handles the implementation of IT systems and controls to facilitate business operations and protect the business' data.
- **Sales and marketing staff** responsible for the sale of the company's products and services, development of marketing strategies and opportunities, and managing relationships with customers.
- **Supply chain managers** responsible for managing the procurement of goods and services that the company needs for its operations, including for purchase of raw materials for production purposes.
- **Other officers** depending on the nature of the business.

The business plan will help you focus on what types of employees you require, depending on your business requirements, your budget, regulatory requirements, etc.

Directors and officers (D&O) liability insurance

South African law permits a company to taken out D&O insurance cover for its directors and officers (D&O). Companies can purchase D&O insurance to protect their directors and officers from personal liability arising from their actions or omissions in their official capacities.

D&O insurance typically covers:
- Legal defence cost.
- Settlements and awards.
- Personal liability of directors and officers.
- Criminal defence costs.
- Regulatory investigations.
- Wrongful termination of employment.
- Extradition costs.

The Companies Act allows companies to indemnify their directors and officers for losses incurred because of their actions or omissions in their official capacities. However, there are certain limitations. For example, companies cannot indemnify directors and officers for losses arising from wilful misconduct, or breach of trust.

D&O liability insurance provides directors and officers with assurance that they will be financially protected while performing their duties and helps to protect their personal assets.

Companies should seek advice from their attorneys and insurers when taking out such policies. The company should advise their insurer timeously whenever a claim under the D&O policy arises.

Beneficial ownership disclosure requirements

CIPC has implemented a process of creating a beneficial ownership register, the purpose of which is to have a comprehensive database of natural persons who ultimately own or control all legal entities. This information empowers law enforcement agencies with essential details during investigations. This requirement is part of the country's efforts to combat money laundering, financing of terrorism, and other financial crimes.

Current regulations:

- **General Laws (Anti-Money Laundering and Combating Terrorism Financing) Amendment Act of 2022.** This Act, passed in 2022, mandates the CIPC to collect and maintain a register of beneficial ownership information for companies and CCs.
- **CIPC User Guidelines.** The CIPC has published guidelines outlining the requirements for companies to comply with the beneficial ownership reporting obligations.

A beneficial owner is an individual or natural person who directly or indirectly owns 5% or more of a company or exercises effective control over it. This determination also applies in cases where ownership or control is carried out through a series of entities or other arrangements.

Companies must submit information about their beneficial owners, including:
- Name.
- Identity number or passport number.
- Date of birth.
- Country of residence.
- Nature and extent of beneficial ownership (eg percentage shareholding, voting rights).

As of 1 April 2024, companies and CCs must submit their beneficial ownership declaration when filing their annual return. CIPC will not accept the filing of annual returns if the beneficial declaration forms are not submitted. See *Chapter 15* for more details on annual returns, in addition to fines, penalties and other administrative sanctions.

Retention period of records

Under the Companies Act, there are various retention periods depending on the type of records. For purposes of this chapter, the following should be noted in terms of the relevant retention periods:
- Register of company secretaries and auditors – indefinite.

- Notice of meetings including AGM, shareholder meetings, director meetings, resolutions and all supporting documentation, and communications to shareholders – seven years.
- All other company records that are not specifically mentioned in the Companies Act or other laws should be retained for at least seven years after the financial year-end in which the record was created.

The above is not a comprehensive list.

We recommend that you seek legal advice for specific queries related to your record-keeping and retention periods. See also *Chapter 59* on record-keeping and specifically the section on *Record retention periods*.

FUNDING AND FINANCIALS

"Financial statements are like a window into the soul of a business."
~ Warren Buffett

"Understanding financial statements is like speaking a new language that unlocks the secrets of business."
~ Carl Richards

In the upcoming chapters, we will cover the following topics:

- Explore why financial planning is fundamental for the success and sustainability of your business.
- Examine different avenues available to fund and expand your business. This will include exploring traditional banking loans, venture capital, crowdfunding, and other financing options.
- The significance of having a well-crafted business plan. We will discuss the essential components of a business plan and how it serves as a roadmap for your business' future growth and development.
- Understand the legal requirements for preparing and presenting annual financial statements in compliance with South African laws and regulations. We will also explain the concept of the public interest score and its relevance in determining whether a company's financial statements require auditing or independent review, or in some cases, neither.
- The process and importance of opening a dedicated bank account for your business operations. We will discuss the benefits of separating personal and business finances and provide guidance on selecting the right financial institution for your needs.

These chapters aim to equip you with valuable insights and practical knowledge to effectively plan your finances, explore funding opportunities, meet legal obligations related to financial reporting, and establish a solid financial foundation for your business.

Chapter 17: Financial planning and access to funding

When starting a business in South Africa, it is vital to go beyond having a vision and a product or service. Comprehensive financial planning and knowledge of funding opportunities are essential. In the following chapters, we will emphasise the importance of financial planning, outline the reasons why it is indispensable, and explore the various avenues for accessing funding in the South African business landscape.

Although you do not need to be a financial expert, understanding essential financial statements is vital. This requires being open to learning key financial terminology and grasping the basic concepts of financial statements.

If you have not studied finance or have limited experience in financial matters, approaching this area may seem daunting. However, a solid understanding of key financial terms is fundamental to the success of any business venture. Overcoming fears or a disinterest in financial matters is necessary. Embrace financial literacy as part of the continuous learning mindset required of all business owners.

The importance of financial planning

Financial planning plays an essential role in the success and sustainability of a business. We will discuss the importance of financial planning and explore the budgeting process below.

Risk mitigation

The South African business environment presents various risks, such as economic fluctuations and regulatory changes. Financial planning serves as a risk management tool, enabling businesses to identify potential pitfalls and develop strategies to mitigate these risks effectively.

Resource allocation

Efficient financial planning involves allocating resources to different areas of the business. By providing the necessary financial support to each department, businesses can enhance operational efficiency and not misallocate resources, which can lead to inefficiencies and hinder overall performance.

Goal-setting and measurement

Financial planning is associated with setting realistic financial goals. Establishing these goals allows businesses to track their progress, make informed decisions, and stay on course towards achieving their objectives. Through regular measurement and evaluation, businesses can adapt their strategies as needed to ensure continued alignment with financial goals.

Decision-making

Informed decision-making relies on accurate financial data. A well-structured financial plan provides decision-makers with insights and analysis, enabling them to navigate challenges, seize opportunities, and strategically steer the business forward. It helps ensure that decisions are based on a solid understanding of the financial implications and potential outcomes.

Budgeting process

The budgeting process involves creating a detailed financial plan for a specific period, typically one year. It entails forecasting revenues, estimating expenses, and setting targets for financial performance. The budgeting process helps businesses allocate resources effectively, monitor financial activities, and control costs. It also allows for periodic evaluation of actual performance against the budgeted figures, facilitating adjustments and corrective actions if needed.

The budgeting process should involve collaboration among stakeholders led by the finance team, and include sales and marketing, production managers, supply chain and procurement, and consider the needs of all other departments in the organisation. Consideration of market conditions and of potential risks and opportunities plays a vital role in both the budgeting and risk management process. Regular review and revision of the budget in response to changes in the business environment or internal factors are essential to maintain accuracy and relevance.

Access to funding in South Africa

Securing funding is often a pivotal step in transforming a business idea into a reality. In the context of South Africa, entrepreneurs can explore a myriad of funding options, each with its own set of considerations.

Personal savings

One of the most common, yet sometimes overlooked, sources of funding is personal savings. Entrepreneurs often inject their own funds into the business to kickstart operations. While this may not be feasible for every entrepreneur, those with personal savings can leverage this option to invest in their business without incurring debt. Carefully consider the use of personal savings based on the forecasted startup and on-going operational costs of the business. The business plan, discussed in the next chapter, will help you determine the feasibility of using personal savings, or using a combination of savings and debt.

Bank loans and financing

Commercial banks in South Africa are integral players in providing financial support to businesses. Entrepreneurs and companies seeking loans or financing must present a compelling case, demonstrating the viability of their business, the intended use of funds, and a clear repayment plan. Building a strong relationship with the chosen financial institution is key to successful collaboration.

South Africa has a sophisticated banking system and there are many banks from which you can seek guidance. Banks offer flexible business accounts with preferential terms to startup and small businesses, but loans are always based on the risk posed to the banks in the event of the borrower defaulting. Banks may require security against such defaults (such as guarantees, suretyships from credible third parties or the pledging of assets), which may pose a challenge for entrepreneurs and small companies.

You should leverage your current bank and/or account manager to establish the feasibility and application process for obtaining a loan.

Government agencies providing loans and other support

The South African government actively supports entrepreneurship through various grants and subsidies. These financial incentives are often directed towards specific industries, economic development initiatives, or addressing societal challenges. Entrepreneurs must carefully research and understand the eligibility criteria and application processes associated with these opportunities.

The **Development Bank of Southern Africa (DBSA)** is a key financial institution that supports development projects in the Southern African region. Entrepreneurs and companies involved in infrastructure or development initiatives may explore funding options provided by the DBSA, which often prioritises projects with a positive impact on regional economic growth and sustainability.

The **Small Enterprise Development Agency (SEDA)** is a South African government agency of the Department of Small Business Development, dedicated to promoting entrepreneurship and the development of small businesses. It provides a range of services, including business development support, access to finance, and training programmes.

The **National Empowerment Fund (NEF),** which falls under the Department of Trade, Industry and Competition, is a government agency that aims to support Black economic empowerment in South Africa. It offers financing solutions, equity funding, and business support to Black entrepreneurs and businesses.

The **Industrial Development Corporation (IDC)** is a government-owned development finance institution in South Africa falling under the auspices of the Department of Trade, Industry and Competition. It provides financial and non-financial support to businesses in various sectors, including manufacturing, agricultural processing, and infrastructure.

The **Technology Innovation Agency (TIA)** is a public entity that supports the development and commercialisation of technology and innovation in South Africa and falls under the auspices of the Department of Science and Technology. It provides funding and support for technology-focused startups and entrepreneurs.

Khula Enterprise Finance is a government-backed agency falling under the Department of Trade and Industry that facilitates access to finance for small, micro and medium-sized businesses (SMMEs) in South Africa. It offers various financial products, including guarantees, loans, and equity funding.

The **Land Bank** in South Africa is a state-owned development finance institution that provides financial services specifically geared towards commercial and emerging agriculture, aiming to empower farmers across the country.

Approach the relevant agency for details on the application process.

Supplier and enterprise development loans

In the South African context, Black-owned businesses (and with revenue of less than R50 million, ie small businesses) can explore funding opportunities through supplier and enterprise development loans, which are provided by larger private companies seeking to support Black businesses within their supply chain. These initiatives are designed to empower historically disadvantaged entrepreneurs by providing financial support and fostering growth by way of interest-free or low-interest-rate loans and other business support. If you are operating within an existing supply chain or wish to become part of another larger company's supply chain, you should enquire about such programmes, which often come with specific eligibility criteria and support mechanisms. See *Chapter 50* for more details on the topic of Broad-Based Black Economic Empowerment.

Incubators and accelerators

Numerous incubators and accelerators operate in South Africa, supporting startups and small businesses with mentorship, workspace, and sometimes funding. Examples include 22 on Sloane, The Innovation Hub, Uvu Africa and mLab Southern Africa.

Venture capital and private equity

Businesses with high growth potential often explore partnerships with venture capital (VC) or private equity (PE) firms. These investors inject capital into the business in exchange for equity, making this option particularly relevant for startups aiming for rapid expansion. Entrepreneurs and existing companies must carefully prepare a compelling business case to attract VC or PE interest.

The primary distinction between VC and PE lies in their target businesses. VC investors typically focus on startup enterprises that they perceive as having significant growth potential. Their goal is to nurture these businesses, potentially leading them to go public, or facilitating the sale of their stake at a later stage to other companies like PE.

On the other hand, PE funding is directed towards established businesses with solid balance sheets and the potential for robust returns on investment. The objective here is to enhance the business' performance and secure a profitable exit, whether through a sale, merger with other businesses, or public listing of the company.

In both cases, investors typically seek a shareholding in the company as well as membership on the board. While this aligns with the investors' goal of actively participating in the company's success, it may pose a challenge for current business owners or entrepreneurs who desire full ownership and control. Therefore, companies need to carefully consider what they are willing to relinquish in exchange for VC or PE investment. This decision involves a strategic balance between gaining the financial support needed for growth (and the prestige of being backed and guided by a VC or PE) and maintaining the desired level of ownership and control within the company.

To learn more about the VC and PE industry, you can contact the Southern Africa Venture Capital and Private Equity Association (SAVCA), the African Private Capital Association (AVCA), to name a few.

Crowdfunding and angel investors

The digital era has spawned alternative funding channels such as crowdfunding, where entrepreneurs can present their ideas to a global audience. Additionally, angel investors, high-net-worth individuals seeking investment opportunities, play a crucial role in supporting early-stage businesses. Entrepreneurs should craft compelling business cases and leverage online platforms to access these funding sources.

Crowdfunding platforms support different models of investment. In reward-based crowdfunding, backers receive non-financial incentives such as products or services. In equity crowdfunding, investors contribute funds in exchange for equity shares in the business along with board membership. Debt crowdfunding involves investors lending money to the business, expecting repayment with interest.

Angel investors typically invest their personal funds in startups or early-stage businesses. They may opt for an equity stake, becoming shareholders in the business and board membership. Alternatively, they might choose convertible debt, a form of a loan that can convert into equity under certain conditions, providing flexibility for both the investor and the business.

There are several angel investor networks in South Africa that connect investors with entrepreneurs seeking funding. These networks often provide not just financial support but also valuable mentorship and expertise. Examples include the Angel Investment Network, Johannesburg Angel Investor Network (JoziAngels), DazzleAngels focusing on female angel funding, to name a few. The South Africa Business Angel Network (SABAN) is the non-profit professional association for early-stage investors.

Private loans

Apart from PE, VC, crowdfunding and angel investors, there are other sources of private funding particularly for small business and Black-owned business. You should do careful due diligence on such companies and be comfortable with the loan and related agreements.

Research and development loans

Entrepreneurs and companies who have an innovative idea requiring research and development funding may seek financing and support from universities and other higher education institutions, or government organisations like the Council for Scientific and Industrial Research (CSIR, which is part of the Department of Science and Innovation). These institutions have access to both private and government donor funds and grants. Some of the issues to consider when exploring this alternative include ownership of the final product, confidentiality, and intellectual property protection.

Existing shareholders providing loans and additional equity investments

For non-startup businesses, eg an existing company or a foreign company looking to establish a local subsidiary company, or partners in a partnership, or members of a close corporation, it is possible to seek funding from the existing owners. This can be done by way of shareholder or member loans to the business, or by way of further equity (capital) injections. The use of loans is a form of debt financing; businesses should record such loans in a loan agreement, be at arms-length, and the lenders should receive interest in addition to the capital repayment. The equity funding option would mean the issuing of new shares to the shareholders who would pay for such shares. New investors could also accept shareholding in the business that could dilute existing shareholders' investments. Both loan and equity options would help inject capital into the company to grow the business and would avoid the expensive cost and time of seeking loans from third parties.

Key considerations

- Most lenders will only make loans to companies that have been in business for at least a few years. They will require audited or independently reviewed financial statements so they can establish the going concern, financial stability, and the current and future profitability of the borrower.
- For entrepreneurs and less established companies who do not have such security, seeking loans from third parties may be a challenge unless you have an innovative idea that has potential for growth.
- The process for seeking loans, whether public or private, can be long and arduous. Be patient and resilient.
- Most black-owned businesses will be able to get preferential terms from government agencies, and from enterprise and supplier development initiatives by larger companies for existing or new suppliers that contribute to their supply chain.
- Conduct your own research into the different funding options available in South Africa.
- Do not rush into signing a loan agreement or sell shares in your company without carefully reviewing the relevant agreements and obtaining legal and financial advice if needed.
- Know the payment terms and pay on time. If you run into payment issues, seek a revised payment schedule with your lender timeously.

- A business plan is critical to prepare when applying for loans as it shows the potential lenders details about your company, financial status and requirements, and other business information.
- In all cases where the lender charges interest, and based on the turnover of the borrower, the requirements of the National Credit Act of 2005 (NCA) must be adhered to and not exceed the maximum permissible interest rate. See our summary of the NCA in *Chapter 49*. In addition, depending on the annual turnover of the borrower, the Consumer Protection Act of 2008 may be applicable – see *Chapter 48 for more information*.

Chapter 18: The business plan

A business plan is a written document that should outline the goals, objectives, strategies, market analysis, and financial projections of a business. It should serve as a roadmap for the business owner, providing a comprehensive overview of the company's status and future direction. If you are seeking funding to grow your business, investors and lenders will want to see your business plan so they can better understand your business, your current situation and needs analysis, and your vision of where the company is heading. Entrepreneurs/startups and existing businesses looking to expand their venture can also make use of a business plan.

Below we set out the main components of a business plan.

Executive summary

The executive summary should encapsulate the essence of the business. It should provide a snapshot of the mission, vision, and the fundamental issue the business seeks to address through its product and service offering. Despite its brevity, the executive summary should captivate the reader's attention and convey the unique value proposition of the business.

Business description

This section should provide a detailed overview of the business, including its structure, legal status, and the core products or services offered. It should set the stage for a deeper exploration of the business' identity and its place in the market.

Market analysis

A thorough market analysis is crucial for understanding the business environment, identifying opportunities, and assessing potential challenges. Entrepreneurs should understand industry trends, customer behaviour, and competitor landscapes. This section should demonstrate a nuanced understanding of the market dynamics.

Organisation and management

The people behind the business are as paramount as the business itself. This section should introduce the key players in the business including shareholders, directors, and management, detailing their roles, responsibilities, and relevant qualifications. It must provide insight into the team's capacity to successfully drive the business forward.

Products and services

The heart of any business lies in its offerings. Entrepreneurs should use this section to delve into the details of their products or services. This includes features, benefits, and the unique selling proposition that sets the business apart in the market.

Marketing and sales strategy

A well-thought-out marketing and sales strategy is essential for attracting and retaining customers. Entrepreneurs should outline their approach to reaching their target audience, pricing strategies, and promotional activities. This section should demonstrate a clear understanding of the competitive landscape and the methods for capturing market share.

Financial projections

One of the most critical sections, financial projections should provide a roadmap for the business' financial trajectory. This includes income statements, balance sheets, and cash flow projections. We will go into more detail on each of these in the chapter on financial statements. Historical data, such as financial statements, should be used by the business to substantiate assumptions. Realism is key; overly optimistic projections may undermine the credibility of the business plan and astute lenders will quickly lose interest.

Funding request

For businesses seeking funding, this section needs to clearly articulate the financial needs of the business. It must outline the amount of funding required, the specific purpose of the funds, and the anticipated return on investment for potential investors. Entrepreneurs should be transparent and realistic in their funding requests, aligning them with the financial requirements of their business plans.

Implementation plan

Your implementation plan must outline the action steps and timelines to execute the business strategies and achieve the defined goals after receiving the funds. For example, if the purpose of the funding is to market your products, then explain how you will do so, on which platforms and how much of your funds will you use for each platform, and over what period. If your funding request is for research and development, then how will you spend it and over what period.

Appendix

The appendices should serve as a repository for supplementary information that supports the content of the business plan. This may include resumes of key team members, detailed market research data, legal documents, or any other pertinent information. While not a primary focus, the appendix should enhance the completeness and credibility of the business plan.

Summary

The correlation of financial planning and access to funding is pivotal for the success of any business. A thorough understanding of the intricacies of financial planning provides entrepreneurs and businesspersons looking to grow their venture with the foresight to navigate challenges and capitalise on opportunities. Simultaneously, tapping into the diverse array of funding options requires a strategic approach, clear communication, and a compelling business case. The business plan, as a dynamic blueprint, not only attracts potential investors but also serves as a guiding force, ensuring that the business remains on a trajectory toward sustainable growth. Entrepreneurs who master these facets enhance their resilience and adaptability, positioning themselves for success in the dynamic South African business landscape. Do not think of the business plan as static – as your business and business needs evolve, continuously tweak the plan so it reflects up-to-date information.

Spend time making your plan look like an engaging document with good and accurate visual information. Own the business plan and make it personal, because no one knows your business better than you.

Chapter 19: Relevance of the Public Interest Score

All companies must accurately prepare annual financial statements reflecting their financial position, including assets, liabilities, income, and expenses. The concept of the 'public interest score' determines whether financial statements require an audit, independent review, or neither for smaller businesses. Under specific circumstances, small companies may use simplified financial statements (prepared by appropriately qualified persons) called management accounts instead of full financial statements. This usually requires approval from relevant parties and involves presenting less detailed financial information primarily for internal use. For purposes of this chapter, we discuss the requirements related to financial statements.

Public companies and SOCs always need an independent audit of their annual financial statements while the requirement for private companies depends on their public interest score. If a private company requires an independent review, it does not need an audit, and vice versa. However, companies with internal skills can prepare their own statements by appropriately qualified persons, but depending on their public interest score they may need to be audited or reviewed (ie there is a difference between the preparation of the financial statements verses whether it needs to be audited or independently reviewed).

Even if a company's public interest score is below the audit threshold, complying with relevant audit requirements is mandatory if the MoI mandates an audit. Companies can choose to audit their financial statements regardless of the score or MoI requirements.

The public interest score also determines the need for a Social and Ethics Committee in private companies.

Difference between an independent review and an audit

An independent review of financial statements is conducted by an independent registered accountant according to prescribed accounting standards. It provides limited assurance and is meant to simplify the review process and reduce costs for small businesses. The review involves reviewing account balances, limited sampling, and cross-checking of data. Management must provide accurate records and cooperate with the review. The reviewer must be independent, registered with a professional body, and not be involved in the company's day-to-day affairs.

On the other hand, **an audit** is the most rigorous review process performed by a registered external auditor. It is mandatory for public companies, SOCs, and companies with a higher social impact or risk, determined by the public interest score. The audit involves extensive examination of source data, accounting policies, rigorous sampling, access to records, and meetings with directors and management. It provides reasonable assurance that the financial statements are free from material misrepresentations.

The benefits of an audit include enhanced credibility for investors, improved governance through identification of weaknesses in internal controls and risk management, and reduction of financial risk by detecting fraud or irregularities.

Accounting standards

All financial statements must comply with certain accounting standards (except in a few instances for owner-managed private companies) such as International Financial Reporting Standards (IFRS), IFRS for Small to Medium Enterprises (IFRS for SMEs) or South African GAAP (Generally Accepted Accounting Standards). Listed companies may also have to comply with other accounting standards (eg US-listed entities must comply with US GAAP).

How to determine if a private company needs to have its financial statements independently reviewed or audited

Assuming the MoI of a private company does not require an audit, such company will need to determine if an independent review will suffice or an audit. This determination is based on the number of points the company scores in terms of the public interest score.

Public interest score

The public interest score is a requirement defined by the Companies Act and measures a company's social footprint and potential impact on the public. If a company's score exceeds a certain threshold, it must have either an independent audit or independent review of its financial statements, although in some cases neither may be required. Companies need to calculate their public interest score annually. The score is determined based on the average number of employees, liability to third parties, turnover, and the beneficial interests of individuals in the company's securities.

For private companies, the consequences of the score are as follows:
- A score of 350 or higher necessitates an audit of the financial statements.
- A score between 100 and 349 would require an audit if the financial statements were prepared internally. However, if an independent registered accountant prepared the statements, an audit would not be required.
- A score below 100 means that a private company does not have to have its financial statements audited unless it chooses to do so or its MoI requires it.

It is important to note that there is an exception for owner-managed companies with a public interest score below 100, where every shareholder participates in managing the business. They are exempt from any audit or independent review requirement.

However, there are additional circumstances where an audit is still required for a private company, even if their public interest score falls between 100 and 349 or is below 100 in the case of an owner-managed business. These circumstances include having assets exceeding R5 million and turnover exceeding R20 million in the previous year or holding assets in a fiduciary capacity for unrelated third parties with a value exceeding R5 million during the year.

As one can see, the determination of whether an independent review or an audit (or neither) is required for a private company is not straightforward as it is dependent on the annual public interest score and other circumstances. To try and summarise the requirements for private companies see the following table:

Public interest score of the private company	Audit required	Independent review required	What accounting standards apply?
Above 350	Yes	Not applicable	IFRS or IFRS for SMEs
100 to 349	Yes (IF the financial statements were *internally* prepared)	Yes (IF the financial statements were prepared by an independent registered accountant, then it qualifies as an independent review)	IFRS, IFRS for SMEs or SA GAAP
1 to 99 where financial statements are *independently* compiled	No	Yes (except for owner-managed companies – see below)	IFRS, IFRS for SMEs or SA GAAP
1 to 99 where financial statements are *internally* compiled AND the company is owner-managed	No	No	Reporting standards as determined by the company but must be complete and accurate

Public interest score of the private company	Audit required	Independent review required	What accounting standards apply?
1 to 99 for owner-managed business but assets exceed R5 million, and turnover exceeds R20 million	Yes	No	IFRS or IFRS for SMEs
1 to 99 for owner-managed business but company holds assets in fiduciary capacity for third parties of over R5 million	Yes	No	IFRS or IFRS for SMEs

The public interest score is calculated based on the previous financial year-end, which determines the regulatory requirements for the upcoming financial year. Each company should calculate and document its public interest score, typically handled by the company secretary with input from finance and human resources and approved by directors. Directors of small or sole-owned businesses can perform the calculation themselves.

The score can change annually, affecting compliance requirements. For example, a private company with a score of 80 may not need an audit or review in year 1. If the score increases to 380 the following year, an audit is required. If it decreases to 250, an audit or independent review may still be necessary for the subsequent year. Regular score calculation ensures ongoing compliance with the law.

If unsure, it is recommended to seek advice from a registered accountant or company secretarial service provider. Understanding the public interest score helps determine whether financial statements require auditing or reviewing; this will be explored further in the next chapter.

Chapter 20: Annual financial statements

In this chapter, we discuss the requirements for annual financial statements (AFS) and for auditing or independent review of the AFS. This only applies to companies in terms of the Companies Act. Sole proprietors are not required to produce AFS (except if they are a financial service provider regulated by the Financial Sector Conduct Authority, the FSCA). However, sole proprietors may choose to produce management accounts as these may be required by their customers as part of the customer's due diligence requirements or by financial institutions if the sole proprietor is seeking funding.

In the previous chapter, we discussed how to calculate the public interest score to determine if a private company needs an audit, an independent review, or neither.

Annual financial statements

AFS gives a comprehensive overview of a company's financial performance and position at the end of its financial year. AFS is important for assessing the company's health and viability. For audited or independently reviewed companies, the AFS typically includes:

- **Directors' report.** Summarises the company's operations, financial performance, and prospects, including a going concern statement.
- **Company secretary's confirmation.** Confirms that all statutory filings have been made, such as the annual return.
- **Auditor's or reviewer's report.** Provides an independent assessment of the financial statements' reliability.
- **Income statement.** Presents revenues, expenses, and net profit or loss.
- **Balance sheet.** Shows assets, liabilities, and equity.
- **Cash flow statement.** Tracks cash inflows and outflows.
- **Notes to the financial statements.** Offers further explanations and details.

The company must prepare the AFS within six months of the financial year-end, signed by directors or an authorised director, and presented at the AGM if applicable. AFS compliance is essential under the Companies Act, and provides transparency to shareholders, stakeholders, lenders, and others for evaluating the company's financial status and making informed decisions.

Audited financial statements

Companies must file audited AFS with the CIPC along with their annual returns in certain circumstances. This requirement applies to the following entities:

- Public companies.
- SOCs.
- Private companies with a MoI stipulating that audited financial statements are needed.
- Private companies with a public interest score of 350 or higher, or a public interest score between 100 and 349 with internally prepared financial statements.
- Private companies holding assets exceeding R5 million and a turnover surpassing R20 million, even if their public interest score is below 100.
- Companies managing assets exceeding R5 million in a fiduciary capacity for third parties during the financial year, even if their public interest score is below 100.
- Companies choosing to have their financial statements audited based on a shareholder or board resolution, irrespective of the MoI requirements.

The audited financial statements should provide additional details on:

- Remuneration, pensions, securities/shares, and other benefits provided to directors and key personnel holding prescribed offices, along with contract details.
- Loans or securities granted to directors and officers.
- Other information required by law or relevant regulatory bodies.

Public companies, being listed entities, also need to include a sustainability report, information on compliance with the King Code on Corporate Governance, and any other disclosures mandated by the stock exchange.

The audited financial statements must be prepared by registered accountants or can be prepared internally if the company has the necessary ability and then audited by an independent auditing firm.

For submission to the CIPC, companies should provide the audited financial statements in the designated XBRL format. Seeking assistance from registered accountants, auditors, or company secretarial support is advisable to ensure proper filing.

Companies not required to submit audited financial statements can decide whether to include their AFS with their annual return to the CIPC. Note that under specific circumstances, small companies may use simplified financial statements called management accounts instead of full audited financials. This usually requires approval from relevant parties and involves presenting less detailed financial information primarily for internal use. Such management accounts must still be prepared by appropriately qualified persons. Speak to your accounting advisors for clarification on any queries.

Importance of financial literacy: Understanding financial statements

Financial literacy is indispensable for business success as it enables you to understand essential financial concepts, assess your company's health, determine profitability, and make informed decisions. While you do not need to become an expert, continuously learning about financial concepts is important. You can enhance your financial literacy through online or in-person courses offered by platforms like Udemy, SkillShare, and universities, or for free on YouTube. Understanding your company's finances and key metrics is vital for building a thriving business. We strongly recommend a basic understanding of financial statements as part of a constantly learning mindset – it is critical to the success of your business that you are familiar with financial statements, and in particular, the balance sheet, income statement and cash flow statements.

Retention period of records

Under the Companies Act, the retention period for financial statements, and any supporting documentation (such as records that formed part of any audit or independent review) must be retained for a period of seven years.

We recommend that you seek legal advice for specific queries related to your record-keeping and retention periods. See also *Chapter 59* on record-keeping and specifically the section on *Record retention periods*.

Chapter 21: Business bank account

Companies must open a business account in the name of the company. On registering the company with CIPC, you have the option to open the bank account via the BizPortal but you do not have to do it through that platform. Sole proprietors and partnerships do not need to create a separate bank account but depending on the complexity of the business, and to keep things separate between your personal and business transactions, it is advisable to open a separate bank account.

South Africa is fortunate to have a sophisticated and competitive banking industry and there are many options available to you when considering who to bank with and the type of business account to create.

Opening a bank account for companies, sole proprietors, and partnerships in South Africa involves specific documentation and processes. While the requirements may vary slightly between banks, here are the general requirements for each type of business entity.

Companies

Documentation

- Completed bank application form.
- Certified copies of the company's registration document (eg Certificate of Incorporation, MoI).
- Copies of identity documents or passports of directors and signatories.
- Proof of business address (utility bill or lease agreement).
- Tax clearance certificate.
- Company resolution authorising the opening of the account and specifying authorised signatories.
- Business profile and business plan may be required by the bank.
- Financial statement or audited financial statements, if applicable. For startup businesses such statements will not yet be available so banks may have further enquiries and requirements.
- Anticipated transaction volumes and types of transactions.

Sole proprietors

Documentation

- Certified copy of the owner's identity document or passport.
- Proof of residence (utility bill or lease agreement).
- Business registration certificate (if applicable).
- Tax clearance certificate.
- Business profile and business plan may be required by the bank.

- Information about the nature of the business and anticipated transaction volumes.
- Personal financial statements of the owner.

Partnerships

Documentation

- Certified copies of the partnership agreement.
- Copies of identity documents or passports of partners.
- Proof of business address (utility bill or lease agreement).
- Tax clearance certificate.
- Business profile and business plan may be required by the bank.
- Information about the nature of the business and anticipated transaction volumes.
- Financial statements of each partner.

General guidance

- Banks may require a minimum deposit and/or for a minimum amount to be maintained.
- If you are seeking a revolving credit facility and/or bank loans, additional documentation and due diligence will be required by the bank together with security for such facilities (such as owners standing as surety or pledging of assets).
- It is advisable for the account signatories or representatives to visit the bank in person to initiate the account-opening process.
- Complete all documentation ahead of time if possible and take all relevant documentation.
- Understand the bank account features and fee structure.
- Choose the right bank by considering the service offering, fees, accessibility of the bank, and any pre-existing banking relationship you have or assigned account manager before deciding,
- Most banks provide competitive offerings for small and startup businesses and some offer accounts on a pay-as-you-use (PAYU) basis (which includes low monthly fees, pay only for what you use, no minimum deposits, improved cash flow management and monitoring, and easy to open functionality).
- We recommend that businesses facing pending tax liabilities, such as VAT and provisional tax, consider opening a separate savings account. This allows for the segregation of funds owed to SARS, ensuring they are readily available for payment when due, and prevents mixing business income with amounts owed to the revenue authority.

The main banks you can consider are:
- ABSA
- African Bank
- Bank Zero

- Bidvest Bank
- Capitec
- FNB
- Investec
- Mercantile Bank
- Nedbank
- Sasfin
- Standard Bank
- Tyme Bank.

Note that the banking industry is a regulated industry; banks will conduct thorough due diligence on applicants, credit and background checks, and other checks as part of their 'know your client' requirements.

TAXATION

"Taxation is the price we pay for a civilized society."
~ Oliver Wendell Holmes Jr.

"The tax collector is the only person in the world who can take half your earnings, and thank you for the privilege."
~ Finley Peter Dunne

Businesses in South Africa are subject to various tax requirements that impact their financial obligations and compliance. In the following chapters, we will explore the major tax requirements that businesses must consider, helping you understand the key tax types and their implications. The tax and tax collection methods we will discuss are:

- Corporate income tax.
- Personal income tax.
- Provisional tax.
- Value-Added Tax (VAT).
- Pay As You Earn (PAYE).
- Unemployment Insurance Fund (UIF).
- Skills Development Levy (SDL).
- Customs code for import and export.
- Customs duties.
- Capital Gains Tax (CGT).
- Dividends tax.
- Donations tax.
- Securities transfer tax.
- Small Business Corporations tax.
- Other taxes.

Chapter 22: Tax requirements - introduction

The South African Revenue Service (SARS), a department of the Ministry of Finance, is responsible for the administration of tax laws in South Africa.

The SARS online login is at *https://secure.sarse-filing.co.za/app/login*. Its contact number is 0800 00 7277.

If not already registered, you can register from the above link.

For owner-managed companies, note that your personal income tax registration profile and your company profile are separate, but you can still access them from the same home page – ensure you select the correct profile to access your company profile. Individual taxpayers including sole proprietors and partners in a partnership will only have a personal income tax profile.

If you appoint external tax advisors, then they will have access to your company tax profile and be registered with SARS as your tax agent. Note this is different from being a public officer for tax purposes – see the section on *Public Officer* in *Chapter 16*. It merely means the tax advisor has access to your profile, can do filings on your behalf, and is authorised to represent you in any filings and communications with SARS. You should always remain familiar with what the tax advisors are doing on your behalf.

The tax season for *individuals* (including sole proprietors and partners in a partnership) commences on 1 March of each year and ends on the last day of February of the following year. The tax season for *companies* depends on their financial period as determined when they register their company and select their financial year-end. Put differently, a company's financial period is essentially its tax season. For example, if when registering the company, an October year-end is selected, the financial period will run from 1 November of each year to 31 October of the following year. The financial year-end is therefore, in this example, 31 October of each year. Tax filings for companies depend on its financial period. The financial period may be known in some countries as the fiscal period, accounting year, financial reporting period, tax year or similar terms. Although individuals have no flexibility to determine their tax season, companies do when they register their companies. They may also amend their financial period by making the necessary filings with CIPC.

Unless otherwise stated, all taxes and tax rules are governed by the Income Tax Act of 1962, the Tax Administration Act of 2011 and/or related regulations and schedules.

Tax percentages, income tax tables, rebates, thresholds, deadlines, timelines and other details are subject to change, sometimes annually. We have provided the information in the following chapters for the 2024 tax year and for illustrative purposes. It is important that you check for any changes.

Taxation can be very complicated. If you are not familiar with tax issues, it is a good idea to hire experts in tax and accounting to guide you. While it is not mandatory to have a tax expert represent you in interactions with SARS, we suggest you consider it especially if you are not a tax expert yourself or are not confident in handling tax matters. Tax and accounting advisors will not only understand the tax laws and processes and guide you through the requirements, but they will be able to free up your time to concentrate on your business, file the relevant tax returns, advise you on how to save on tax in a compliant manner, provide strategic business and financial planning, help mitigate against penalties and fines for incorrect or late filings and keep your business tax healthy. Although such advisors will come at a cost, we believe it is a saving overall and a worthwhile investment – plus you can claim such cost as a business expense. Speak to peers about reputable advisors or conduct online research – ensure you verify the credentials and registration with tax and industry bodies of such tax and accounting advisors. The following chapters nevertheless provide you with a general understanding of what each tax involves.

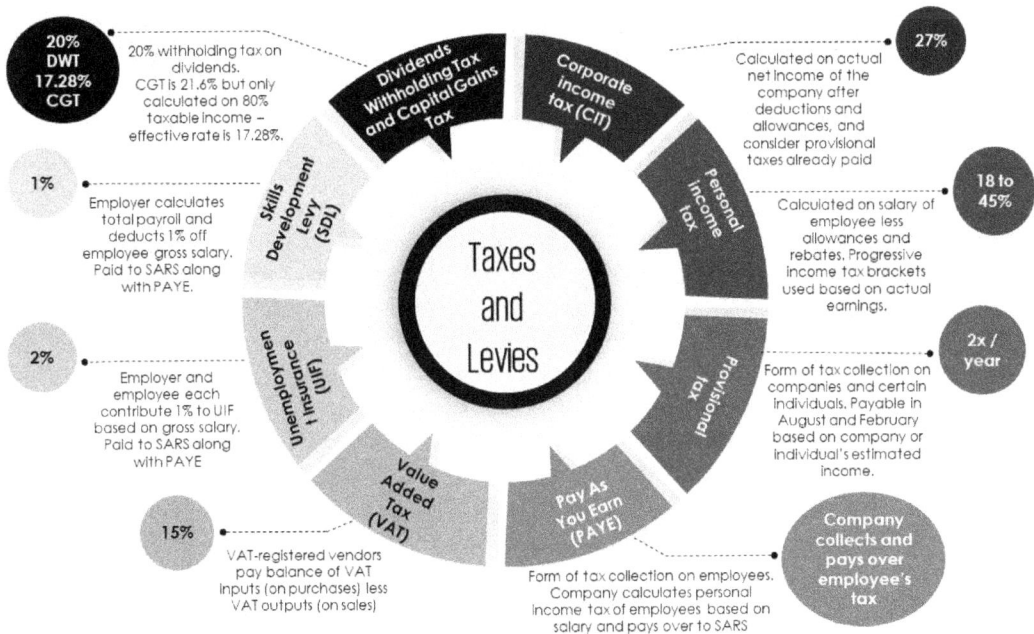

20% DWT 17.28% CGT — 20% withholding tax on dividends. CGT is 21.6% but only calculated on 80% taxable income – effective rate is 17.28%.

1% — Employer calculates total payroll and deducts 1% off employee gross salary. Paid to SARS along with PAYE.

2% — Employer and employee each contribute 1% to UIF based on gross salary. Paid to SARS along with PAYE

15% — VAT-registered vendors pay balance of VAT inputs (on purchases) less VAT outputs (on sales)

Skills Development Levy (SDL)

Unemployment Insurance (UIF)

Value Added Tax (VAT)

Dividends Withholding Tax and Capital Gains Tax

Corporate income tax (CIT)

Personal income tax

Provisional tax

Pay As You Earn (PAYE)

Taxes and Levies

27% — Calculated on actual net income of the company after deductions and allowances, and consider provisional taxes already paid

18 to 45% — Calculated on salary of employee less allowances and rebates. Progressive income tax brackets used based on actual earnings.

2x / year — Form of tax collection on companies and certain individuals. Payable in August and February based on company or individual's estimated income.

Company collects and pays over employee's tax — Form of tax collection on employees. Company calculates personal income tax of employees based on salary and pays over to SARS

Chapter 23: Income tax

In this chapter, we will discuss both corporate income tax and personal income tax, which is administered by SARS. The tax year in South Africa runs from 1 March to the last day of February of the following year. This period is relevant to all individuals (including individual provisional taxpayers) and companies with a February financial year-end. For companies with a financial year-end other than February, the tax season aligns with the respective financial period. For instance, if a company has a September year-end, its tax season for 2024 would run from 1 October 2023 to 30 September 2024.

Corporate income tax

The corporate income tax rate for companies is 27% (previously 28%) except for Small Business Corporations and companies eligible for turnover tax (see *Chapter 29*). When registering a company with CIPC, a company income tax number is automatically assigned and recorded with SARS for tax purposes. No separate registration for corporate income tax is required. The Income Tax Act and regulations govern both corporate and personal income tax.

A company's income tax (CIT) liability is based on its net income, also known as taxable income. To arrive at this figure, businesses are allowed to deduct certain expenses from their gross income. These allowable deductions include a wide range of operational costs, including the cost of goods sold (CoGS), employee salaries, rent, utilities, and depreciation (which reflects the gradual wear and tear of equipment and property, not the initial purchase price). In addition, capital losses, interest on loans (with limitations), donations to approved charities, and expenses incurred for research and development, or marketing are generally deductible, if they are considered ordinary and necessary for the business. It is important to remember that specific rules and limitations might apply to certain deductions. Consulting a tax and accounting advisor is always recommended to ensure compliance with the latest regulations and maximise allowable deductions.

To calculate the corporate income tax, subtract the total allowable expenses from the gross profit, and apply the corporate tax rate (currently 27%). For example, if your company has a gross income of R2.5 million and allowable expenses of R1.8 million, resulting in a net income of R700 000, the corporate income tax payable would be R189 000 (R700 000 x 27%). The tax liability, however, is not payable in one lump sum to SARS but rather, due to the provisional tax system, is paid in two tranches (in some cases with an optional third payment) – we discuss this in more detail in *Chapter 24*.

Income tax returns for companies

All companies must submit their annual income tax returns (IT14 form) to SARS within 12 months of the company's financial year-end. For instance, if a company's financial year ends on 30 September, it must file the IT14 form for the 2024 tax year no later than 30 September 2025.

A company selects its financial year-end when registering with CIPC. If the company wishes to change its financial year-end, it can do so by completing the CoR 25 form, accompanied by a board resolution confirming the change request and payment of the relevant fee, and submit the documents to CIPC.

The company should file its income tax return using the SARS eFiling system. It should include details of the company's income, expenses, deductions, and credits, along with supporting documentation such as financial statements and audit reports, if applicable. The company should also consider the provisional tax amounts already paid during the year, as explained in *Chapter 24*. If the income tax return reveals that the company underpaid provisional tax compared to its actual income, it will have to pay additional taxes, possibly incurring penalties and interest. On the other hand, if the company overpaid provisional taxes, SARS would refund the amount due to the company.

It is worth noting that income tax returns do not need to be filed with CIPC, only with SARS.

Personal income tax

This book discusses personal income tax because many small businesses are owner-managed, with directors, shareholders, sole proprietors, and partnership partners drawing a salary from the business. Understanding the relationship between corporate income tax and personal income tax is essential to avoid complications and understand how running the business affects you personally, and vice versa. It is important to maintain a clear separation between the company's interests and your personal affairs. Individual income tax returns (IT12 forms) are filed within a specified period after the tax year has ended – for non-provisional taxpayers, the filing is generally done in October after the end of the tax season; for provisional taxpayers, it is filed in January of the following year.

South Africa has a progressive rate of personal income tax, meaning that you pay an increasing amount of tax the more income you make (also referred to as 'bracket creep' based on the personal income tax brackets as per the table below). The income tax return for individuals, including sole proprietors and partners in a partnership, is referred to as an IT12 form that gets submitted to SARS.

For the 2024 tax year (ie covering the period 1 March 2023 to 29 February 2024), personal income tax is calculated as follows:

Individuals must pay tax if they earn more than:
- R95 750 if 65 years or younger.
- R148 217 if older than 65 but younger than 75.
- R165 689 if aged 75 and older.

The current applicable tax table for personal income tax for the 2024 tax year (being 1 March 2023 to 29 February 2024) is as follows:

Taxable income in Rands	Tax rate in Rands calculated on taxable income
1 to 237 000	18%
237 101 to 370 500	42 678 + 26% of taxable income above 237 100
370 501 to 512 800	77 362 + 31% of taxable income above 370 500
512 801 to 673 000	121 475 + 36% of taxable income above 512 800
673 001 to 857 900	179 147 + 39% of taxable income above 673 000
857 901 – 1 817 000	251 258 + 41% of taxable income above 857 900
1 817 001 and above	644 489 + 45% of taxable income above 1 817 900

Note: There are no changes to the income tax table for the 2025 tax year (1 March 2024 to 28 February 2025). During the annual budget speech by the Minister of Finance to Parliament, adjustments in the tax tables, and other related tax matters, is communicated.

For example, if an owner-managed company pays its director a salary of R600 000 then that director's personal income tax calculation will be: R121 475 + {(R600 000 - R512 800) x 36%} = R31 392 + R121 475 = R152 867. It is the company's responsibility to pay this tax directly to SARS via the PAYE system (see *Chapter 26*). *Note: This example does not consider rebates, UIF and other deductions and is purely for illustrative purposes.*

The Income Tax Act allows for various allowances, deductions and rebates, which will reduce an individual's personal income tax:
- **Travel allowances** being deductions for travel expenses incurred in the course of employment.
- **Medical scheme contributions and medical expenses** paid on behalf of oneself, the spouse, and dependent children.
- **Retirement contributions** (including contributions to a retirement annuity, pension fund and/or provident fund) of the greater of 27.5% of the person's taxable income for the year or R350 000 per annum. Note that you can always make contributions to your retirement savings above these thresholds, but they will not be tax deductible in that tax year; the excess contributions can, however, be rolled over to the following tax years.

- **Income tax rebate** is a reduction in your payable tax amount granted according to specific criteria (eg age) to provide some financial relief. For the 2024 tax year, individuals can benefit from three main income tax rebates. (1) The primary rebate, amounting to R17 235, applies to all natural persons. (2) Taxpayers aged 65 and over are eligible for a secondary rebate of R9 444. (3) Those aged 75 and over can claim a tertiary rebate of R3 145. It is worth noting that individuals who reach 75 years old or older qualify for all three rebates.

All allowances, deductions and rebates must (unless otherwise defined under the tax laws) be actual costs and supported by documentation that will need to be filed with the tax returns.

Startups and owner-managed businesses must understand the implications of both corporate income tax and personal income tax when determining their salary. It is crucial to strike a balance between maintaining business profitability and ensuring a reasonable salary that reflects the effort put into managing the business. Managing these factors effectively is important for the financial success of the business, and to ensure fair compensation for the work involved.

You should seek financial advice if you have any queries or appoint accountants and tax advisors to structure your affairs, so you remain compliant with your tax obligations.

Tax efficiency: Sole proprietor vs forming a company

Entrepreneurs and small businesses will need to carefully consider whether to conduct their business in their own name or by forming a company. What will be the taxable income from conducting their business is a key tax consideration. In short, if the individual's business places them in a lower tax bracket, then it is more tax efficient not to form a company and obtain the tax efficiency from the taxable tables and rebates applicable to individual taxpayers. In contrast, if the individual falls into a higher tax bracket, then it will make sense to form a company as this will be more tax efficient. Note that tax efficiency is only one consideration when deciding whether to conduct your business as a sole proprietor or to form a company – other considerations like any risk to your personal assets, for example, need to be factored into your decision. You should speak to your financial or tax advisor to decide what best suits your needs.

Chapter 24: Provisional tax

Provisional tax is not a separate type of tax but rather a mechanism for the collection of income from companies and certain individual taxpayers. Its purpose is to divide the tax payments into periods instead of requiring a single large payment at the end of the tax year. This approach is designed to be more manageable for taxpayers, avoiding the burden of paying a significant amount at once. The key characteristic of provisional tax, compared to income tax, is that it is based on the business estimating its taxable income and then paying the relevant amounts to SARS when it falls due. When the business files its income tax returns (IT12 form for individuals and IT14 form for companies), the actual income will get reported to SARS. Should the estimations be reasonably accurate, this will avoid SARS levying penalties and interest for underestimation of taxable income.

Requirements for provisional tax

Companies are automatically regarded and registered with SARS eFiling for provisional tax (unless exempt from provisional tax, for example under SBC tax as discussed in *Chapter 29*), while individuals are regarded as provisional taxpayers under certain circumstances.

The following should be considered by individuals, including sole proprietors and partners in a partnership, when assessing if they are required to be registered for provisional tax:

- Any income derived from an employer who is not registered for PAYE and does not withhold PAYE to pay it over to SARS. See *Chapter 26* for more details.
- Any foreign income or foreign employment where you do not qualify for the R1.25 million exemption. Alternatively, any foreign income or foreign employment that exceeds such amount in a particular year of assessment.
- You trade as a sole proprietor, independent contractor, or freelancer.
- You earn rental or investment income. Note that for the 2024 tax year, the first R23 800 for individuals under 65 years of age, and R34 500 over the age of 65, are exempt from tax.
- If you are a director of a company or member of a CC and derive remuneration from such a position, then speak to your accounting or tax advisors for clarification about your specific circumstances.
- Should you be employed by multiple employers who provide IRP5s. Note that the accumulation of the various salaries can push you into higher personal income tax brackets.
- SARS informs you that you are a provisional taxpayer. If you believe this to be an error, clarify this with SARS timeously.
- Partners in a partnership must consider their own individual circumstances by considering any of the above qualifying criteria for provisional tax registration.

The requirement to register and pay provisional tax for individuals (including sole proprietors and partners in a partnership) depends on meeting the applicable tax threshold. For the 2024 tax year, the threshold is R95 750 for individuals under 65 years of age. However, if the combined income from interest, dividends, foreign dividends, rental income, and other sources is less than R30 000, there is no requirement to register for provisional tax. It is the responsibility of individual taxpayers to assess annually whether they are provisional taxpayers or not, and to take appropriate action. In case SARS accidentally deregisters a provisional taxpayer, the taxpayer must rectify the situation.

To register for provisional tax (for individual taxpayers), log in to the SARS eFiling system and follow the relevant instructions under *Home – User – Tax Types – Provisional Tax (IRP6)*. Provisional tax filings (IRP6 forms) can be completed on the SARS eFiling system by following the instructions under *Returns – Provisional Tax*. The filing process involves completing and submitting the relevant IRP6 forms for the corresponding period. Payments can be made through SARS eFiling or at any bank by depositing the funds into the relevant SARS account and using the appropriate reference number for proper allocation. Ensure you make the tax payments timeously to avoid the levying of penalties and interest.

It is worth remembering that the tax season for individuals, and companies with a financial year-end in February, runs from 1 March of one year to 28 February of the following year (or 29 February in a leap year). All non-provisional individual taxpayers file tax returns (IT12 forms) in accordance with the tax seasons, with tax filings due in about October of each year. Individual provisional taxpayers will need to submit their annual provisional tax filings (IT12 forms, based on estimated income) generally in January of the following year, after the end of the tax year. Therefore, if an individual has a salaried income where an IRP5 form is issued, as well as other non-salaried income which would require the taxpayer to register as a provisional taxpayer, such individual will have to submit income tax returns as a non-provisional taxpayer in October, and annual provisional tax returns (based on estimates) being in January, 11 months after the end of the relevant tax season. This is particularly important for sole proprietors, partners in a partnership and owner-managed companies (and others) who fall into both categories (non-provisional and provisional) to comply with the relevant requirements and timelines.

Companies that have a financial year ending in February are required to submit their tax returns (IT14 form) within 12 months after the conclusion of their financial year, which means by the end of February in the year following the financial year-end. For companies with a financial year-end other than February, the deadlines for provisional tax (IRP6 forms) and income tax returns (IT14 form) are determined in accordance with the companies' respective financial year-end.

First and second provisional periods

Before we explain how to calculate provisional tax, it is important to understand the different provisional tax periods. Companies and affected individual taxpayers are required to submit provisional tax returns (IRP6 forms) and make payments in two instalments known as the first period of assessment and the second period of assessment.

For individuals and companies with a February financial year-end:
- The first provisional tax assessment and payment is due by the last business day of August (six months into the tax year).
- The second provisional assessment and payment is due by the last business day of the following February (the end of the tax season).
- For example, for the 2024 tax year (which covers the period 1 March 2023 to 29 February 2024), the first provisional period of assessment and payment would have been 31 August 2023 (the last business day of August 2023) while the second provisional period of assessment and payment would have been 29 February 2024 (being the last business day of February 2024).

In the case of companies with a financial year-end other than February:
- The first provisional assessment and payment is due six months into their financial year (on the last business day of that period).
- The second provisional assessment is due on the last business day at the end of their financial year-end.
- For example, consider a company with a financial year ending September 2024 (ie the financial year of the company commences on 1 October 2023 and ends on 30 September 2024). The first provisional period of assessment and payment for this company would be due no later than 29 March 2024, being the last business of March 2024 (ie 6 months after its financial year commences), and the second provisional period of assessment and payment would be due on 30 September 2024, being the last business day in September 2024.

Third provisional period

There is an optional third provisional tax payment, often referred to as a *top-up payment*. The purpose of this optional payment is to prevent penalties and interest imposed by SARS for underestimation of tax liabilities during the first and second provisional periods of assessment.

For individuals and companies with a financial year-end in February:
- The optional third provisional tax payment is due on the last business day of September, which is seven months after the end of the tax year.
- In the 2024 tax year example above, for individual provisional taxpayers and companies with a year-end of February 2024, the third optional provisional tax payment would, therefore, be due and payable to SARS no later than 30 September 2024.
- For individual provisional taxpayers, their annual income tax return (IT12 form) would be due no later than a date set by SARS for January of the year following the end of the tax year. For the 2024 tax year, individual provisional annual returns (IT12 form) are due on 23 January 2025 (in contrast, non-provisional individual taxpayers must submit their annual income tax return in October following the end of the tax year – in our example, it would be October 2024 for such non-provisional taxpayers).

- For companies with a February financial period, their tax returns (IT14 form) would be due no later than 28 February 2025 for the 2024 tax period.

For companies with a financial year-end other than February:
- The optional third provisional tax payment must be submitted within six months after the end of the year of assessment.
- For example, consider a company with a financial year ending on 30 September 2024. The optional third provisional payment for this company would need to be completed by the last business day of March 2025, being 31 March 2025. In this case, the income tax return to SARS (IT14 form) would be due by no later than 30 September 2025 (12 months after the company's financial year-end).

By making the optional third provisional tax payment, individuals and companies can rectify underestimations discovered after the first and second payments. This voluntary payment helps adjust the tax liability if the initial estimates were lower than the actual amounts owed and to avoid penalties and interest before SARS makes its assessment. In an ideal scenario, accurate estimations during the first and second provisional tax payments would eliminate the need for the third voluntary payment.

Summary of provisional tax and annual income tax periods

This table summarises the periods of assessment for provisional and income tax:

Periods of provisional and income tax	Due date (Individuals & February year-end companies)	Due date (Companies with non-February year-end)	Example of company with September 2024 financial year-end (1 Oct 2023 to 30 Sept 2024)
First period of assessment and payment (IRP6 form)	Last business day of August (within the tax year).	Six months after company financial year-end. Last business day for the period end.	29 March 2024. Last business day for the period.
Second period of assessment and payment (IRP6 form)	Last business day of February (within the tax year – end of the tax year).	Last business day of the company's financial year-end. Last business day for the period end.	30 September 2024. Last business day for the period.
Third (optional) payment (IRP 6 form)	Last business day of Sept (following year – seven months after the end of the tax year).	Within six months of the company's financial year-end. Last business day for the period end.	31 March 2025. Last business day for the period.

Periods of provisional and income tax	Due date (Individuals & February year-end companies)	Due date (Companies with non-February year-end)	Example of company with September 2024 financial year-end (1 Oct 2023 to 30 Sept 2024)
Income tax annual returns	For individual non-provisional taxpayers – generally October. For example, the 2024 tax year would be from 1 March 2023 to 29 February 2024. The income tax returns for individuals would be due generally in October 2024. IT12 form.	12 months after the company's financial year-end.	30 September 2025. 12 months after financial year-end.
	For individual provisional taxpayers – generally January of the following year (11 months after the end of relevant tax season). IT12 form.		
	For companies – 12 months after the end of the company's financial year period. IT14 form.		

Calculation of provisional tax

During the first period of assessment, provisional taxpayers:

- Estimate their full year's gross taxable income (including salaries before PAYE deductions and other income sources) and apply the relevant tax rate. The tax rate will be 27% for companies (except for the relevant rate applicable for SBCs and those eligible for turnover tax – see *Chapter* 29) or the applicable individual tax brackets.
- Divide the calculated tax amount by half as it is for the first half of the year.
- Deduct employees' tax (PAYE will already have been withheld and paid over to SARS), allowable credits (eg medical aid contributions), and rebates (eg travel expenses for business) for that six-month period.
- Pay the calculated amount to SARS along with an IRP6 form containing details for the period.

Remember that the calculations are based on estimated income and not actual income, which you will report later in your annual tax return.

The second period of assessment considers:

- The total estimated taxable income for the full year with the relevant tax rate applied (as described above). Remember the estimation during this second period is now based on more up-to-date information compared to the assessment under the first period,
- Deduct employees' tax, credits, and rebates as described above but for the full year.
- Subtract the amount of tax already paid in the first period from the total calculated tax for the full year.
- Pay the calculated amount to SARS along with an IRP6 form containing relevant information.

Note: Even if you estimate no income for a particular period, it is essential to submit a nil IRP6 return. This demonstrates to SARS that your business is still active, you are complying with tax laws, maintaining accurate records, and creating a paper trail of your compliance.

The third voluntary payment (if needed) is calculated by:

- Considering the total estimated (or actual) taxable income for the full year.
- Subtracting the total employees' tax paid, allowable credits, rebates, and amounts paid in the first and second periods.
- Paying any resulting tax liability to SARS along with an IRP6 form containing relevant information.

Remember that the third payment is optional and used to settle any underestimation of tax liability in the previous periods to avoid the levying of penalties and interest. You can use your actual income if you have filed your tax return early or received a SARS assessment. Ideally, accurate and reasonable estimations during the first and second provisional tax payments would eliminate the need for the third voluntary payment. However, unforeseen circumstances can sometimes affect income throughout the year, which justifies making the third voluntary payment and IRP6 return.

Penalties and interest

Although provisional tax is based on estimates of taxable income, you need to ensure that the estimates are as close as possible to the actual taxable income to avoid penalties and interest being levied by SARS for underestimation. The onus is therefore on the taxpayer to be diligent and ensure the estimates are based on what the reasonable income will be rather than a thumb suck.

Here's a simplified overview of potential penalties:

- **Underestimation.** A penalty may apply if your provisional tax payments fall below a certain percentage of your actual income.
  - **Over R1 million in actual income.** Your provisional tax payments should be at least within 80% of your actual income.
  - **Less Than R1 million in income (individuals).** Your payments should be at least 80% of your actual income, considering the 'basic amount'. The basic amount is the individual taxpayer's taxable income assessed by SARS for the latest preceding year of assessment less the amount of any taxable capital gain. The basic amount is not applicable for companies.
- **Penalty amount.** The penalty is typically 20% of the difference between the expected tax based on your estimates (IRP6 forms) and the actual tax owed based on your final tax return (ITR12 form for individuals or IT14 forms for companies).
- **Interest** may also be charged on any underestimation of provisional tax.

Other penalties and interest can be charged for late, incorrect or no filing of provisional tax returns.

Please note that these are simplified examples, and specific calculations may vary depending on your situation. For a more detailed understanding and assistance with provisional tax calculations, and to avoid penalties and interest, consult timeously with tax and accounting advisors.

Understanding the difference between income tax and provisional tax

Although provisional tax is a method of advance tax collection and payment to SARS, it is essential to understand that a company (or the individual, as the case may be) still needs to file its annual income tax returns (ITR12 form for individuals or IT14 forms for companies) within the specified timelines mentioned above. Provisional tax payments are separate from the actual income tax return, which is filed within 12 months of the company's financial year-end or in January of the following year in the case of individual provisional taxpayers and reflects the company's or individual's actual financial circumstances.

The income tax return serves to reconcile the estimated payments made through provisional tax with the actual financial performance of the company or the individual. Based on this reconciliation, additional tax payments (including possible penalties and interest, as mentioned above) may be required if there was an underpayment, while any overpayments made will result in a refund from SARS. By filing the income tax return, the company or the individual ensures that the estimated provisional tax payments align with its actual tax liability.

Provisional tax – summary

This chapter is a simplified explanation and there are many nuances to provisional tax. It is therefore important to obtain expert tax and accounting advice in case of any queries or uncertainties.

Here are some key recommendations:

- **Understand your tax obligations.** Familiarise yourself with the requirements and deadlines for provisional tax in South Africa. Be aware of the tax seasons, filing dates, and payment due dates based on your financial year-end.
- **Estimate your income as accurately as possible.** Provisional tax is based on estimated income. It is important to make realistic estimations to avoid underpayment of tax. Regularly review and update your income projections throughout the tax year.
- Maintain **good financial records.** Keep detailed records of your income, expenses, and deductions. Accurate financial information will help you make informed estimates for provisional tax calculations and facilitate the preparation of your tax returns.
- To **effectively manage cash flow**, it is important to consider the impact of provisional tax payments. Creating a budget and cash flow plan will help ensure that sufficient funds are available to meet your provisional tax obligations. Regularly monitoring cash flow and making necessary adjustments is crucial. To prevent cash flow challenges, it is advisable to allocate a monthly amount based on accurate estimations and set it aside in a separate bank account, like how VAT amounts are handled (refer to the *Summary* section in Chapter 25). Keeping provisional tax funds separate from the primary business account promotes estimation accuracy, enhances budget planning procedures, and mitigates risks to business cash flow.
- Explore legitimate **tax planning measures** to minimise your tax liability. This may include utilising allowable deductions, tax credits, and incentives provided by the South African tax system. Consult with tax and accounting advisors to identify tax planning opportunities specific to your situation.
- **Stay updated** on tax legislation. Tax laws and regulations can change over time. Stay informed about any updates or changes to South African tax legislation that may impact your provisional tax obligations. Regularly review tax updates and publications from SARS or consult with tax and accounting advisors to stay up to date.
- **Review and file tax returns** on time. Review your tax returns carefully, ensuring accuracy and compliance with all requirements. File your returns on time to avoid penalties and interest charges. Consider engaging professional accounting and tax advisors to assist with the preparation and filing of your tax returns.
- If a business fails to submit provisional returns (IRP6 forms), it may face penalties, interest charges, and the risk of **deregistration** from the provisional tax system. Avoid such deregistration by filing the IRP6 forms timeously.

- Even if a business has not made any income during any period of assessment, submit a **nil return** to avoid the business being deregistered and to remain compliant with tax laws.
- In certain circumstances, registration and payment of provisional tax is not required. Speak to your tax and accounting advisors for more information.
- Remember the exact dates for filings can **vary each year** as determined by SARS; tax percentages, thresholds, tax tables, etc may also change periodically.

Chapter 25: Value-added tax

Value-Added Tax (VAT) is an indirect tax levied on the consumption of goods and services in South Africa, serving as a crucial source of government revenue. It is governed by the Value-Added Tax Act of 1991. The current VAT rate is 15% for standard-rated goods and services, although certain goods and services may qualify for a zero rate (0% VAT) or are VAT-exempt altogether.

VAT requirements

Mandatory VAT registration is required for businesses who have sold goods or services exceeding R1 million in the previous 12 months. Registration as a VAT vendor must be completed within 21 days of surpassing this threshold. Furthermore, voluntary VAT registration is possible if taxable supplies in the past 12 months amounted to more than R50 000. VAT registration is carried out through the SARS eFiling platform, following the instructions provided under *Registration – VAT Registration*. SARS will issue you with a ten-digit VAT number beginning with the number 4.

Once registered as a VAT vendor, it is compulsory to charge VAT on all taxable supplies of goods or services provided for consideration (ie sales) in South Africa. VAT vendors must issue VAT invoices that clearly show the VAT vendor number issued by SARS, the applicable VAT percentage (ie 15% or 0%) and amount. This creates a *VAT chain* where each VAT vendor registered in the supply chain charges VAT on their sales (VAT output) and can claim VAT incurred on their purchases from VAT registered suppliers as a credit (VAT input) to reduce their VAT liability. VAT vendors collect VAT on behalf of SARS, and it is not part of the income of the business.

For goods that are subject to zero rate, it is still necessary to issue VAT invoices and show the VAT percentage as 0%. Zero-rated VAT goods and services allow the VAT vendor to still claim the VAT input charges from its suppliers even though no VAT output is charged to customers. Examples of goods and services that are subject to zero rate for VAT are essential foods (like fruit, vegetables, maize meal, brown bread, eggs, milk, powder), basic sanitation, public transport, some medial and welfare services, paraffin, exported goods, etc.

When a vendor makes a VAT-exempt supply, they do not apply VAT to the transaction and cannot claim a deduction or credit for the VAT paid on goods and services used for that exempt supply. As a result, vendors consider the VAT they paid, without any deduction or credit, as an additional cost. They recover this cost by including it in the amount they charge for the VAT-exempt supply. Examples of goods and services that are VAT-exempt are certain instances of finance interest charges, residential rentals, educational services, etc.

Foreign companies supplying electronic services digitally to South African residents may need to register for VAT and apply VAT charges on invoices if they exceed a threshold of R1 million in a 12-month period. This applies when at least two of these conditions are met – payment from a South African bank account, recipient with a South African address, or service supplied to a South African resident. In contrast, if a South African VAT registered vendor is making sale of goods or services to a foreign company then no VAT is chargeable as it will be considered an export, and exports are not subject to VAT given there is no local consumption of the goods and services – the invoice will be zero-rated so input VAT can still be claimed.

Although VAT compliance is onerous, its primary advantage for businesses that are registered is that they can claim back the VAT input costs from their suppliers.

VAT categories

SARS applies five categories of tax periods for VAT vendors in South Africa – categories A, B, C, D, and E. Each category has different criteria based on the type of business, the value of taxable supplies, and the frequency of submitting VAT returns.

- **Category A.** Every two calendar months, ending on the last day of January, March, May, July, September, and November. SARS will determine whether a vendor falls within this category.
- **Category B.** Every two calendar months, ending on the last day of February, April, June, August, October, and December. SARS will determine whether a vendor falls within this category.
- **Category C.** Every calendar month. A vendor will fall within this category (1) if the total value of taxable supplies made by the vendor has exceeded or is likely to exceed R30 million in any consecutive period of 12 months, (2) the vendor has applied in writing to be placed in this category, or (3) the Commissioner determined that the vendor falls within this category due to the vendor repeatedly failing to perform any obligations as required by the VAT Act.
- **Category D.** Every six calendar months, ending on the last day of February and August (or any other month where written application is made to SARS and approved). This category applies mainly to a vendor who carries on farming activities, where the total value of taxable supplies is less than R1.5 million for a period of 12 months or is a micro business that is registered in terms of the Income Tax Act.
- **Category E.** every 12 calendar months, ending on the last day of the vendor's year of assessment (or any other month where written application is made to SARS and approved). This category applies to a vendor that is a company or a trust fund that carries on activities of letting of fixed property or renting of movable goods or the administration or management of companies that are connected persons to the vendor.

Note: A VAT vendor can apply to SARS to change its allocated tax period provided it meets the relevant criteria. Speak to SARS directly or accounting or tax advisors for further information if needed. Most individuals and small companies will fall into either category A or B and hence their VAT201 returns would be due every two months. A category A company's VAT201 02 form for

March, for example, would therefore disclose the VAT inputs and outputs for the months of January and February of that year.

VAT201 returns

A VAT return (VAT201 form) must be submitted, and payment made by the last business day of the month following the end of each applicable VAT cycle (depending on the category you fall into). If payment is made manually then it is due on the 25th day of the month following the end of each applicable VAT cycle. The VAT201 will disclose the total VAT inputs (the VAT you were charged by your VAT registered suppliers) and the VAT outputs (the total VAT you charged on the sale of goods and services at 15% or 0%, as the case may be). If the VAT input exceeds the VAT outputs, then SARS will pay you a refund of the difference; if the VAT output exceeds the VAT input, then you will need to pay SARS the difference within the prescribed period as described above. If you are dealing with a supplier that is not VAT registered, you cannot claim any VAT input; in contrast when you become VAT registered, you must charge all your customers VAT even if they are not VAT registered, although there may be circumstances where VAT is not required to be charged (for example, your customer is based overseas and is not required to be VAT registered in South Africa). Due to the complexities of VAT regulations, especially regarding international transactions, we strongly recommend seeking advice from your tax and accounting professionals for any specific questions.

Failure to make timeous VAT201 returns and payments could result in penalties and interest being levied by SARS. Penalties are 10% of the amount payable and interest is levied at the standard charge for interest. Even if you have not made any taxable supplies or incurred any input tax in a particular period (depending on your category), you should submit a nil return to maintain compliance and avoid potential penalties for non-filing of the VAT returns.

VAT compliant invoicing

All businesses (including those that are not VAT registered) should adopt good practices of issuing invoices as proof of their sales. For VAT registered vendors, VAT invoicing is an essential requirement to remain compliant with SARS and to correctly calculate your VAT output. Similarly, if you are a VAT registered vendor, you should obtain VAT invoices from your suppliers to calculate your VAT input. These invoices serve as proof of transactions and allow businesses to calculate their VAT input and output, while for SARS, they ensure proper VAT collection. The SARS requirements for invoicing for VAT purposes is as follows:

- **Mandatory information:**
    - **Title.** Clearly label the document as a Tax Invoice, VAT Invoice, or Invoice.
    - **Supplier details.** Name, address, and VAT registration number of your business.
    - **Recipient details.** Name, address, and VAT registration number (if applicable) of the customer.
    - **Invoice date.** The date the invoice was issued.

- **Unique invoice number.** A unique identifier for tracking purposes.
- **Supply description.** Clear and concise description of the goods or services provided.
- **Quantity.** Number of units of each item supplied.
- **Taxable supply value.** The value of the supply before VAT.
- **VAT rate.** The applicable VAT rate (15% or 0%, as described previously).
- **VAT amount.** The calculated amount of VAT charged.
- **Total amount.** The final amount payable, including VAT.

- **Additional requirements:**
  - **Currency.** All amounts must be in South African Rand (ZAR).
  - **Serial numbering.** Invoices should be consecutively numbered.
  - **Record-keeping.** All invoices must be retained for five years.
  - **Electronic invoicing.** While not yet mandatory, consider exploring electronic invoicing options for easier record-keeping and reporting.

Invoice vs payment basis

When registering for VAT, businesses in South Africa are automatically enrolled as vendors on the *invoice basis*. This means that VAT must be declared and paid to SARS based on the date of invoice issuance, regardless of when payment is received from customers. This can be challenging particularly for small businesses and startups if customers make delayed payments exceeding 30 days or if the agreed payment terms extend beyond that period.

Alternatively, the *payment basis* provides a more flexible option. Under this approach, VAT declaration and payment to SARS occur only after the customer settles the issued invoice. This offers significant benefits for effectively managing a business' cash flow.

It is important to note that not all businesses are eligible for the payment basis. Qualifying VAT vendors for this option include natural persons (or partnerships consisting solely of natural persons) whose total taxable supplies (i) did not exceed R2.5 million (exclusive of VAT) in the previous 12 months and (ii) are not expected to exceed that amount in the next 12 months. Non-resident suppliers of specific electronic services or intermediaries facilitating such supplies also qualify. Unfortunately, companies cannot opt for this payment basis. This creates a hurdle for small businesses and startups registered as companies and paying VAT. Unlike eligible entities, companies must pay VAT to SARS even before receiving customer payments if their payment terms are lengthy (eg 60 days or more). This mismatch between VAT liability and customer payments can strain their cash flow unless they have ample reserves to bridge the gap.

If a business qualifies for the payment basis, it needs to apply to SARS for a transition from the invoice basis to the payment basis. Once approved, the business can pay the VAT to SARS upon receipt of payment from customers. If the criteria are not met or the application is rejected, it is crucial to set aside the VAT portion from received payments and pay to SARS when due. Small businesses should also consider negotiating more favourable payment terms with their customers to alleviate cash flow burdens.

VAT – summary

In conclusion, we acknowledge that VAT, like any other taxes can be complex, so seeking assistance from accounting or tax advisors is advisable to ensure proper fulfilment of VAT obligations and accurate and timeous filing of VAT returns.

To ensure your VAT compliance, consider the following recommendations:
- **Register promptly** for VAT once you exceed the relevant threshold.
- Ensure that all **invoices** accurately reflect the correct VAT registration number for invoices issued to your customers and invoices received from your suppliers. VAT invoices must meet the other requirements set out by SARS as mentioned above.
- Ensure **consistency between your turnover and financial statements**, as this is regularly checked by tax authorities. Any discrepancies between these figures and your VAT returns may raise concerns and prompt enquiries from SARS.
- **Inflating your claims** can have adverse consequences for your business. Inflated input claims can inaccurately reduce your VAT liability or result in an excessive refund, which is considered a criminal offence.
- **Reclaim VAT paid on bad debts** by writing them off; consult your professional accountant for guidance on the process.
- **Include VAT on all quotes**, whether it is 15% (normal VAT rate on taxable supplies) or 0% (on applicable goods and services). It is necessary to include VAT on every quote provided to customers and clients to properly calculate VAT outputs and inputs.
- Retain **documentary evidence** to justify zero-rating. If you do not charge VAT, you can still claim VAT on supplied items. However, it is vital to maintain proof of eligibility to avoid potential issues with SARS.
- If you are eligible for the **payment basis**, ensure you timeously apply to SARS to change your status from the invoice basis.
- **Submit VAT returns** regardless of whether you calculate any VAT liability or payment due to SARS. Even if no VAT is due to SARS or expected to be refunded, registered vendors must still submit their VAT returns, known as nil returns. This demonstrates that the business is still operating and fulfils its tax compliance obligations. It also contributes to good record-keeping practices.
- Treat all VAT amounts received from your customers, and not paid over to SARS yet, as separate by placing it in a **separate bank account** and then paying it over to SARS when due. For example, if you are a Category A vendor and you receive payment from customers in a particular month before it is due for payment to SARS, set it aside in the secondary account until it is due for payment.
- **Use the window period** of 30/31 days to submit your return after the relevant period ends. Timeously review your VAT report (inputs and outputs) and gather the necessary information early to avoid hasty submissions that may contain errors resulting in potential fines and penalties by SARS.

- **Timely submission** of VAT returns is essential to **avoid interest and penalties** imposed by SARS. Penalties can be 10% of the VAT liability and interest charged at the prescribed rate, as well as administrative penalties.
- Maintain a **comprehensive record** of all VAT returns and supporting documentation in case of audits or substantiation/proof requests from SARS.
- The **retention period** of VAT documentation is five years from submission of the relevant filings to SARS (this includes the supporting documentation).

Chapter 26: Pay-as-you-earn and employer registration

Pay As You Earn (PAYE) is not a tax itself but a method for employers to collect income tax on behalf of SARS from their employees. PAYE involves deducting income tax from employees' salaries at the time of payment. The frequency of salary payments can be weekly, fortnightly, or monthly, based on company practices or, in the case of self-employed individuals / owner-managed businesses, whenever they pay themselves a salary. However, the relevant filing to SARS, called the EMP201 form, must be filed monthly.

The calculation of PAYE is based on each employee's taxable income. This includes their gross income minus allowable deductions, such as medical and retirement contributions, travel allowances (subject to specific rules), and approved expenses. The tax amount is determined by the individual's applicable income tax bracket, as per the official individual tax tables for the relevant year – see the *Personal Income Tax* section in *Chapter 23* for the 2024 tax table.

The EMP201 form summarises the total amount of PAYE paid by the employer each month for all employees (as well as amounts for UIF, SDL and other amounts), while the IRP5 form, provided annually, reflects the total PAYE withheld for each employee. To calculate PAYE, the employer needs to:

- Multiply the employee's taxable earnings, including any taxable fringe benefits (such as retirement fund contributions, subject to certain limits, medical aid, travel allowances, etc) by 52 weeks, 26 weeks, or 12 months, or other payment period (depending on the pay frequency) to obtain an annual amount.
- Cross-reference this annual sum against the SARS tax tables for individual taxpayers to calculate the employee's annual tax.
- Divide the employee's annual tax by the same work period to determine the monthly PAYE tax to be withheld.

For example, if an employee has a regular monthly income of R28 000, the annual tax calculation would be: R28 000 x 12 = R336 000 (adjusted if the employee worked fewer than 12 months during the year). The employer then applies the relevant tax table to determine the tax payable and divides it by 12 (or the relevant work period) to calculate the monthly PAYE to be deducted from the employee's salary.

The benefits of PAYE include:

- Simplifying tax collection for SARS by ensuring employers deduct and remit taxes periodically and regularly.
- Assisting employees by automatically paying their income tax liability and spreading it over time rather than requiring a lump sum at the end of the tax year.
- Ensuring a steady revenue stream for the government.

The PAYE system imposes significant responsibilities on employers, including the accurate deduction of taxes, prompt payment of taxes, and regular filings with SARS. The EMP201 form must be submitted, and amounts paid to SARS by the 7th day of the following month. For example, PAYE for the month of February would need to be paid over, and the EMP201 form submitted to SARS no later than 7 March. Penalties on late or incorrect filings, or delayed payment, can be 10% of the tax liability, interest at the prescribed period and administrative penalties.

Effective December 2023, foreign employers operating in South Africa through a permanent establishment (PE) must register with SARS and withhold and pay PAYE for their employees to SARS. This change aligns foreign employer responsibilities with domestic ones, ensuring consistency between the two. Previously such PEs were exempted from having to withhold PAYE for their employees and paying the relevant amounts to SARS. While UIF and SDL obligations remain unchanged (ie the employer must still pay UIF and SDL unless exempted), affected PEs should review their payroll processes and register with SARS if necessary to avoid non-compliance. A PE should not be confused with external companies (see *Chapter 10*) – an external company is registered with CIPC as a company that is an extension of its foreign parent company under certain circumstances. A PE is where a foreign company has a physical presence (but not a legal entity presence) in South Africa that conducts or intends to conduct business for a period, creating a taxable nexus and necessitating registration with SARS for employee PAYE compliance, in addition to other laws.

Employers who fail to pay PAYE on time are subject to penalties and interest. It is important for employees to review their payslips carefully, as they can also be held liable for any incorrect or non-payment of PAYE, such as if the wrong tax bracket is used. In such cases, employees should raise their concerns with the employer, who should thoroughly review and address the concerns. Employees also have the option to contact SARS directly to raise any queries or concerns.

Employees should note that they remain responsible for paying their income taxes to SARS. If there is underpayment of PAYE, SARS can recover the outstanding amounts from the employee in addition to sanctioning penalties and interest on the employer. Individual taxpayers are also accountable for declaring all additional taxable income received outside of employment during the tax filing season, and they must pay any additional taxes owed after SARS has assessed the amounts due. Under PAYE regulations, even if no salaries are paid in a particular month, it is still mandatory to submit a nil return on the EMP201 form to SARS. This demonstrates your business' ongoing operation and compliance with tax laws, while also maintaining a record of your payroll activity.

Employer registration for tax purposes

When employing others for your company, you must register as an employer with SARS via the SARS eFiling platform by logging in and following the instructions after clicking on *Registrations – Employer Registration*. You will then be given an Employer Registration Number (ERN). Once you are a registered employer with SARS, you will need to follow these requirements:

- Deduct PAYE (see below).
- Register for UIF (if not already done when you registered your company) and pay amounts due.
- Register with the Compensation Fund for COIDA (Compensation for Occupational Injuries and Diseases) if you have not already done so when you registered your company and pay amounts due.
- File monthly EMP201 declaration to SARS showing total amount of PAYE, UIF, SDL and employment tax incentives deducted from employees' salaries for the prior month and paid over to SARS. The EMP201 must be filed no later than the 7th day after the end of the relevant month, eg the March EMP201 must be submitted no later than 7 April.
- File employer reconciliation declarations with SARS, EMP501 form, twice a year (known as the interim and final EMP50). The Interim EMP501 declaration is due on 31 October for the period 1 March to 31 August while the final/annual period is due on 31 May for the full year 1 March to 28/29 February. The EMP501 form is a reconciliation of all EMP201 declarations for the relevant period showing all deductions for the period for employees iro PAYE, UIF and SDL.

Even if you are the sole business owner of the business and sole employee, you must follow the above requirements as soon as you begin to draw a salary. If you also employ others on a temporary or casual basis, you will need to register as an employer.

The employer must also issue all employees with an annual IRP5 form showing all PAYE and other deductions – the IRP5 form allows the employee to complete their annual tax submissions. See *Chapter 39* for more details.

Fringe benefit tax

Fringe benefit tax (FBT) is imposed on non-cash benefits provided by employers to their employees or their family members. These benefits are considered part of the employee's taxable income and affect the calculation of PAYE. Examples of FBT include the provision of assets at a reduced price or for free, private use of company assets (such as a company vehicle), long-service awards, subsidised meals or meal vouchers, residential accommodation, low-interest loans, contributions to insurance policies, subsistence allowances for business travel, payment of debt on behalf of the employee, medical aid contributions, retirement fund contributions, and more.

Employers need to calculate the cash value of the fringe benefit using prescribed formulae and add it to the employee's remuneration as part of the employee's taxable income. These fringe benefits are reported on the employee's IRP5/IT3(a) certificate issued annually and are identified by a SARS 4-digit code starting with the number 38.

Fringe benefits are taxable for employees as they directly benefit from the non-cash benefits provided by the employer. Employees must declare these benefits in their tax returns using the relevant information from their IRP5. Certain fringe benefits, such as retirement fund and medical aid contributions, may be eligible for allowable deductions, but specific limits and requirements are set by SARS.

Employers must submit annual employer reconciliation declarations (EMP501) to SARS, providing details of all taxable benefits provided to employees during the year. It is important to note that the rules and regulations governing FBT can be complex and subject to change. Employers should seek advice from qualified accounting or tax advisors to ensure compliance with relevant laws and regulations.

Chapter 27: Unemployment Insurance Fund and Skills Development Levy

Unemployment Insurance Fund

Unemployment Insurance Fund (UIF) acts as a social security safety net for all employees, offering financial support during times of unemployment, maternity leave, paternity leave, adoption leave, and temporary work incapacity. It helps employees, and their dependents, to weather unexpected storms and reduces poverty and inequality in the country.

Registration and contributions

Whether you are starting a company with one employee or running a larger business, registering for UIF is mandatory. This can be done when registering your business with CIPC or later once you start hiring employees by registering at *https://ufiling.labour.gov.za/uif/*. Both the employer and employee contribute 1% each, making up a total contribution rate of 2% of the employee's gross salary. However, contributions have a ceiling that is reviewed annually. As of March 2023, the maximum earnings ceiling is R212 544 per annum, or R17 712 per month. This means the maximum monthly contribution for both employer and employee combined is R354.24, with each paying R177.12. Employees earning less than the maximum ceiling rates will pay 1% of their actual gross salary and the employer will pay a matching 1%. Employers cannot deduct more than 1% of the employee's gross salary for UIF purposes.

What is gross salary?

Gross salary, or earnings, includes all forms of remuneration earned from the employer including basic salary, overtime (if applicable), bonuses and allowances, and before any deductions but excludes commissions. Put differently, it is the amount that the employer uses to calculate the PAYE.

Benefits and eligibility

Employees meeting certain criteria can claim UIF benefits when facing unemployment. The amount received depends on their previous income. Remember, these benefits are not available for voluntary resignations but are meant to support you during involuntary situations like retrenchment, dismissal, or contract termination. Even in cases of constructive dismissal, where the employer creates a difficult work environment, you can claim UIF benefits, but you will need proof of your situation from the CCMA.

Benefit duration and calculation

UIF benefits typically last for a maximum of 12 months, with a system of 'credit days' determining who qualifies for the full duration. You earn one credit day for every four days you work as a contributor. So, to receive the full 12 months of benefits, you will need to have worked as a contributor for at least four years. The benefit amount itself is calculated on a sliding scale, ranging from 38% to 60% of your salary for the first 26 weeks, depending on your income level. From week 27 to 52 (the remaining half of the maximum benefit period), you will receive a flat rate of 20%. Importantly, lower-income earners receive a higher percentage of their salary as benefits.

Staying updated on the latest UIF information, especially the annual adjustments to the contribution ceiling, is important for accurate deductions and claims.

The UIF amount should be paid by the employer to SARS monthly, no later than the last day of the following month from when the salaries were paid. The payment must be made along with the required EMP201 form. Although the amount is paid to SARS, the UIF programme is administered by the Department of Employment and Labour.

The UIF calculations can be complex, and there are exceptions to consider. If you have any queries, it is advisable to seek legal advice.

The applicable legislation is the Unemployment Insurance Act of 2001, the Unemployment Insurance Contributions Act of 2002, and the Income Tax Act of 1962. Once registered for UIF, you will receive a unique UIF reference number.

Skills Development Levy

The Skills Development Levy (SDL) is imposed on all employers who are registered with SARS for PAYE, to fund the development of skills in the workforce such as apprenticeships, learnerships, on-the-job training, vocational training and education, short courses, and workshops. The SDL helps improve the productivity of the workforces thereby enhancing not just the individual companies and employees but the economy.

The SDL rate is 1% of the employer's payroll. It is calculated on each employee's remuneration before deductions for income tax, UIF, medical aid, and retirement contributions. This includes salaries, overtime, leave pay, bonuses, and commissions. The SDL amount should be paid by the employer to SARS monthly, no later than the last day of the following month from when the salaries were paid. The payment must be made along with the required EMP201 form. However, if the business' *anticipated* annual payroll for the next 12 months is less than R500 000, you are exempt from paying the SDL. This also means you do not need to register for SDL with SARS if the payroll is below this threshold.

The applicable legislation is the Skills Development Levies Act of 1999. Once registered for SDL, you will receive a unique SDL reference number.

Chapter 28: Dividends tax

A dividend is an amount declared by the board of directors and paid to shareholders from the profits earned in a specific year. Dividends tax is the tax applied to such dividends. In South Africa, the current dividend tax rate is 20%. The tax is withheld by the company declaring the dividend, and the net amount (after deducting dividend tax) is paid to the shareholders. As the dividend tax is already paid by the company, shareholders are exempt from paying income tax on the received amount. However, they must still declare the dividends or verify the accuracy of any disclosed dividends in their individual tax returns.

Dividends tax applies to both ordinary dividends and special dividends. Ordinary dividends are paid out of current profits while special dividends are paid out of accumulated profits.

All companies must register for dividends tax via the SARS eFiling system if they declare and pay dividends, and complete and submit DTR01 (information to record the dividends tax transactions) and DTR02 (dividends tax return) forms. Dividend returns, whenever a dividend is declared, needs to be filed with SARS, providing details such as the total amount of dividends paid, the amount of dividends tax withheld, the names of shareholders receiving dividends, the number of shares held by each shareholder, and the amount of dividends paid to each shareholder. This registration and reporting process helps ensure the company's compliance with tax laws, timely payment of dividends tax, simplification of the company's income tax return, and enables SARS to monitor dividends paid to shareholders within the economy. The withheld dividend tax must be paid over to SARS the month after the dividend has been declared.

Dividends tax vs drawing a salary

When considering whether to declare a dividend or draw a salary, owners of a small company should be cautious and not rush into deciding. While the dividends tax rate may appear lower at 20% compared to personal income tax, there are key factors to consider.

Salaries are considered allowable expenses and reduce the company's profits, consequently lowering the tax liability. On the other hand, dividends are paid out of the company's profits, without reducing the company's expenses.

Let us consider an example where a director owner wants to draw R200 000:

If the R200 000 is taken as a salary, it would reduce the company's profit and the associated tax liability. However, if the R200 000 is declared as a dividend, the following would occur:

- Corporate income tax of 27% would be charged on the R200 000 (R54 000) bringing the amount to R146 000.

- Dividends tax at 20% would then be applied to the R146 000 (R29 200) leaving the actual amount to be paid to the shareholder after all taxes at R116 800.
- In this scenario, the effective rate of the dividend tax is (R200 000 - R116 800) / 100 = 41.6%.

It is important to note that the effective dividend tax rate is higher than initially perceived due to the application of corporate income tax before distributing the dividends. Make sure to consider this effective tax rate and consult with your accountant or tax advisor, as the decision between salary and dividend depends on numerous factors and individual circumstances. This does not mean declaring dividends will never make sense. You need to explore your personal tax situation with your accountant and tax advisor, and when it makes sense to draw just a salary or a salary and a dividend. This is especially the case if you fall into the highest income tax bracket (45%) where a happy balance can be reached between drawing a salary and declaring a dividend. For those below the highest income tax bracket, drawing a salary is the most tax-effective choice but seek proper advice before making any decision.

Here are some further considerations for entrepreneurs and small businesses when considering drawing a salary or declaring a dividend:
- **Profitability.** If the business is highly profitable, paying a salary may be more tax-efficient.
- **Going concern.** Sufficient funds should be left in the company to meet future commitments and ensure sustainability.
- **Cash flow needs.** Dividends offer more flexibility for managing personal cash flow.
- **Retirement planning.** If you are self-employed, a salary may be necessary to make contributions to a retirement fund.
- **Tax efficiency.** In most cases, salaries are more tax-efficient than dividends. While the dividend tax rate is 20%, the effective rate can be higher due to corporate income tax on profits before distribution.
- **Salaries reduce taxable income.** As mentioned earlier, drawing a salary reduces the company's taxable income, resulting in a lower overall tax liability.
- **Dividend flexibility.** Dividend payments offer more flexibility than regular salaries, depending on the individual shareholder's circumstances.

It is important to note that the scenario described above specifically applies to owner-managed companies, where dividends and salaries can have a complex interplay. For companies with corporate or individual shareholders where salaries are not relevant, these considerations may not be applicable.

Chapter 29: Small business corporation tax and turnover tax

Small business corporation tax

Small business corporations (SBC) is not a type of company under the Companies Act – they are private companies (including close corporations, co-operatives, and personal liability companies) that are given certain benefits for tax purposes, where applicable criteria are met. The criteria to meet the SBC status is, among other criteria:

- Must be a private company registered with CIPC.
- Gross income less than R20 million per annum.
- All shareholders are natural persons.
- The shareholders must not hold shares or interests in other companies (subject to certain exceptions).
- Must not hold investment income over 20% (subject to certain exceptions and conditions).
- Not be a subsidiary of another company nor a member of a group of companies.

Advantages

- A preferential rate on the taxable income of the SBC. For example, for the 2024 tax year, the tax rates are as follows:

Taxable income (Rand)	Tax rate (Rand) calculated on taxable income
1 to 95 750	0% of taxable income
95 751 to 365 000	7% of taxable income above 95 750
365 001 to 550 000	18 848 + 21% of taxable income above 365 000
550 001 and above	57 698 + 27% of taxable income above 550 000

- The SBC can immediately write off all plant and machinery bought for the business that is brought into use for the first time (except for farming and mining purposes).
- Accelerated depreciation allowances on movable assets, based on certain criteria. Unlike standard depreciation for other companies, which spreads the cost of an asset over years, SBCs can deduct the depreciation costs of assets over shorter periods: 50% in year one, 30% in year two, and 20% in year three. This translates to improved cash flow, as businesses retain more money for investment and growth. It also lowers taxable income in the short term. Keep in mind though, this speeds up the reduction of the asset's value on the accounting books, potentially leading to less depreciation benefit later.

Consider consulting a tax and accounting advisor to see if accelerated depreciation aligns with your business' long-term tax strategy.

The purpose of these tax reliefs to SBCs is to support small businesses as they grow by improving their cash flow and liquidity. Once they stop meeting any of the criteria set out above, they will have to follow the normal tax requirements for all other companies. Companies that meet the criteria for SBC status do not need to submit a separate application to SARS. However, when filing their annual income tax return (IT14 form), they should declare that they meet all the requirements for SBC status. SARS may then confirm or deny SBC eligibility based on the information provided.

Disadvantages

Although SBCs are beneficial to small businesses and startups, they have some major drawbacks:

- Professional or personal service businesses are disqualified from being an SBC. Professional service businesses include areas of accounting, actuarial science, architecture, auctioneering, auditing, broadcasting, consulting, draftmanship, education, engineering, financial service broking, health, journalism, law, management, etc. However, if the company qualifies in all other respects and permanently employs three or more people who are not shareholders or connected/related to the shareholders of the business then the company can qualify as an SBC. Owner-managed companies providing professional services that do not employ others will not be able to claim SBC status and associated benefits.
- Enhanced reporting requirements by the SBC to SARS including audited financial statements.
- Ensuring compliance with key criteria such as shareholders not having interests in other entities, the company not having investment income of more than 20% (subject to certain exceptions), and turnover not exceeding R20 million.
- SBCs must still comply with all other tax requirements such as IRP6 provisional tax submissions, VAT, PAYE, capital gains tax, dividends withholding tax, etc.

Turnover tax

Turnover tax (also known as TOT) is a simplified tax system specifically designed for micro businesses, including sole proprietors, partnerships, companies, or CCs, with a 'qualifying turnover' of less than R1 million per year, with the first R335 000 being exempt from tax (ie tax-free). Unlike traditional corporate income tax, which is based on the profit (income minus expenses), turnover tax is calculated based on the business' turnover. Turnover is the total revenue from sales, while profit is the income remaining after subtracting expenses from revenue. Turnover tax simplifies the administration process for business owners as they do not have to keep detailed expense records or calculate deductible expenses for tax purposes. It also creates significant tax savings for micro businesses. Furthermore, turnover tax replaces income tax, VAT, IRP6 provisional tax returns, capital gains tax and dividends withholding tax. However, micro businesses must still fulfil PAYE, UIF and

SDL requirements. Micro businesses can elect to register for VAT in which case they must comply with all VAT requirements.

Based on the current tax table for micro businesses, in a simplified example, if the business had a turnover of R800 000.00 then its taxable income would be R6 650.00 + 3% of income above
R750 000.00, which results in a tax liability of just R8 150.00. This is a significant tax advantage for micro businesses. The turnover tax range is currently between 1% and 3% based on a sliding scale with 3% applying to the highest turnover bracket.

Registration for turnover tax requires completion of the TT01 application form and following other SARS requirements. If the business turnover exceeds the R1 million threshold in a subsequent year, it will no longer qualify as a micro business. However, depending on the circumstances, it may qualify for SBC tax purposes, discussed in the section above.

It is important to note that not all businesses are eligible for turnover tax, and specific criteria set by SARS must be met to register for this special tax dispensation. Determining eligibility requires a careful assessment of the qualifying requirements. It is advisable to seek advice from an accountant or tax professional who can guide you through the registration process and provide a proper assessment based on your business' circumstances.

Chapter 30: Customs duty

Customs code for import and export

A customs code is an eight-digit unique number issued by SARS upon application by a company. It is required for companies involved in importing or exporting goods, with few exceptions. All companies, including foreign companies, who engage in importing and exporting goods to and from South Africa are required to register with SARS.

The registration process for customs involves completing a customs trader registration form, also known as the DA185 form, and providing proof of company registration, proof of address, and/or affidavits by company representatives. The application can be done through the SARS eFiling system, and accounting firms can assist with the registration process.

Once a customs code is issued, it must be used on all documentation related to the import and export of goods. In addition to shipping costs incurred by courier or transportation companies, payment of duties, fees, and other applicable charges is necessary.

It is crucial to maintain complete and accurate records and establish transparency with SARS to ensure compliance and avoid penalties. Documentation related to the import and export of goods typically includes bills of entry, invoices, and transport documentation. Logistics companies such as DHL, Aramex, FedEx, etc can also provide guidance on the requirements. Due to the potential complexity of the application process and the import-export procedures, it is advisable to seek assistance from suitable advisors to prevent penalties or delays in the shipment of goods.

The relevant legislation governing customs is the Customs and Excise Act of 1964.

Customs duty

Customs duty, also known as import duty, is a tax imposed on goods imported into a country. Its main purposes are to protect local industries by increasing the cost of imported goods and to generate revenue for the government.

In South Africa, the calculation of customs duty involves several factors. The Harmonised System (HS) code is used to classify imported goods internationally with each code having a specific duty rate. Importers must declare the value of the goods on their customs declaration, which includes the cost of the goods, insurance, and freight charges.

The applicable duty rate depends on the HS code and any relevant trade agreements. South Africa has free-trade agreements with certain countries, offering lower duty rates for goods originating from those countries. To calculate the customs duty, the declared value of the goods is multiplied by the duty rate.

SARS is responsible for administering customs duties. It handles tasks such as classifying goods, determining duty rates, collecting customs duty, and enforcing customs regulations. Importers must pay the calculated customs duty before the goods can be released from customs, which is typically done at the port of entry or a designated customs warehouse. Payment can be made electronically through the SARS eFiling platform or by bank deposit or by appointed agents / logistics companies appointed by you to handle the importation.

There are certain exemptions from customs duty, such as for personal effects and low-value gifts. Additional duties known as anti-dumping and countervailing duties may be imposed on imported goods if they are found to be dumped or subsidised.

Importers have the option to hire customs brokers to handle the customs clearance process on their behalf. VAT should also be considered when importing goods.

For specific queries regarding customs duty, dutiable rates, and the overall process, logistics companies are a valuable source of guidance and information.

Chapter 31: Other taxes and rules

In this chapter, we discuss other tax types and tax rules that may apply to your business.

Capital Gains Tax

Capital Gains Tax (CGT) is a tax imposed on the profits obtained from the sale of assets by companies and individuals, including sole proprietors and partners in a partnership. Since 3 November 2023, the CGT rate for companies is 21.6%, but only 80% of the capital gain is included in the taxable income, resulting in an effective rate of 17.28% (ie 21.6% x 80% = 17.28%). Resident companies are liable for CGT on the disposal of assets both within and outside of South Africa, although exceptions apply.

When calculating the CGT liability, the company can apply certain deductions, including the base cost of the asset, capital improvements made to the assets, and selling expenses.

The CGT liability must be paid to SARS within 12 months of the financial year-end in which the capital gain was realised.

Securities transfer tax

Securities transfer tax (STT) is levied at a flat rate of 0.25% tax on the transfer of securities like stocks, bonds, and derivatives. This tax, payable by the transferor, includes shares and depositories of a company or member's interest in CC, whenever such securities are bought, transferred, cancelled, or redeemed, and includes both listed and unlisted entities. The requirements of who is responsible to pay the STT and in which period it is payable is different based on listed or unlisted entities so seek the guidance of a tax practitioner where needed. Where the value of the STT is less than R100.00, STT will not apply, or put in another way, where the value of the shares or interest transferred is less than R40 000.00 no STT is payable due to the R100 exemption (R40 000 x 0.25% = R100). STT, when due, is payable to SARS within the relevant period.

The relevant law is the Securities Transfer Tax Act of 2007.

Transfer duty tax

Transfer duty tax applies whenever there is a transfer of property from one person or entity to another. The exact duty is based on a sliding scale and tax tables depending on the value of transaction with the maximum rate being 13% (plus a fixed amount). The tax due is payable to SARS within six months of the sale being completed. There are various rules related to transfer duty and some complexities related to how VAT applies so ensure you speak to a tax practitioner for advice.

The relevant law is the Transfer Duty Act of 1949.

Donations tax

Donations tax of 20% on the value of donations applies in South Africa, up to a value of R30 million, and 25% above R30 million. The donor is responsible for the tax payment to SARS by way of an IT144 declaration, and the payment is due no later than the month after the month in which the donation is made. All South African resident taxpayers, however, have an annual donation exemption of R100 000 per year below which no donation tax applies. Exemptions against paying donation tax exist for donations made to PBOs (see the section on *Public benefit organisations* in *Chapter 5*) for which the resident taxpayer can claim a tax deduction from their taxable income provided the donation does not exceed 10% of the donor's taxable income. The PBO must issue a Section 18A certificate to the donor for the donor to qualify for the deduction. The donor must file the Section 18A certificate as part of their annual tax declaration. The beneficiary of the donation has no tax obligations but must declare the donation in their annual tax filing IT12 form as 'amount considered non-taxable'.

Employer tax incentive

To address the high unemployment levels in South Africa, particularly among the youth and those with less experience or skills, government introduced the Employer Tax Incentive (ETI) in 2014 (currently due to end in 2029) for eligible employers. The purpose of the ETI is to reduce the cost of hiring young people for employers by creating a cost-sharing mechanism with government. This is achieved by reducing the amount of employee's tax (ie PAYE) that the employer needs to pay over to SARS in respect of qualifying employees' remuneration. This ensure that the employees receive more income.

To qualify, the employer must be registered with SARS for PAYE (see the relevant section above) and be in good standing (ie all tax returns must have been submitted and there are no outstanding tax debts due to SARS). Eligible employees must be between the ages of 18 and 29, have a valid South African identity document (or be an asylum seeker or refugee in terms of relevant legislation), not be connected to the employer, and may be permanent or part-time employees. Certain other criteria need to also be met. A sliding scale to calculate the relevant ETI is used and relevant information on the employer's monthly EMP201 return must be submitted to SARS.

The relevant law is the Employment Tax Incentive Act of 2013.

Thin tax rules

Thin capitalisation rules are tax regulations aimed at preventing companies from artificially reducing their tax liability through excessive debt financing. These rules limit the amount of interest a company can deduct for tax purposes on debt owed to 'related parties' typically defined as foreign-connected companies or individuals. The intent is to prevent companies from shifting profits to low-tax countries by borrowing heavily from related parties, paying high interest rates, and deducting those interest payments from their taxable income in South Africa.

SARS applies the thin capitalisation rules through the Income Tax Act of 1962. Under these rules, a company's debt-to-equity ratio is compared to a benchmark ratio. If the company's debt-to-equity ratio exceeds the benchmark ratio, the tax deduction for interest on the excess debt may be limited or disallowed by SARS. The current benchmark ratio in South Africa is 3:1 meaning the total debt of a company should not be more than three times its equity.

The specific application of thin capitalisation rules can be complex and involve numerous factors, including the nature of the business, the relationship between the company and the related party, and the terms of the loan agreement. Companies facing thin capitalisation issues should consult a qualified tax advisor to understand their specific situation and compliance requirements. SARS has issued guidance on the application of thin capitalisation rules.

Transfer pricing

Like most countries, South Africa has adopted strict rules around transfer pricing. Transfer pricing refers to the pricing of transactions between related parties, such as subsidiaries and parent companies, or two branches of the same company found in different countries. SARS oversees this via the Income Tax Act of 1962 and relevant regulations. These regulations aim to ensure that related-party transactions are conducted at arm's length, meaning the price charged or paid for goods, services, or intangible assets should be the same as the price that would be charged or paid between two independent parties in an open-market transaction.

Objectives

- Ensure fair and correct determination of taxable income for related-party transactions.
- Prevent multinational companies from shifting profits to low-tax countries through artificial pricing arrangements.
- Promote fair competition in the South African market.

Key principles

- **Arm's length principle.** Transactions between related parties should be priced at the same level as would be agreed upon by independent parties in an open-market transaction.
- **Best method principle.** The most appropriate transfer-pricing method should be used, depending on the specific circumstances of each transaction.

Common transfer-pricing methods

- **Transactional methods.** These methods compare the price of the related-party transaction to the price of similar transactions between independent parties. Examples include the comparable uncontrolled price (CUP) method and the resale price method (RPM).
- **Profit-based methods.** These methods compare the profitability of the related-party transaction to the profitability of independent companies in comparable

businesses. Examples include the transactional net margin method (TNMM) and the profit split method (PSM).

Compliance requirements

- Companies engaged in related-party transactions exceeding a certain threshold are required to prepare and submit transfer-pricing documentation to SARS.
- This documentation should prove that the transfer prices used are consistent with the arm's length principle and the best method principle.

Consequences of non-compliance

- SARS may adjust the taxable income of a company that is found to be in violation of the transfer-pricing rules.
- This can lead to additional tax liabilities, penalties, and interest.

Understanding transfer-pricing regulations is critical for multinational companies operating in South Africa to ensure compliance and avoid potential tax penalties. Seek the advice of tax practitioners for advice on transfer pricing issues.

Other taxes

There are other specific types of taxes that may apply to your business. Some examples include estate duty, diamond export levy, air passenger tax, mineral and petroleum resources royalties, withholding tax on interest, etc. Speak to your tax practitioner or accountant for specific information. SARS also issues useful guidance documents, which you can locate on its website.

Also bear in mind that local municipalities have specific levies and fees based on the location of your business.

Chapter 32: Tax compliance and concluding remarks

Tax compliance status

SARS issues a Tax Compliance Status (TCS) to show that you are in good standing. Third parties that want to do business with you may require a TCS PIN, which they can use to check that you are in good standing. The TCS certificate contains the PIN number, and you can provide this to the third party who in turn can verify your status with SARS. You can request your TCS via the SARS eFiling system. The PIN is only available for a certain period (one year) so you will need new PINs after expiry. You can cancel your PIN at any time (however, the third parties will then not be able to verify your TCS, which could inhibit them from doing business with you). Companies typically want to ensure they are dealing with a tax-compliant vendor or customer for the following reasons:

- To follow their own governance requirements by reducing the risk of doing business with a company that is not compliant with tax laws.
- To follow industry regulations or best practices (eg listed entities may want to prove higher degrees of due diligence to follow their overall commitment to good governance as per listing requirements and the King Code on Corporate Governance).
- To protect their reputation by proving their commitment to do businesses with companies that are of good standing.

Non-compliance with tax laws

We have not always discussed the specific consequences of non-compliance with each aspect of tax laws but briefly it can be summarised as follows:

- Investigations by SARS into the affairs of the company including verification of documentation or audits of the financial affairs of the company.
- Imposition of penalties and fines if there has been non- or under-payment or delayed payment of any taxes due by the company, or failure to register when needed to do so for certain taxes.
- Criminal prosecution of the company and its directors in the case of fraud, tax evasion, or other serious offences involving dishonesty or gross negligence.
- Revocation of the company's tax clearance certificate, which may adversely affect its ability to do business with customers and other third parties.
- Deregistration of the company if it fails to submit returns, including nil returns, which can pose difficulties when the company wants to recommence submission of return.
- Seizure of the company's assets by SARS for non-compliance. This, however, can only be done following a court order.

Retention period of records

Under the various taxes and relevant laws mentioned in the preceding chapters, there are different retention periods depending on the type of records. For purposes of this chapter, the following should be noted in terms of the relevant retention periods:

- **Income Tax Act.** For records related to EMP201 (monthly PAYE records) and EMP501 (annual PAYE reconciliation records) submissions – five years.
- **Value-added Tax Act.** Relevant records – five years.
- **Securities Transfer Act.** Relevant records – five years.
- **Transfer Duty Act.** Relevant records – five years.

The above is not an exhaustive list of records, and you should seek tax advice for specific queries. See also *Chapter 59* on record-keeping and specifically the section on *Record retention periods*.

Summary

South African tax laws can be challenging, particularly for small businesses and startups without internal expertise. Compliance with tax laws is vital for the success and sustainability of any business.

Here are some recommendations:

- Having a basic understanding of tax types and requirements contributes to a constant learning mindset.
- Considering the complexity of tax regulations, we highly recommend partnering with qualified tax and accounting advisors. These professionals can file your returns on time, ensure you stay compliant, and identify opportunities to utilise legitimate tax benefits that can save you money in the long run. While there is a cost associated with this service, the potential savings and peace of mind often outweigh the expense.
- Proactive tax management is key to avoiding cash flow strain. For example, regularly estimate and set aside funds throughout the year for both provisional tax payments (based on estimated liability and tax rate) and VAT obligations (net of inputs and outputs). This consistent approach ensures you have the funds readily available to meet tax deadlines without having to scramble to find the funds and placing your cash flow, and business, in distress.
- Maximise the tax-deductible expenses you are entitled to – speak to your tax and accounting advisors timeously about this.
- Consider strategically timing large business expenses to potentially lower your tax burden. This could involve bringing forward equipment purchases or improvements to claim depreciation benefits in the current year or delaying non-essential expenses until the next year. Remember, prioritise business needs over tax benefits, and ensure you have the cash flow to manage these decisions. Consult your tax and accounting advisors to analyse your situation and determine the best timing strategy for planned expenses.
- Small businesses should take advantage of the preferential tax regimes such as SBC tax and turnover tax, where they meet the qualifying criteria.

- Pay your taxes on time to avoid penalties, interest, and unnecessary complications with revenue authorities.
- Maintain proper documentation of all transactions and keep them easily accessible.
- A variety of affordable accounting and tax software tools are available to simplify the tasks of tax calculation, tax return preparation, and monthly account statement generation for businesses. Examples include Pastel, Xero, Sage, and QuickBooks, among others. Should you decide to work with an accounting firm, they typically have access to such software, enabling them to efficiently prepare your tax and accounting documentation. See also the section on *Payroll and financial management* in *Chapter 60*.
- Register and update your tax registrations as required. De-register when permitted by law.
- Act transparently and communicate openly with your advisors and tax authorities. In case of errors, consider utilising the voluntary disclosure programme, and plan to settle any outstanding amounts. Speak to your advisors whenever you are considering this.
- If your company undergoes a verification or audit by SARS, remain calm and provide the necessary documentation to support your compliance. Regularly communicate with your advisors on the matter.
- Read the guides provided by SARS on various tax topics to better understand your obligations and stay informed.
- If cost constraints prevent you from appointing advisors, be prepared to invest your own time and effort in dealing with SARS, including providing information, submitting filings, and making timely payments.
- Tax laws and regulations and requirements can change over time, so refer to the latest official sources or consult with qualified tax and accounting advisors for specific and up-to-date information.
- Remember the tax filing dates, tax percentages, thresholds, tax tables, etc may also change from time to time so check with your tax or accounting advisors for up-to-date information.
- To avoid penalties, interest charges, and potential deregistration by SARS, it is advisable to submit nil tax returns whenever a filing deadline approaches. This applies even if your company has not conducted any business activities, has no taxable income, or is currently dormant. Regularly filing nil returns demonstrates compliance with SARS regulations, prevents the accumulation of penalties and interest, and safeguards your company's registration status. Additionally, consistent filing helps maintain good standing with SARS, making it easier to obtain tax clearance certificates needed for business loans, government tenders, and other purposes.
- Ensure you have a locally registered public officer as required by SARS.
- You do not need to be a tax law expert unless you already are or feel comfortable handling tax matters, as tax laws can be complex and require significant time to understand fully. Instead, consider hiring qualified and reputable accounting and tax advisors to help you comply with tax regulations. Many accounting firms offer both accounting and tax services, so you will not

need separate advisors. This approach ensures better coordination and more accurate advice and planning for your tax and business matters.

- A summary table of the most important issues related to taxes, as well as the taxes, is provided below for ease of reference.

Tax type	Description	Relevant forms & due dates
Corporate Income Tax (CIT), excluding companies eligible for preferential tax under Small Business Corporation Tax and Turnover Tax	Tax on company profits.	Company determines its financial year, which acts as its tax season. IT14 form filed annually within 12 months of the financial year end. Tax rate: 27%.
Small Business Corporation Tax	Reduced tax rate for qualifying small businesses based on profit.	IT14 form filed annually within 12 month of the financial year-end. Progressive tax rate based on taxable income. Varies from 7% to 27%. See SARS table.
Turnover Tax	Simplified tax system for small businesses based on their turnover.	IT14 form filed annually within 12 months of the financial year-end. Tax rate: 1% to 3% of turnover.
Personal Income Tax (range based on tax bracket)	Tax on individual income from various sources.	Tax year 1 March of each year to last day of February of following year. ITR12 form – submitted annually by individual taxpayers. Deadlines vary (typically end of October for non-provisional taxpayers and January of following year for individual provisional taxpayers). Tax rate range: 18% to 45%. See SARS table. IRP5 form provided by employers to employees annually.

Tax type	Description	Relevant forms & due dates
Provisional Tax	Tax paid in advance by companies and certain individuals based on estimates of taxable income.	IRP6 forms – for individuals and companies with a February year-end: First payment end of August, second payment end of February – both within the tax year; optional third payment end of September following the end of the tax year. IRP6 forms – for companies with year-ends other than February: First payment six months after the start of the company's financial year, second payment at the end of its financial year, optional third payment six months after the end of the financial year-end.
PAYE	Tax withheld by employers from employees' salaries and paid directly to the government.	EMP201 – monthly, by the 7th or last working day. Based on individual salary scales. Discloses PAYE, SDL, UIF and other deductions. EMP501 – biannual reconciliation of PAYE, SDL, UID and other deductions for the period. Due end-October (for half-year) and end-May (for full-year.
Dividends Tax	Tax on dividends paid by companies.	DTR01 and DTR02 forms – Dividends Tax Declaration. Forms filed within one month of dividend declaration and dividend tax withheld by company is paid to SARS. Tax rate: 20%.
UIF	Contributions to support employees during unemployment.	UIF Declaration via EMP201 form – monthly, by the 7th. 2% of remuneration (1% employee, 1% employer).
SDL	Levy imposed for funding education and training as per the Skills Development Act.	SDL Declaration via EMP201 form – monthly, by the 7th. 1% of payroll above R500 000.

EMPLOYMENT AND LABOUR LAWS

"Treat your employees as if they were your most valuable customers."
~ Richard Branson

"The only real competitive advantage is people."
~ Anne M. Mulcahy

"The best and most sustainable competitive advantage a company can have is a reputation for being a great place to work."
~ Brian Chesky

In the next chapter, we will discuss important considerations and requirements regarding labour and employment.
- Explore how to assess and determine the appropriate employment structure for your specific business needs.
- Understand the specific legal obligations and regulations related to employment in South Africa.
- Examine the responsibilities and legal rights that employers have in relation to their employees and vice versa.
- Understand the rights and legal obligations that employees have within the employment relationship and effectively manage and resolve employee-related matters, such as disputes, disciplinary actions, etc.

This chapter aims to provide comprehensive guidance on labour and employment matters to ensure compliance with the relevant laws and foster a productive working environment for both employers and employees.

Chapter 33: Employment and the regulatory environment

In this and the following chapters, we discuss the most important factors for you to keep in mind when employing others. For sole business owners, the same principles below will apply whenever a) you draw a salary and therefore become an employee of the company, and b) you employ others for your company.

Employment laws

Employment is an essential part of any business. Employers need employees to help them achieve their business goals, and employees need jobs to support themselves and their families.

Employment also helps to:
- Grow and sustain the economy through job creation.
- Contribute to tax revenue through payroll taxes, income generation and consumer spending,
- Reduce social welfare costs.
- Develop human capital.
- Grow investment.
- Act as a catalyst for entrepreneurship and innovation.
- Enhance competitiveness at a local and international level.
- Reduce unemployment.
- Increase social stability.

In South Africa, there are several mandatory requirements that employers must comply with when hiring and employing staff. These requirements are set out in a variety of laws and regulations, including the Basic Conditions of Employment Act of 1997 (BCEA), the Labour Relations Act of 1995 (LRA), and the Employment Equity Act of 1998 (EEA).

The **BCEA** sets out the minimum basic conditions of employment for all employees in South Africa, and includes maximum working hours, minimum wages, types of leave and their requirements, public holidays, maternity leave, and termination of employment. It also regulates other matters such as the prohibition of child and forced labour, and discrimination in the workplace.

The **LRA** regulates the relationship between employers and employees. It covers a wide range of topics such as the right to freedom of association and collective bargaining, the right to strike, the right to fair labour practices, unfair dismissal, and resolution of disputes. The LRA also established the CCMA, which is a statutory body that helps to resolve labour disputes between the employer and the employee.

The **EEA** aims to promote employment equity in the context of South Africa's past discriminatory practices against Black people, woman, and people with disabilities. This legislation requires employers to take certain steps to ensure that their workforce is representative of the population. This includes taking steps to address past discrimination, and to promote the advancement of the designated groups as mentioned above including the youth.

The main differences between the BCEA, LRA and the EEA is that the BCEA sets out the minimum basic conditions of employment, while the LRA regulates the relationship between employers and employees, and the EEA aims to promote employment equity.

Relevance of earning thresholds

Employment laws aim to protect all employees, with a particular focus on safeguarding the most vulnerable individuals. To provide enhanced protection, the law sets a threshold based on the employee's annual earnings. As of 1 March 2023, the threshold is set at R241 110.59 (approximately R20 093.00 per month). The previous earnings threshold was R224 080.48. Effective 1 April 2024, the earnings threshold will increase to R254 371.67 (approximately R21 198 per month). This means that employees earning below the revised threshold are entitled to full protection under the BCEA, LRA, and EEA.

The term *earnings* refers to the gross salary before deductions (such as income tax, retirement contributions, and medical aid, including employer contributions), but excludes items like commissions, overtime pay, allowances, achievement awards, etc.

Employees who fall below the threshold can claim benefits under the BCEA, such as ordinary working hours, overtime pay, average working hours, meal intervals, rest periods, and other entitlements (double-pay for work on Sundays and public holidays). In case of disputes, eligible employees can refer their matters to the CCMA instead of the courts. Even employees earning above the threshold can access the CCMA for claims of unfair discrimination.

However, employees earning above the threshold generally have limited access to the CCMA for other types of disputes and may need to resolve them through the courts (such as the Labour Court or High Court). But there are exceptions, and they may still access the CCMA for specific issues like unfair dismissal at certain stages or violations of basic employment conditions.

Under the LRA, employees earning below the threshold who have been employed for three months or under successive fixed-term contracts can claim permanent employment status. Regarding the EEA, employees earning below the threshold who have referred a conciliation matter to the CCMA have the automatic right to refer the dispute to arbitration, while those earning above the threshold do not have this automatic right. It is important to note that the EEA also covers other aspects beyond automatic referral to arbitration, and its impact on employees above the threshold can be complex. We recommend seeking professional legal advice for specific situations.

Constitutional protection of employee rights

The South African Constitution of 1996 also sets out the rights of employees including:

- The right to freedom of association, and the right to form and join a trade union.
- The right to collective bargaining.
- The right to strike.
- The right to fair labour practices.
- The right to equal pay for equal work.
- The right to safe and healthy working conditions.
- The right to maternity and paternity leave.
- The right to annual and sick leave.
- The right to be treated with dignity and respect.
- The right to be protected from unfair dismissal.

The LRA, BCEA and EEA all give effect to the constitutional rights of employees.

In addition to these mandatory requirements, there are also several codes of good practice that employers are encouraged to follow. These codes provide guidance on how to create a fair and equitable workplace, and how to avoid discrimination and harassment.

Employer rights

The reason for protecting the rights of employees is that there is a power imbalance between employees and employers, and so the Constitution and labour laws seek to redress this by protecting the rights of employees. This does not mean that employers have no rights.

The employer's rights can be summarised as follows:
- Manage their businesses as they consider proper including protecting their property and employees.
- Hire and discipline, including dismiss employees, subject to following the applicable legal requirements and disciplinary code.
- Set wages and working conditions subject to compliance with the BCEA and any applicable collective agreements.
- Engage in collective agreements to decide wages and working conditions for employees with the relevant trade unions.
- Apply the principles of lock-out and no-work-no-pay in case of any strikes.
- Enforce contractual obligations on employees, such as restraints of trade.
- Freedom of association and freedom of expression.

Employers and employees must always follow the law, act in accordance with their contractual obligations, and treat each other fairly.

Factors to consider when deciding whether to employ others

When deciding whether to employ others, businesses should consider the following factors:

- **Size and complexity of the business.** Larger and more complicated businesses, and those that are heavily regulated, have a greater need for employees.
- **Human capital requirements.** Businesses should consider the skills, knowledge and experience they need from employees,
- **Owner capabilities** (particularly among small companies, sole proprietors, and partnerships). Businesses should identity the skills, knowledge, and experience that the owners do not have that would justify employing others.
- **Compliance requirements.** Some laws and regulations require businesses to employ persons with specific qualifications.
- **Cost.** Businesses should factor in the cost of salaries, benefits and taxes when considering whether to employ others and this should form part of the budget.
- **Tax incentives.** The *ETI* referred to in *Chapter 31* was specifically created as a tax incentive for employers to employ specific categories of workers.
- **Budget.** Businesses should ensure that they have the financial resources to employ and retain others.
- **Compensation.** Businesses should offer employees a competitive salary and benefits package to attract and retain their employees while also considering their budgets and financial resource constraints.
- **Outsourcing vs employment.** Businesses should consider whether it is more cost effective to outsource certain tasks to third-party companies who have the necessary qualifications and experience rather than hiring employees.
- **Business plans.** Businesses should consider their future growth plans when making hiring decisions and make appropriate changes to the budgets in their business plans. A critical part of any business plan is considering the human capital requirements to grow the business.
- **Other relevant factors.** Businesses should consider any other relevant factors that are important to them, such as their company culture and values, when making hiring decisions and the legal requirements to ensure a representative workforce (eg to meet the requirements for Broad-Based Black Economic Empowerment purposes).

Understanding the context of unemployment in South Africa

South Africa has a high unemployment rate, especially among the youth. In 2022, the official unemployment rate was above 33%, but the youth unemployment rate was over 60%. This means that more than half of all young people in South Africa are unemployed. The Black population group is the most impacted when it comes to unemployment.

There are several factors that contribute to high unemployment in South Africa, including:

- **A mismatch between the skills of the workforce and the needs of the economy.** Many young people in South Africa do not have the skills that are in demand by employers. This is due to several factors, including a poor education system, and a lack of access to training and development opportunities.
- **A lack of economic growth.** South Africa's economy has been growing slowly in recent years, which has led to fewer job opportunities.
- **An elevated level of inequality.** South Africa is one of the most unequal countries in the world. This means that a small number of people control a large share of the country's wealth, which leaves less wealth and opportunity for the rest of the population.

The high unemployment rate in South Africa has several negative consequences causing poverty, crime, and social unrest. It also reduces the country's economic growth potential.

The South African government has identified unemployment as a priority issue with several initiatives, including:

- **Investing in education and training.** The government is investing in education and training to ensure that unemployed and particularly young people have the skills that they need to find jobs.
- **Promoting economic growth.** The government is working to promote economic growth to create more job opportunities. The *ETI* mentioned in *Chapter 31* is an example of this.
- **Addressing inequality.** The government is working to address inequality through several measures, such as land reform and social grants.

However, more needs to be done to address the problem of high unemployment in South Africa, especially among the youth. The government, businesses and civil society need to work together to create a more inclusive economy that provides opportunities for all.

By considering the unemployment levels faced in the country, companies will be able to proactively contribute to addressing the unemployment challenges when making their hiring decisions. It also contributes to companies being responsible corporate citizens.

Chapter 34: Employment contracts and policies

All employees in South Africa should have a written employment contract to provide certainty and clarity for both the employer and the employee, and to avoid disputes on the terms of employment. The contract must set out the terms and conditions of employment, including:

- Personal details of the employee and the employer, including relevant contact details.
- Job title and description of the job including the employee's duties and responsibilities.
- The general location of employment, eg remote, on-site/at the office, or hybrid.
- The start date of employment.
- Any applicable probationary periods.
- The notice period for either party to terminate the contract, including procedures to be followed in case of termination, grounds of dismissal (eg resignation, retirement, or for misconduct).
- Salary and benefits due to the employee including, where applicable, things like medical aid, pension or retirement fund contributions, travel and car allowances, bonuses, employee incentives, commissions, and any other benefits.
- The working hours.
- Leave, including annual leave, sick leave, and family responsibility leave.
- Compliance with the company's code of conduct and applicable laws by the employee.
- Confidentiality requirements.
- Any applicable non-compete or restraint of trade requirements.
- Any other terms and conditions the employer needs.

Consult with a labour/employment lawyer for the drafting of a template employment contract for your company that will take into consideration all the legal requirements.

Termination of employment

Employers must follow certain procedures when terminating an employee's employment. The procedures vary depending on the reason for termination. For example, if an employer is dismissing an employee for misconduct, the employer must give the employee a notice to attend a disciplinary hearing and comply with any disciplinary code adopted by the company, in addition to complying with the labour laws. Termination for retrenchment must follow the necessary legal process with consultation and alternative job positions being explored before termination is deemed necessary. Employees who voluntarily resign must serve out any applicable notice period unless the employer agrees to a shorter notice period.

Confidentiality

Employees must maintain the confidentiality of any information they obtain while employed and not disclose it to third parties without their employer's consent. This obligation to keep information confidential applies even after the employment relationship ends. This means that employees are not allowed to share confidential information or take any proprietary documents or information with them when they leave the company. Moreover, employees are prohibited from using such confidential information to set up their own business.

An employer must protect the personal information of an employee in accordance with the employment contract and applicable laws such as the Protection of Personal Information Act of 2013.

Restraint of trade

A restraint of trade is a contractual term that prevents an employee from joining a competitor or starting a business that will be in competition with the company or soliciting customers from the former employer. Such restraints are legal under South African law subject to being reasonable and enforceable. The determination of what is reasonable and enforceable is based on:

- The nature of the employer's business.
- The employee's position and responsibilities.
- The scope and duration of the restraint.
- The geographical territory covered by the restraint.

The courts in considering whether the restrain is reasonable and enforceable will consider the legitimate business interest of the company (such as protecting confidential information or proprietary information being used by the former employee and/or being divulged to its competitors) and balance it against the limitation on the employee's freedom to earn a living and associate with others. The employee's position within the company and their actual knowledge are key factors in considering whether the restraint is reasonable. Any restraint must be in writing and be specific to the employee's role within the company, specify the duration of the restraint and its geographical application. Blanket restraints for all employees without having regard for their specific position will not be regarded as reasonable. An unlimited or excessive duration of the restraint and applying it to a wide geography will also be considered unreasonable.

You should consult a labour lawyer when drafting a restraint of trade and carefully consider which employees or categories of employees to whom the restraint will apply. There is no general requirement to pay an employee for a restraint of trade after they leave the company.

Discrimination

Discrimination in the workplace is prohibited in South Africa. This means that employers may not discriminate against employees based on their race, gender, religion, sexual orientation, pregnancy, marital status, family responsibility, ethnic or social origin, colour, age, disability, religion, HIV status, conscience, belief, political opinion, culture, language, birth, or any other arbitrary or protected ground. Employers must create an inclusive workplace that is free from such forms of discrimination.

Harassment

Harassment, and sexual harassment in particular, in the workplace is also prohibited in South Africa. This means that employers must take steps to prevent and address harassment in the workplace.

Policies

Depending on the size, type and complexity of your organisation, consider adopting the following policies (which you should communicate and make available to all employees). Tailor the policies to suit the requirements of your organisation and implement the policies consistently and fairly. Ensure all policies follow legal requirements (including codes of good practice) and seek the help of human resource advisors in case of any queries or to draft the relevant policies.

- **Workplace health and safety policy.** Implement measures to ensure a safe and healthy work environment, including risk assessments, safety protocols, emergency procedures, and occupational health programmes.
- **Environmental policy.** Outline the company's commitment to environmental sustainability and employee responsibility.
- **Substance abuse policy.** Set standards for workplace behaviour regarding alcohol and drug use.
- **Equal opportunity, diversity, and non-discrimination policy.** Clearly define expectations for fair treatment, equal opportunity, and embracing diversity and non-discrimination based on factors such as race, gender, age, disability, religious or political views, sexual orientation, marital or pregnancy status.
- **Anti-harassment and bullying policy.** Establish a zero-tolerance policy against any form of harassment, bullying, or intimidation and provide mechanisms for reporting and addressing such incidents.

- **Leave policy.** Outline the types of leave (annual, sick, maternity/paternity, etc) employees are entitled to, as well as the procedures for applying, granting, and managing leave.
- **Grievance and disciplinary procedures.** Establish a fair process for addressing employee grievances, complaints, and disciplinary matters, ensuring transparency and procedural fairness.
- **Social media and information technology usage policy.** Set guidelines on the appropriate use of social media and company technology resources, including email, internet, and data privacy considerations.
- **Training and development policy.** Promote continuous learning and skills development by offering training opportunities, career development programmes, and support for professional growth.
- **Flexible working policy.** Define guidelines for flexible work options such as remote work, flexitime, compressed work weeks, and job sharing, while balancing business needs and employee work-life balance.
- **Confidentiality, intellectual property, and data protection policy.** Safeguard sensitive company information including intellectual property, client data, and personal employee information by setting guidelines to ensure confidentiality and follow data protection laws.
- **Performance management policy.** Establish a structure for regular performance evaluations, goal setting, feedback mechanisms, and recognition programmes to drive employee performance and development.
- **Remuneration policy.** Structure salaries, benefit packages, bonuses, and overtime compensation in a fair and consistent manner.
- **Retrenchment and redundancy policy.** Outline the procedures and support mechanisms in case of retrenchment or redundancy, including consultation, selection criteria, and any applicable severance packages.
- **Whistleblower policy.** Encourage employees to report any unethical activities or misconduct by providing a confidential and protected reporting mechanism to address concerns.
- **Employee assistance programme (EAP).** Provide confidential counselling and support for employees facing personal or professional challenges.
- **Employee handbook.** An all-encompassing document outlining working conditions, benefits, conduct expectations, disciplinary procedures, and grievance processes. Reference and/or include the code of conduct.

Chapter 35: Collective agreements and trade unions

Collective agreements

Collective agreements, or collective bargaining agreements, are written agreements between the trade union or worker representative body and an employer or employer organisation that regulates the terms and conditions of employment of workers. Collective agreements are legally recognised and protected under South African law and are binding for the duration of the validity period of the agreement. The collective agreement typically covers wages, working hours, leave, benefits, disciplinary procedures, and dispute resolution procedures. Such agreements play a significant role in South Africa's labour relations system as they ensure, for the benefit of employers and employees, an agreement is reached on the various labour issues for a set period. Although the negotiations are well known to be difficult, the advantage is that it creates certainty for the employer by ensuring there is no need to negotiate individual terms of employment for those employees who fall under the collective agreement, at least for the duration of the agreement.

Collective agreements can be negotiated at the sectoral, enterprise or individual plant level. Sectoral collective agreements are negotiated between trade unions and employer organisations at the industry level and apply to all workers in that industry. Enterprise collective agreements are negotiated between trade unions and employers at the company level and apply to all workers at that company. Plant collective agreements are negotiated between trade unions and employers at the plant level and apply to all workers at that plant. The applicable collective agreement should be available to all employees from the relevant trade union or the employer.

The main benefits of collective agreements are that they:
- Provide certainty to employers, employees, and the trade unions on the terms of employment for a specific period.
- Improve wages and working conditions for employees by setting out minimum standards for pay and other benefits.
- Reduce conflict in the workplace by providing a framework for resolving disputes between workers and employers.
- Increase productivity by creating a more stable and harmonious work environment.
- Improve the competitiveness of companies by helping to attract and retain skilled workers.
- Promote fair and equitable labour relations in South Africa.

The existence of a collective agreement does not mean that a company does not need to have individual employee contracts in place. A collective agreement is between the trade union and the employer. The employee contract is specific to the employee and will cover specific terms that are supplemental to the collective agreement.

Trade unions – rights and obligations

Trade unions have played a historic role in the fight against apartheid and the protection of workers' rights. They continue to play a key role in protecting employee rights under the Constitution and labour laws. Trade unions have the right to:

- Protect the rights of workers as enshrined in the Constitution and labour laws.
- Organise and represent workers.
- Bargain collectively with employers on wages and other working conditions.
- Strike and picket.
- Represent workers in grievance and disciplinary hearings.
- Represent workers in arbitration and litigation matters at the CCMA.

Equally, trade unions must abide by the Constitution and labour laws (and other laws generally), including that they too must not engage in unfair labour practices such as:

- Intimidate or coerce employees to join a trade union or force them to participate in trade union activities like strikes and pickets.
- Discriminate against employees based on their membership (or non-membership) of, or support for, a trade union or an employers' organisation.
- Prevent employees from entering or leaving the workplace or from performing their duties.
- Damage an employer's property.
- Disclose confidential information about the employer.
- Enter into collective agreements with clauses requiring employees to join a trade union or pay dues to the union as a condition of employment, prevent employees from resigning from the union, and prevent the employer from managing the business.

If the trade union fails to comply with its legal obligations, it could result in them compensating affected parties or other legal consequences.

Any industrial action, such as a strike, must follow the relevant process and adhere to prescribed timelines. For example, only if the process of mediation followed by arbitration before the CCMA fails to resolve a dispute, may a strike be legally declared, and 48 hours' notice served on the employer. However, the LRA allows trade unions to give no notice if it is in response to unfair labour practices by the employer. Any illegal strike can result in an employer seeking an interdict from the Labour Court prohibiting the strike from going ahead.

Employers do not have to pay workers who engage in any industrial action (such as when they join a strike or engage in a protected lock-out) for such number of days that they are not working (unless a collective agreement requires payment even during a strike). At the same time, employers cannot retaliate against workers who are engaged in a lawful strike or other industrial action, but they can act against employees who are engaged in any unlawful activity or cause damage to company property.

Chapter 36: Employee leave entitlements

Employers are required to provide certain types of leave (paid leave) while other types are not mandatory (unpaid leave). Companies are free to provide leave benefits that are in addition to legally prescribed requirements and often do so to attract and retain employees.

Regardless of the type of leave, all employers should bear in mind that the law does not allow any form of discrimination based on sex, gender or sexual orientation, and members of the LGBTQI+ communities enjoy the same benefits as heterosexual people. For instance, a spouse in terms of South African law means both those in a heterosexual or same-sex relationship.

Paid leave

All employees in South Africa are entitled to paid leave, including annual leave, sick leave, and family responsibility leave as per the BCEA. The amount of paid leave that an employee is entitled to depends on their length of service and should be contained in their employment contract.

Employers must keep accurate records of leave entitlements and usage as this is subject to review or audit by the Department of Employment and Labour to ensure compliance with the LRA and the BCEA.

Paid leave is a mandatory standard required by law and employers are free to grant additional leave days, which should be in the employment contract.

Annual leave

Annual leave is due to any employee who works more than 24 hours in a month for the employer and is based on an annual leave cycle of 12 months calculated from the day the employee commences employment with the employer. Employees are entitled to, and cannot be denied, annual leave in the leave cycle as follows:

- 21 consecutive days on full remuneration for employees who work five days a week.
- Public holidays must not count towards annual leave.

Although the employee is entitled to request leave at any time, subject to the above, the employer can reject such application for leave based on the operational requirements of the company. For example, if an employee in the finance department wishes to take leave during the preparation of the annual financial statements, or any audit, then the company can reject such application.

Sick leave

Sick leave is based on an employee's date of commencement of employment or the completion of the prior sick leave cycle. Employees are entitled to:

- Six weeks sick leave per 36 months for employees who have been employed for at least six months, and based on a five-day working week, meaning a total of 30 days in a three-year leave period.
- One day sick leave for every 26 days worked for employees who have been employed for less than six months.

The employer is entitled to demand a medical certificate as proof of sickness. Such certificate must be issued by a medical practitioner, or such other person registered as a professional to diagnose and treat patients in accordance with applicable laws and regulations.

Family responsibility leave

Family responsibility leave is three days in any year for employees who have been employed for at least four months and work more than four days per week. Such leave is based on full pay and the employer cannot reject such leave unless exceptional circumstances exist. Typical examples of such leave are the illness or death of a close family member, need to attend to an urgent family matter (like a child's school play or family wedding), or to care for sick or elderly family members. Close family members include spouse or partner, parents and grandparents, children including stepchildren and adopted children, siblings, in-laws, nieces, and nephews. Employers should act reasonably in granting such leave to avoid any adverse finding by a labour tribunal that rejecting the application was unreasonable.

Unpaid leave

In addition to mandatory paid leave which employers must abide by, South African law (in terms of the BCEA and UIF Act) recognises certain kinds of mandatory unpaid leave which employees are entitled to, and which employers must recognise. Employees claiming such unpaid leave will be entitled to claim unemployment benefits under UIF – see the section on *UIF* in *Chapter 27* for details on the entitlement, requirements, and process to be followed. Employers are free to pay such leave or part of it, and this should be in the employment contract.

Parental leave

The BCEA grants the following unpaid parental leave, which is claimable by an employee-parent from the UIF:

- Fathers of a newborn child are entitled to ten consecutive days of unpaid leave (note, not working days).
- One parent of an adopted child, under the age of two years, is entitled to six consecutive weeks of unpaid leave while the second parent is entitled to ten consecutive days unpaid leave. Similar leave entitlements apply to the biological parents who are parties to a surrogacy agreement (called the

'commissioning parents'). The adopting or surrogate parents will decide between them who will take the six consecutive weeks or ten consecutive days leave.

The employee must give the employer one month's prior notice before taking such leave (as far as possible) and supply proof when required by the employer (such as a healthcare practitioner's certificate).

Maternity leave

Under South African law, pregnant employees (employee-mothers) are entitled to four consecutive months of maternity leave. This leave must begin one month before the expected date of birth of the child, or earlier or later as agreed or needed for health reasons. Employees may not go back to work within six weeks after the birth unless their doctor or midwife says it is safe. Employers must always consider the health and well-being of the mother and child to be paramount.

Unlike other forms of leave such as annual leave, sick leave and family responsibility leave, there is no legal obligation on the employer to pay for maternity leave, although companies may opt to pay for some or all maternity leave. If the pregnant employee gets no or partial payment for maternity leave from the employer, the employee may claim compensation benefits from UIF.

At its maximum, UIF will pay working mothers 17.32 weeks (121 days) of maternity benefits. To qualify for UIF maternity benefits, an employee must have contributed to UIF for at least 13 weeks in the six months before they give birth.

Key considerations to keep in mind regarding maternity leave:
- Employees must give their employer one month's notice of the commencement of maternity leave.
- The employee must be receiving less than the normal remuneration while on maternity leave.
- Employers cannot deny employees their legal entitlement to four consecutive months of unpaid maternity leave, nor must they be subject to any adverse negative consequences for claiming it.
- Employees should not be pressurised by the employer to return to work after giving birth and during the four-month maternity leave entitlement.
- Employees returning to work after maternity leave must resume the job they held prior to going on leave, or substantially the same, and be entitled to the same remuneration and benefits as if they had not been on leave.
- Failure by the employer to adhere to the maternity leave entitlement of employees will give rise to an unfair labour practice.
- The employer must be a registered taxpayer, pay the relevant UIF contributions to SARS before the 7th day of each month, and register all employees on the eFiling system.
- The employee and employer must complete and submit various forms, declarations and supporting documents before the UIF will pay out the benefits due.

- The employee must be on maternity leave prior to submitting the documentation to the UIF or within 12 months after the birth of the child.
- A claim for maternity benefits under UIF does not impact any other entitlement to claim from UIF if the employee becomes unemployed later.
- The benefit payable is a flat rate of 66% considering the difference of what the employer pays the employee and the prescribed rate in the benefit schedule under the Unemployment Insurance Act; however, the total amount received cannot be more than what the employee would have received if she were not on maternity leave.
- Normal annual leave continues to accrue to the employee during maternity leave, and the employer cannot deduct such leave from sick or family responsibility leave.

Claiming UIF benefits can be a laborious process and benefits can be delayed. Seek assistance from reputable UIF claims processing companies to assist you if needed.

Legal challenges to leave rights under the BCEA

In October 2023, in a landmark ruling, the Gauteng High Court (Van Wyk vs Minister of Employment and Labour) found that the existing leave entitlements for maternity leave, parental leave, and leave related to adoption and surrogacy under the BCEA (and corresponding provisions under the UIF Act) are unconstitutional, as it infringes on the rights of parents to dignity, to not be discriminated on the grounds of gender, and does not take into proper account the right of the child to be nurtured by both parents rather than just one. The court found the differing leave entitlements by parents to be unjustified and ruled that all parents should be entitled to the same four-month parental leave with the parents deciding how to divide the leave between themselves. The parents would then inform their respective employers and claim the relevant benefits from UIF.

The court therefore declared certain sections of the BCEA and the UIF Act unconstitutional. Effectively, the court's decision erases the concept of 'maternity leave' which is associated with the mother and replaces it with a single concept of 'parental leave' in respect of the birth of a child, adoption, or surrogacy. In addition, the High Court has given parliament two years to amend the law following the judgment. However, the Constitutional Court needs to approve such declaration of unconstitutionality to ensure consistent application of the law throughout South Africa. The government may also appeal the judgment of the High Court to the Constitutional Court.

In practical terms, for employers and employees, pending the decision of the Constitutional Court and/or any changes made to the BCEA by parliament, the current law in respect of maternity leave and parental leave as described in the above sections is still valid. Employers should, nevertheless, be mindful of changes to these types of leave.

Chapter 37: Overtime pay and minimum wage

Employers and employees must agree on the working times of the employee and record this in the employment contract to avoid any misunderstandings. The BCEA prescribes a maximum number of 45 working hours per week (excluding mealtimes). Employers must pay overtime pay to employees who work overtime subject to the earnings threshold mentioned in *Chapter 33*. Certain categories of employees do not qualify for overtime pay:

- Senior managers (although this is not specifically defined).
- Sales staff who travel to customers' premises and regulate their own working hours.
- Employees who earn more than a regulated amount (currently set at R224 080.48 per annum).
- Employees who work for less than 24 hours a month.

Employers must pay employees eligible for overtime pay 1.5 times their normal wage rate except for Sundays when it is at least double the normal wage rate. The maximum permitted overtime is ten hours per any one week. By agreement between the employer and the employee, leave in lieu of paying overtime pay is permitted. Overtime pay or leave in lieu of overtime pay being due must be taken by the employee within prescribed periods.

The basis for prescribing maximum working hours and overtime pay entitlements is to ensure that employers comply with relevant occupational health and safety requirements and protect the well-being of their employees. Even where employees earn above certain amounts or are senior managers, the employer has an obligation to consider the health, safety, and wellbeing of the employees. Employers cannot force employees to work beyond the prescribed limits and without their agreement. Forced labour is specifically prohibited under the BCEA, Section 48.

Minimum wage

All employees in South Africa are entitled to be paid a minimum wage. Government sets the minimum wage and reviews it annually. As of 1 March 2023, the minimum wage is set at R25.42 per hour but there are exceptions for industries that may have different wage requirements and/or in terms of applicable collective agreements.

Chapter 38: Compensation Fund (workman's compensation)

The Compensation Fund is a government agency that provides compensation to employees who are injured or contract diseases while at work. If an employee dies because of an occupational injury or disease, then the dependents are entitled to claim death benefits from the Fund. The Fund and Compensation for Occupational Injuries and Diseases Act of 1993 (COIDA) therefore act as a form of social security for employees and their dependents in the event of death, by providing financial support due to occupational injuries, disease, and death.

All employers in South Africa are required to register with the Compensation Fund. Registration can take place when you register your company with CIPC but the requirement to register with the Compensation Fund is distinct and separate from the company registration process. Alternatively, you must register with the Compensation Fund when you begin to employ people.

COIDA sets out the requirements for employers to register with the Fund and to pay contributions, and the circumstances under which an employee may claim from the Fund. The Compensation Fund and COIDA fall under the authority of the Department of Employment and Labour.

The contribution to the Fund by the employer is based on the risk level of the relevant industry (known as the industrial classification system) in which the employer operates, and results in a particular prescribed tariff that will apply to the company's industry. Assessment fees to the Fund are then calculated based on a percentage of the annual earnings paid to employees (the rate is calculated per R100 of the employee earnings in a particular year). To put it more simply: the assessment fee due to the Fund by the employer in a year = (total employee earnings / 100) x compensation fund assessment tariff applicable to the company's industry.

Example

An employer operates in an industry with a prescribed compensation fund assessment tariff of 2% with total annual earnings paid to the employees of R1 000 000 for the assessment period.

To calculate the assessment fee, you would use the following formula:
Assessment Fee = (Total Employee Earnings / 100) x Compensation Fund Assessment Tariff

Applying the numbers:
1. *Total Employee Earnings = R1 000 000*
2. *Compensation Fund Assessment Tariff = 2% (or 0.02 when expressed as a decimal)*

Therefore:
Assessment Fee = (R1 000 000 / 100) x 0.02 = R10 +-000 x 0.02 = R200

In this example, the employer would owe R200 as the assessment fee to the Compensation Fund for that year, based on the employer's total employee earnings and the industry-specific assessment tariff.

Certain categories of employment are not subject to COIDA, and specified maximum and minimum thresholds apply. For the 2023/24 period, the maximum earnings on provisional assessment is set at R563 520 per annum per employee (Government Gazette 48065 of 17 February 2023). The assessment tariff is reviewed annually.

Employers must make an annual payment of their contributions to the Fund based on Return of Earnings (ROE). The due dates for these contributions can vary, but generally, the process is:

- **Assessment period.** The assessment period for the Compensation Fund typically runs from the beginning of March until the end of February of the following year.
- **Submission of earnings.** Employers must submit a ROE form to the Compensation Fund. This form details the earnings of all employees for the assessment period. The deadline for submitting this form is usually in March or April of each year, but the specific date can vary and should be confirmed annually.
- **Issuance of assessment notice.** Once the ROE is processed, the Compensation Fund issues an assessment notice to the employer, showing the contribution amount due.
- **Payment due date.** The due date for payment is typically set for 30 days after the assessment notice is issued. However, it is important to check the specific due date on the assessment notice, as this can vary.

A letter of good standing will also be issued if the employer is compliant.

Benefits provided by the Fund to employees related to occupational injury or disease:

- Payment of reasonable medical expenses.
- Temporary disability benefits.
- Permanent disability benefits.
- Death benefits for the dependents/family members.

The Fund will investigate all claims received on application by the affected employee (or the dependents in case of death), and if successful, will pay the relevant benefit.

Note that COIDA is a no-fault compensation system, which means that an affected employee (or the dependents) is entitled to compensation without having to prove fault on the part of the employer or any other third party that caused the death, injury, or disease. The employer must timeously report all reportable incidents to the Compensation Fund, provide any required documentation and cooperate in any investigation.

Failure to follow the requirements with the Act and the Fund, including non- or overdue payments, can result in the Fund imposing penalties.

Chapter 39: Individual tax reporting and IRP5 form

Payroll taxes

We have discussed the requirements for employers to register with SARS, and for PAYE, UIF, SDL, COIDA, etc in *Chapters 26* and *27*. We discussed the requirements to register with the Compensation Fund in the previous chapter.

IRP5 / IT3a

An IRP5 form is a tax information certificate provided annually by an employer to its employees so they can submit their personal income tax returns to SARS. The certificate summarises the employee's earnings and deductions for the relevant tax year including:

- Employer's details and tax number.
- Employee's details and tax number.
- The tax year.
- Employee's total income including any lump sum payments such as for bonuses.
- Total income tax deducted (ie PAYE) and other deductions, eg UIF and SDL.
- Any fringe benefit amounts.
- Other deductions such as medical aid and retirement fund contributions.
- Other information.

Unlike the EMP201 form filed monthly with SARS (as discussed in *Chapter 26*), which provides an aggregate overview of tax deductions for all employees but is not shared with them individually, the IRP5 form is a personalised document issued to each employee. It details their annual income, PAYE and other amounts withheld or deducted throughout the year, and other relevant tax information for their individual tax filing purposes.

Remember that individuals' income tax year commences on 1 March of each year and ends on the last day of February of the following year with individual income tax returns due in about October of that year (except for individual provisional taxpayers whose tax returns are generally due in January of the following year after the end of the tax season). Tax season for individual non-provisional taxpayers opens in about July or August of the year; the employer must issue the IRP5 so employees can file their tax returns. The employees are responsible for a) disclosing any other income and deductions that do not appear on the IRP5 certificate, and b) paying any additional taxes due. Note that individual provisional taxpayers will have a longer period to complete their tax returns, generally in January following the end of the tax season (see *Chapter 24* for more details on provisional tax).

IRP5 certificates may also be issued by retirement fund institutions in respect of once-off withdrawals, any encashment upon retirement, death claim benefit payments, Section 14 transfers (transfer of retirement fund benefits from one fund to another in terms of the Pension Funds Act of 1956), payments related to a divorce order, income from an annuity or awarded in accordance with a maintenance claim.

An IT3a is issued when no tax was due and provides the reason for no deductions.

Chapter 40: Codes of good practice

Various codes of good practice under the labour laws have been compiled and are available under the Department of Employment and Labour or CCMA websites. Codes of good practice are not legally binding, but they have persuasive value in courts and other labour dispute bodies such as the CCMA. Employers are encouraged to follow the codes of good practice, as they provide guidance on how to create a fair, inclusive and equitable workplace, and how to avoid discrimination and harassment.

Codes of Good Practice have been adopted in the following areas:

- **LRA codes**
  - Collective bargaining, industrial action, and picketing, which provides guidance on the right to collective bargaining, the right to strike, and the right to picket.
  - Dismissal, which provides guidance on the fair dismissal of employees.
  - Dismissal for operational reasons, which provides guidance on the dismissal of employees for operational reasons such as restructuring or retrenchments.
  - Managing exposure to SARS CoV-2 in the workplace 2022, which provides guidance on how to manage the risk of COVID-19 in the workplace.
  - Picketing, which provides guidance on the right to picket by employees.
  - Who is an employee, which provides guidance on who is classified as an employee for the purposes of the LRA.

- **BCEA codes**
  - Arrangement of working time, which provides guidance on the arrangement of working time including working hours, rest periods and overtime.
  - Expanded public works programmes, which provides guidance on the employment of people involved in the expanded public works programmes.
  - Protection of employees during pregnancy.

- **EEA codes**
  - Employment of persons with disabilities.
  - Equal pay and remuneration for work of equal value.
  - HIV and AIDS and the World of Work.
  - Key aspects of HIV AIDS and employment.
  - Integrating employment equity into human resource policies.
  - Preparing, implementing, and monitoring employment equity plans.
  - Prevention and elimination of harassment in the workplace.

These codes are periodically reviewed and updated by the Department of Employment and Labour, and some may be repealed and replaced so ensure you check the relevant websites or seek guidance from human resource advisors if needed.

Chapter 41: Disciplinary codes and dealing with misconduct

Under the LRA, employers are legally required to have a disciplinary code in place and to communicate the code to all employees. The benefits of having a disciplinary code are as follows:

- To ensure free and consistent treatment of employees when they are accused of misconduct. The disciplinary code provides a clear and objective framework for dealing with disciplinary matters.
- To deter misconduct as it ensures that employees know what the consequences of the misconduct will be, which can ensure a more disciplined and productive workplace.
- Giving employees assurance that any misconduct will follow a particular framework that ensures they will be treated fairly and consistently, and that they understand what the consequences will be for misconduct.
- To protect the company's interests by allowing the company to take disciplinary action against employees who engage in misconduct thereby preventing financial or reputational damage.
- The disciplinary code will help any disputes that are referred to a court or a tribunal in determining whether the company has acted fairly.

A well-drafted disciplinary code will include the following elements:

- A definition of misconduct.
- A list of possible disciplinary sanctions depending on the type of misconduct.
- A procedure for investigating and disciplining employees who are accused of misconduct.

When drafting a disciplinary code, it is important to consider the following factors:

- The size and complexity of the business, including whether the business is in a regulated industry, eg finance or mining.
- The types of misconduct that are most likely to occur. For example, in the finance industry, fraud and embezzlement are more likely to occur.
- The company's culture and values, which may be enshrined in a code of conduct.

It is important to ensure that the disciplinary code is fair and reasonable, complies with all applicable laws and regulations, including the codes of good practice where applicable, and that the code is communicated and easily available to employees. The disciplinary procedure should always be fair and transparent, and the deliberations of the disciplinary committee and its findings should be documented.

The person chairing the disciplinary committee must be fair and independent – independent does not mean that the chairperson cannot be employed by the company but rather that the chairperson is not part of the investigation and must act impartially. In more severe cases, the company may choose to appoint an external chairperson. An employee is not entitled to legal representation (unless the chairperson determines otherwise) but is always entitled to be represented at the hearing by a colleague. The chairperson should never be coerced by the company into finding in favour of the company – the facts must speak for themselves as proven by the company as the complainant. An employee representative who is assisting the employee in defending them from the charges of misconduct should not be subject to any retaliatory action for representing the employee.

Seek the guidance of a labour lawyer in drafting a disciplinary code and for assisting the company in understanding the requirements for disciplinary hearings.

Chapter 42: Employee code of conduct

Employers should consider adopting a code of conduct, which is communicated to all employees. A code of conduct essentially explains what the company expects of its employees in the workplace or while representing the employer. The code of conduct also demonstrates to shareholders, customers, suppliers, and other stakeholders the company's commitment to ethical behaviour. Even if your company is owner-managed with no other employees, some customers may require a code of conduct as part of their onboarding process of your company, so they get comfort that your business values align with theirs.

Some of the topics covered in a code of conduct are:
- A message from the board and senior management stating the reasons for having such a code and their commitment to it.
- The importance of employees abiding by the code.
- Key workplace behaviour such as honesty, respecting one another, integrity, and professionalism.
- Commitment to ethical business behaviour such as no bribery, fraud, embezzlement or acts of dishonesty.
- Avoiding conflicts of interest, or where they cannot be avoided, to declare them timeously to management.
- Compliance with applicable laws and regulations such as competition laws, data protection, etc.
- Creating a workplace that is compliant with health and safety requirements and free of substance abuse and violence.
- Commitment to sustainability, social responsibility, and the environment.
- Confidentiality and intellectual property protection, and protection of the company's assets.
- Creating a culture of inclusivity free of discrimination and harassment, including sexual harassment.
- Mechanisms for reporting any violation of the code or applicable laws and a firm policy of non-retaliation against people who make such reports.

Tailor your code of conduct to your specific business, considering the type, size and complexity of your organisation and the industry, and risks prevailing in your business.

Proper implementation and communication of a code of conduct is essential for establishing expected behaviours, integrity standards, and ethical guidelines for employees. It serves as a guide for conducting business and representing the company in an ethical and responsible manner and adhering to applicable laws. Although your organisation may implement workplace policies as detailed in *Chapter 34* and referenced within the code of conduct, it is essential to understand that the code of conduct offers a broad perspective and guiding principles, rather than delving into specific details covered by individual policies.

Detailed policies will address specific areas of concern and provide more comprehensive guidance.

The code of conduct should also form part of the employment contract, be regularly communicated by management to employees and followed consistently. The code should create a positive and productive workplace, and be clear, concise, and written in plain language so it is easy to understand. The code of conduct should form part of any onboarding programme for new employees, and any periodic refresher training done for employees as a reminder of the company's values. You should also consider getting employees to periodically sign confirmation of their adherence to the code of conduct or written reminders that the code is part of the employment contract.

Chapter 43: Retirement and medical aid contributions

Retirement fund contributions

Under South African law, employers do not have to contribute to an employee's retirement fund unless specified by a bargaining council agreement or an employment contract. However, there are strong incentives for employers to do so, including:

- **Tax benefits.** Employers can deduct contributions to retirement funds from their taxable income.
- **Employee retention.** Offering a retirement fund can be a valuable benefit for employees, leading to increased morale and loyalty to the company.

Employees also receive a tax incentive for making contributions to retirement savings as they can claim deductions from their taxable income based on certain limits. The deduction allowed is either up to R350 000 or 27.5% of their remuneration for PAYE purposes or taxable income, whichever is higher. By deducting this amount, their taxable income is reduced, resulting in a lower tax liability. If an employee's contributions exceed the limit, the excess amount can be carried forward to the following year for deduction. When an employer contributes to an employee's retirement fund, it is considered a fringe benefit. However, only a portion of the employer's contribution is subject to fringe benefit tax and included in the employee's taxable income.

Should an employer elect to create a retirement benefit for its employees it has several options:

- Retirement annuity.
- Provident fund.
- Pension fund.

The applicable laws governing retirement savings are the Pension Funds Act of 1956 and the Income Tax Act of 1962, along with their respective regulations. These laws outline the rules and provisions related to employee contributions, tax benefits, and withdrawal options. Notably, recent changes have aligned withdrawal rules across all three main options (pension funds, provident funds, and retirement annuities) allowing a maximum one-third cash lump sum at retirement. This ensures greater consistency and flexibility for employees when planning their future.

Further significant changes are on the horizon with the upcoming two-pot system. This system separates contributions into two portions – an accessible 'savings pot' for short-term needs and a locked 'retirement pot' for long-term security.

South Africa has many service providers across the range of retirement fund options. Consult with a financial advisor for any queries and to stay informed of important changes such as the two-pot system.

Medical aid contributions

South African law does not require employers to contribute to an employee's medical aid unless a collective bargaining agreement provides otherwise. In all other instances, employers may choose to contribute to the employee's medical aid in whole or, which is more normal, in some proportion (eg 50%) with the employee contributing the rest.

- **Tax benefits.** Employers who contribute to their employees' medical aid can deduct those contributions from their taxable income, providing a financial incentive to do so.
- **Employee retention.** Offering medical aid as a benefit can boost employee morale and loyalty, leading to lower turnover rates.
- **Alternatives to employer contributions.** Even if they do not directly contribute, employers can still support their employees' access to healthcare by offering flexible work arrangements or facilitating group medical aid schemes.

South Africa has many open medical scheme plans, and you should consult with your financial advisor if you have any queries. The employer's contribution to an employee's medical aid is considered a fringe benefit and is fully included in the employee's taxable income for fringe benefit tax purposes.

Impact of the National Health Bill

The proposed National Health Insurance (NHI) in South Africa introduces a potential shift in the landscape of employer-sponsored medical aid contributions. While its ultimate impact remains to be seen, understanding the possible impact to businesses is essential.

The NHI aims to offer universal healthcare, gradually reducing reliance on private medical schemes. This could lead to reduced employer contributions to medical aid, as some expenses currently covered by employer-sponsored plans might be handled by the NHI. However, the final details of NHI funding and service coverage are still under development, making the exact impact uncertain.

It is possible that the NHI might coexist with private medical schemes, with medical aid plans adapting to offer supplemental services or cater to specific needs not covered by the NHI. This could still warrant continued employer involvement in medical aid provision, albeit potentially to a lesser extent.

For businesses, keeping informed of developments in the NHI is critical. Remember, the NHI is still in development, and its specifics might change. Therefore, businesses should approach this information with flexibility and adapt as the NHI implementation progresses. Consulting with tax advisors and legal professionals is crucial to understanding the NHI's potential impact on employer contributions, employee taxation, and overall healthcare strategies.

Chapter 44: Employment dispute resolution

Referral of disputes to the CCMA and labour courts

Any matter mentioned in the preceding sections where an employee feels aggrieved by the actions of the employer may be referred to the CCMA or the Labour Court, depending on the type of complaint and subject to the thresholds mentioned in *Chapter 33*.

The CCMA will typically hear matters involving:

- Unfair dismissal.
- The interpretation or the application of a collective agreement such as the right to strike and the right to picket.
- Conciliation, mediation, or arbitration of disputes between trade unions and employer organisations involving collective agreements.
- The right to freedom of association and the right to collective bargaining.
- The right to fair labour practices.
- Unpaid wages.
- Leave issues, eg annual leave, sick leave, parental leave, and maternity leave.
- Basic working conditions such as working hours and rest periods.

The Labour Court typically hear matters such as:

- Disputes about the validity or interpretation of a provision of the LRA/BCEA.
- Disputes about the jurisdiction of the CCMA.
- Appeals against a decision of the CCMA.
- Disputes about the validity or interpretation of collective agreements, including hearing appeals against decisions of the CCMA involving collective agreements.
- Disputes involving public sector employees.

In some cases, a matter may be referred to the CCMA or the Labour Court. For example, a dispute about unfair dismissal may be referred to the CCMA or the Labour Court depending on the circumstances of the case. You should also consider the thresholds mentioned in *Chapter 33* when considering whether a matter is to be brought before the CCMA or the Labour Court.

You should consult a labour lawyer about which tribunal should hear such matters, or generally for all disputes, so that you protect the interests of the company but at the same time act in compliance with the law in the fair treatment of employees.

Chapter 45: Compliance with labour laws and concluding remarks

We have not detailed the specific consequences for non-compliance with each aspect of the labour laws as detailed in the sections above. In short, the consequences can be summarised as follows:

- Investigations and fines levied by the Department of Employment and Labour.
- Fines and penalties by SARS for non- or incorrect payroll and other employee and employer taxes.
- Criminal prosecutions in cases of use of child labour, human-trafficking, or exploitation.
- Referral of disputes to the CCMA or Labour Courts by employees or trade unions for any contravention of a collective agreement and/or for any alleged unfair labour practice.
- In the case of an unfair dismissal, the CCMA or Labour Courts can impose the following sanctions on an employer:
  - Reinstatement of the employee with back-pay.
  - In the case of a procedurally unfair labour practice, up to 12 months compensation.
  - In the case of an unfair labour practice, up to 12 months compensation.
- Reputational damage, which can jeopardise relationships with government and other customers, and potential termination of contracts.
- Low employee morale and productivity.
- Trade union action.

Retention period of records

Under the relevant employment and tax laws, there are various retention periods depending on the type of records. For purposes of this chapter, the following should be noted in terms of the relevant retention periods:

- **BCEA.** The general retention period of relevant records – three years.
- **EEA.** The general retention period for relevant records – five years.
- **LRA.** There are varying retention periods of three years to indefinite depending on the type of records. All employee records are generally required to be retained for the duration of the employee's employment plus three years thereafter (subject to any legal retention periods).
- **COIDA.** Register of earnings and other information – four years.
- **UIF.** Relevant records, as per the Income Tax Act requirements – five years.

Given the varied types of records under employment and tax laws, it is recommended that you seek legal advice for specific queries. See also *Chapter 59* on record-keeping and specifically the section on *Record retention periods*.

Summary

Employment law in South Africa is complicated and tricky to navigate, but it is important for employers to understand the basic requirements to avoid non-compliance, which could attract investigations and sanctions by the Department of Employment and Labour as well as referral of disputes to the CCMA and/or the Labour Courts. You should seek the advice of a labour lawyer in case of any questions or potential actions by the authorities, or in case of any labour case being referred to the CCMA or Labour Courts.

Employers should also consider the codes of good practice to create a fair workplace.

Additional tips for employers

- Keep accurate employee records.
- Pay all payroll taxes timeously and register with the relevant government agencies where needed.
- Conduct regular training on employment law and company policies.
- Have a clear and fair disciplinary code and disciplinary process in place.
- Enforce disciplinary action in a consistent, fair, transparent, and documented manner.
- Adopt a code of conduct to help employees understand the company's expectations.
- Implement appropriate workplace policies suited to your organisation and communicate the policies to employees.
- Be respectful of all employees and employee rights.
- Maintain a balanced and fair relationship with relevant trade unions.
- Create a culture of tolerance and inclusion, free of discrimination and harassment.
- Invest in the culture of the organisation by providing a safe and healthy environment, open and clear communication, and training and development programmes.
- Depending on the size and complexity of your business, hire experienced and qualified human resource personnel and/or appoint suitable advisors to support your compliance with labour laws.
- Consider utilising human resource software or management tools to streamline administrative tasks and improve efficiency.
- Understand your industry's specific regulations as some industries have specific rules and regulations beyond general labour laws.
- Cooperate with the authorities when requested to do so. If you find yourself in a situation where legal matters are involved or if you need guidance, it is advisable to seek legal advice.
- Stay informed about changes in employment and labour laws including changes to thresholds, due dates, etc.

LAWS AND REGULATIONS

"Commercial law is the oil that lubricates the engine of commerce."
~ Lord Denning

"The essence of the free market is not the absence of rules, but of good rules."
~ Milton Friedman

"Laws are like sausages; it is better not to see how they are made."
~ Otto von Bismarck

In the upcoming chapters, we will provide an overview of the South African legal system, commercial laws and other laws so that you understand the legal framework in which businesses operate. The discussion on laws is limited to those laws that will be of general application to all businesses and is by no means an exhaustive list. AI, in this section, we will provide some guidance on records retention.

We have already discussed the companies' laws, and specifically the Companies Act and the role of CIPC in company formation in *Chapters 1 and 4;* the different tax types and the role of SARS in *Chapter 22 to 31; and* the various employment and labour laws, and the requirements for employers in *Chapters 33 to 45.*

Chapter 46: The legal system

In this chapter, we give you an overview of the South African legal system including the source of our laws and the court system for the adjudication of disputes.

South Africa's legal system

Understanding the legal framework in South Africa is important for any business. The following are the key components of our legal system:

- **The Constitution.** This is the supreme law that guarantees basic rights and freedoms and establishes a democratic government. All other laws must comply with the Constitution.
- **Common law.** This is a flexible body of legal principles based on past court decisions. It fills in the gaps where written laws do not exist and adapts to changing circumstances.
- **Statutory law (Acts).** These are laws passed by Parliament to address specific situations. Examples include laws on company formation, taxation, labour, and IP, to name but a few.

How these components work together

- The Constitution is the foundation, and all other laws must respect and consider it.
- Common law provides a framework for resolving disputes and fills the gaps in written laws.
- Statutory law deals with specific areas in detail and can be updated by Parliament.
- When considering the facts of the case before them, the courts must consider the requirements of the Constitution, applicable legislation and the common law.

Additional points for businesses

- Regulatory bodies like SARS (tax) and CIPC (company registration) issue rules following the laws passed by Parliament.
- These regulations have legal force but cannot contradict the main laws or the Constitution.
- Businesses can challenge decisions by regulatory bodies through various avenues.

The court system

In this section, we provide you with an overview of the judicial system.

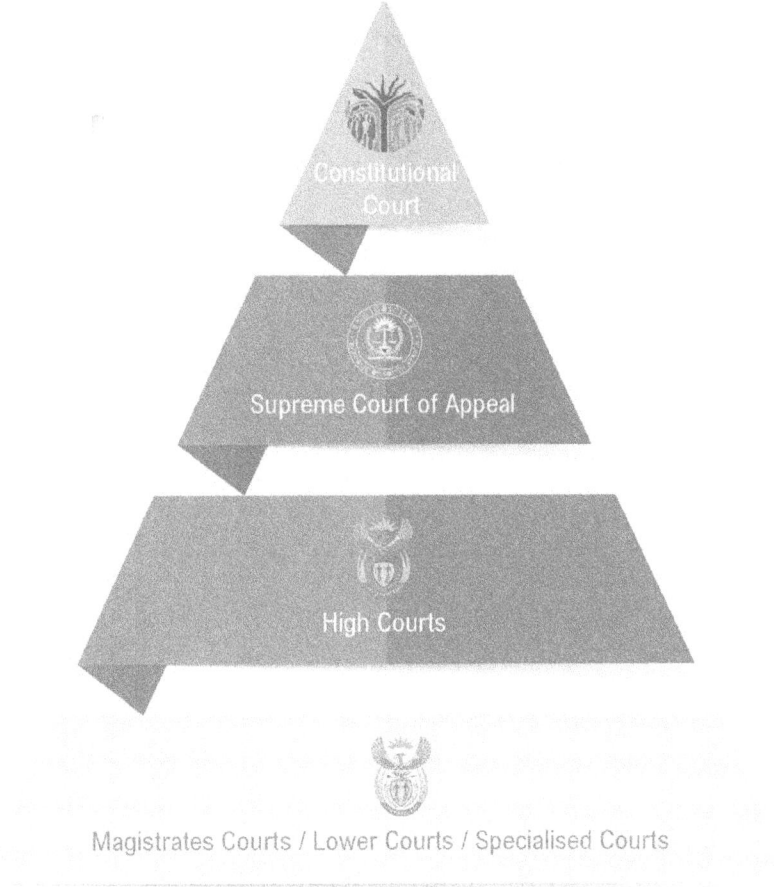

Constitutional Court

Supreme Court of Appeal

High Courts

Magistrates Courts / Lower Courts / Specialised Courts

Constitutional Court

Constitutional Court

* Highest court aka Apex Court
* Final arbiter on all constitutional matters that are referred on appeal (except in case of direct access being granted)
* 11 judges but at least 8 must hear matters
* Based in Johannesburg

- Decides final rulings on all constitutional matters.
- Examples include Bill of Rights disputes and the constitutionality of laws.
- Located in Johannesburg with 11 judges.

Supreme Court of Appeal

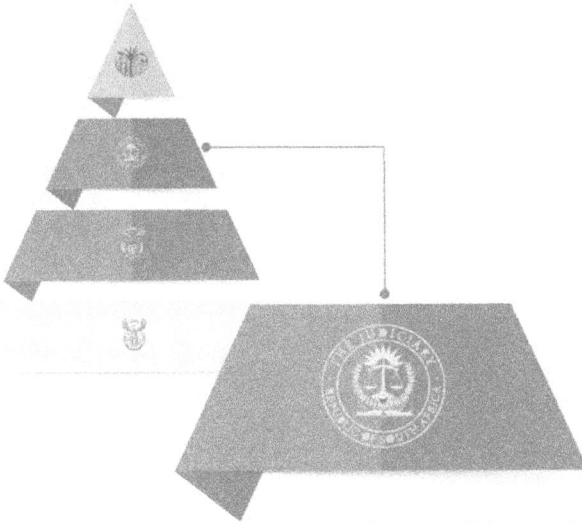

Supreme Court of Appeal

- Highest court on all non-constitutional matters (except for certain matters related to labour and competition law)
- More than 20 appeal judges but at least three or five hear matters assigned by the President of the Supreme Court of Appeal
- Based in Bloemfontein

- The Labour Appeal Court has similar status as the Supreme Court of Appeal in respect of labour matters

- Highest court for non-constitutional matters (except labour and competition law).
- Hears appeals from High Courts.
- Located in Bloemfontein with multiple appeal judges.

Labour Appeal Court (similar to SCA)
- Deals specifically with appeals on labour law matters.
- Decisions can be appealed to the Constitutional Court if a constitutional issue exists.

High Courts

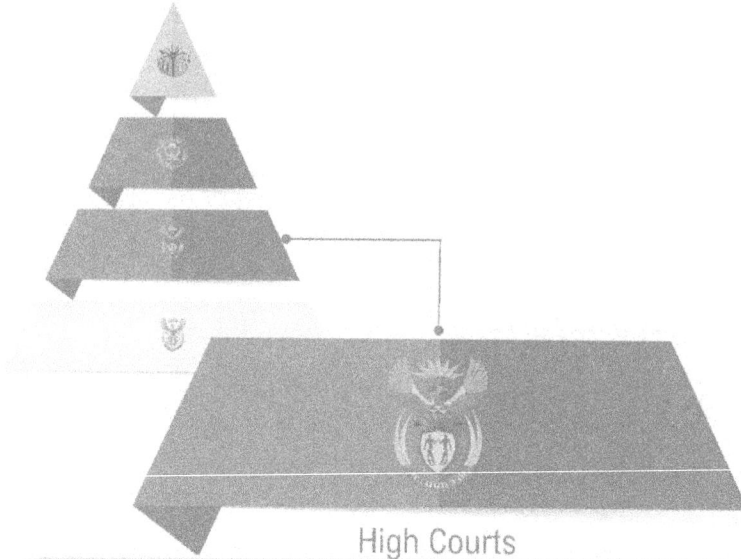

High Courts

- Hears all matters related to its geographical jurisdiction including appeals from Magistrates Courts and where it has authority to hear matters first
- A single judge hears matters assigned to them by the Judge President of the court. An appeal against a judge's decision can be referred to a full bench of that High Court
- Each Province has its own High Court
- Appeals from the High Court are referred to the SCA
- Specialist high courts: Competition Appeal Court (hears appeals from the Competition Tribunal), Labour Court (appeals are heard by the Labour Appeal Court), Land Claims Court, Electoral Court, Tax Court

- Each province has its own High Court and are divided and located as follows:
  - **Eastern Cape** located at Grahamstown with local seats at Bhisho, Mthatha and Port Elizabeth.
  - **Free State** located at Bloemfontein.
  - **Gauteng** located at Pretoria with a local seat at Johannesburg.
  - **KwaZulu-Natal** located at Pietermaritzburg with a local seat at Durban.
  - **Limpopo** located at Polokwane with local seats at Thohoyandou and Lephalale.
  - **Mpumalanga** located at Mbombela with a local seat at Middelburg.
  - **North-West** located at Mahikeng.
  - **Northern Cape** located at Kimberley.
  - **Western Cape** located at Cape Town.
- Handles serious civil disputes, major criminal cases, and some constitutional matters (appeals go to Constitutional Court).
- Hears appeals from lower courts within its province.

Magistrates Courts

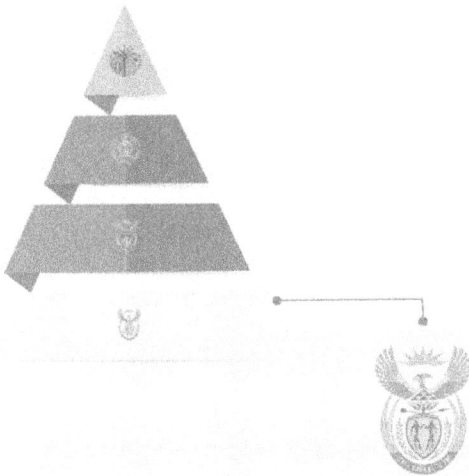

Magistrates Courts / Lower Courts / Specialised Courts

- District court for each geographical district
- Hears matters falling within its authority as per legislation related to certain civil and lesser criminal matters
- Magistrate hears cases assigned by the Chief Magistrate
- Regional court covers a number of districts and can hear matters as per legislation and authority over more serious criminal matters and civil matters up to a certain threshold
- Hears appeals from district and regional courts
- Other courts: Equality Court, Chief's Court, Small Claims Court, Children's Court, Maintenance Court

- Divided into district and regional courts (regional has broader sentencing power).
- Handles smaller civil claims and less serious criminal cases.
- Appeals are referred to the relevant High Court based on the same geographical location of the magistrates' court.

Legal implications for businesses in South Africa

When deciding to refer a matter to the courts, consider the following factors:

- **Dispute value (quantum).** This determines where you file your commercial lawsuit – Magistrates' Court (smaller claims) or High Court (larger claims).
- **Defendant's location.** You can also sue in the court with jurisdiction over the defendant's location.
- **Appeals.** Magistrates' Court decisions are appealed to the High Court. High Court decisions (normally heard by a single judge) can be appealed to a larger High Court panel (three judges) or the Supreme Court of Appeal (SCA).
- **Constitutional Court.** Deals only with matters directly related to the Constitution, even in business disputes.

Specialised dispute resolution

Tax disputes

- Alternative Dispute Resolution (ADR) relating to disputes between a taxpayer and SARS is encouraged (see *Chapter 47*).
- If ADR fails, disputes under R1 million are referred to the Tax Board (which is a tribunal).
- Larger disputes are referred to the Tax Court (which, despite its name, is not a court but rather a tribunal, led by a tax-expert High Court judge).
- Appeals from the Tax Court are referred to the relevant High Court or SCA with permission.
- Only constitutional issues reach the Constitutional Court.

Labour disputes

- Depending on the earnings threshold and nature of the labour dispute between an employer and employee, the matter may be referred to the CCMA or the Labour Court – see *Chapter 33*.
- A CCMA decision may be referred on appeal to the Labour Court.
- Appeals from the Labour Court are heard by the Labour Appeal Court (LAC), which has similar status as the SCA for labour matters only.
- Only employment disputes with a constitutional element reach the Constitutional Court.

Competition law complaints

- Disputes relating to competition law complaints and mergers and acquisitions are handled by the Competition Commission and Competition Tribunal.
- Appeals are referred to the Competition Appeal Court (CAC), a special division of the High Court.
- Appeals from the CAC can only go to the Constitutional Court, not the SCA.

Legal proceedings, no jury system

- Initiated by filing documents with the appropriate court.
- Involves exchanging documents, arguments, and potentially a trial.
- Judgments can be appealed as outlined above.
- Cases are heard by judges, magistrates, or other presiding officers.
- In criminal cases, judges may have expert assessors to assist them.

Factors to consider in litigation

Litigation can be a lengthy and costly process. Consider the following factors:

- **Before commencing litigation.** Carefully evaluate your case with legal and other experts to consider the merits of your case, the documents and witnesses that may be needed and any expert witnesses that may be needed. Consider potential counterclaims from the defendant and inform your insurers (if applicable).

- **Time limits:**
  - **Government claims.** Some laws have strict deadlines for claims against government bodies such as declaring disputes with SARS. Missing these deadlines can bar your claim entirely.
  - **Contractual deadlines.** Contracts may specify timeframes for bringing claims. Pay attention to these to avoid being time-barred.
  - **The Prescription Act of 1969.** This law limits the time you have to sue someone (usually three years from the time you become aware of the claim but other time limits and requirements need to be considered). Missing this deadline can also bar your claim.

Speak to your lawyer about any specific time limits or exceptions that might apply to your situation.

Remember:
- There are other time limits besides the Prescription Act.
- Tax laws and other regulations may also have specific timeframes for claims.

By understanding these time constraints, and consulting your legal, tax and other advisors timeously, you can avoid missing deadlines and jeopardising your legal rights.

Legal advisors: The difference between attorneys and advocates

Understanding the legal system is important, but knowing who to talk to is equally essential. South Africa has a split bar system, similar to the United Kingdom with attorneys and advocates:

Attorneys (solicitors as known in the UK legal system)
- Your first point of contact for legal matters (like a general medical practitioner).
- Handles a wide range of legal issues, with some specialising in specific areas (commercial, family, IP, labour, criminal, etc).
- Can practise independently or form firms/partnerships or personal liability company – see *Chapter 8*.
- Advise clients, handle legal documents, and represent them in lower courts (Magistrates' Courts).

Advocates (barristers in the UK legal system)
- Specialised legal practitioners who argue court cases and give expert legal opinions.
- Instructed by attorneys to use their expertise in court.
- Can specialise in specific legal fields like commercial, competition, family, etc.
- Historically, only argued cases in higher courts (High Courts, SCA, Constitutional Court).

The split bar system (changing landscape)

- Traditionally, attorneys handled general legal matters and referred to advocates for litigation or expert advice.
- In the past, attorneys could go on to become magistrates while advocates could become judges of the higher courts.
- Today, attorneys can represent clients in higher courts and become judges.
- Businesses must still use attorneys first, who may then involve advocates for complex court cases. Even when attorneys refer a matter to advocates, the attorney continues to be involved in the matter.

Who to contact

- Consult an attorney first for most legal needs.
- Your attorney will advise if an advocate is needed for complex litigation.

Benefits and costs

Dual representation (attorney and advocate) can be expensive, but their roles are distinct and complementary.

Regulation

Both attorneys and advocates are regulated by the Legal Practice Council, established under the Legal Practice Act of 2014.

Arbitration and alternative dispute resolution

South African law recognises the right of parties to refer disputes to arbitration and alternative dispute resolution mechanisms rather than bringing the matters to courts. We discuss this in the next chapter.

Summary

The sophisticated nature of the South African legal system necessitates a careful approach when dealing with legal matters. Its rich body of laws and regulations, coupled with a complex court system and alternative dispute resolution methods (discussed in the next chapter), highlight the need for expert guidance. By seeking the assistance of experienced legal advisors, individuals and businesses can ensure they have the knowledge and support needed to effectively navigate the complexities of the legal sphere. This proactive approach can help mitigate risks, protect rights and interests, and ensure compliance with applicable laws and regulations in South Africa.

Chapter 47: Commercial laws

Contracts are the foundation of business dealings. Understanding these core principles can help you navigate commercial transactions smoothly:

- **Freedom of contract.** You can generally agree on terms you see fit, but there are certain limitations.
- **Legality.** Contracts cannot break the law or go against public interest (eg anti-competitive agreements).
- **Capacity to contract.** Both parties must be of legal age and mentally sound to enter a contract.
- **Voluntary agreement.** No pressure, threats, or lies should influence the agreement.
- **Proper contract formation.** Follow the required steps to create a valid contract.

Contract law

South African contract law is a complex and dynamic area of law that is governed by a combination of statutory law and the common law. Specific laws govern contracts, but the common law plays a key role in interpreting and supplementing the provisions of the statutory law. The courts in South Africa also have the power to develop the common law of contract to meet the needs of the changing social and economic environment.

Two sources of contract law

- **Statutory law.** Specific laws like the National Credit Act set ground rules for certain contracts.
- **Common law.** Longstanding legal principles used by courts to interpret and fill gaps in statutory law.
- **The law evolves.** Courts can adjust common law principles to fit the changing business environment.

Examples of contract-related laws

- Alienation of Land Act of 1981 (land purchases).
- Electronic Communications and Transactions Act of 2002 (electronic contracts).
- National Credit Act of 2005 (consumer credit agreements).
- Consumer Protection Act of 2008 (protecting consumers in contracts).

The Constitution is supreme

- All laws, including contract law, must comply with the Constitution.
- Courts can strike down laws or contracts that conflict with the Constitution.

Understanding this structure will help you navigate business contracts in South Africa.

Contract formation

South Africa follows the same principles of contract formation as most other countries.

- **Offer, acceptance, consideration.** These are the building blocks of a valid contract.
- **Offer.** A clear proposal made by one party.
- **Acceptance.** Unequivocal agreement to the offer's terms by the other party.
- **Consideration.** What each party gives or promises in return (money, goods, etc).

Written vs unwritten contracts

- Except for certain types of contracts as described below, there is no legal requirement for contracts to be in writing, ie even a verbal agreement can be a binding contract. Even though not mandatory, written contracts are highly recommended for:
  - Easy proof of terms and existence of the contract.
  - Avoiding misunderstandings.
- Some contracts must be in writing by law:
  - Land sales (Alienation of Land Act).
  - Credit agreements (National Credit Act).
  - Long-term leases (10+ years).
  - Suretyship agreements (common law).
- Not having contracts in writing when required in terms of these laws renders them unenforceable.

Types of contracts

The most common categories of commercial agreements in South Africa include:

- **Sale and purchase agreements** governing the sale and purchase of goods and services between customers and their suppliers, the prices, delivery terms, quality of goods, representations, and warranties.
- **Lease agreements** detailing the terms of property (movable or immovable), vehicles (including fleet management) or equipment rental including rental amount, property description and what it can and cannot be used for, period of lease, terms of any triple net lease, if applicable, etc.
- **Credit or loan agreements** providing for the terms of credit between the borrower and the lender. It will set out the loan amount, interest rates, repayment terms, and any security requirements.

- **Enterprise and supplier development agreements** are specific types of loan agreements given by companies to their suppliers to grow their business in furtherance of BBBEE – see *Chapter 50* for further details.
- **Service Level Agreements (SLAs)** outlining the terms of services to be provided by the service provider to the client including the nature and scope of services to be provided, the length of time, payment terms, intellectual property rights, and any specific obligations or warranties.
- **Employment contracts** showing terms of employment between employers and employees. See *Chapter 34* for more details on what needs to be contained in an employment contract.
- **Collective bargaining agreements** governing the terms and conditions of employment between an employer, or employer group, and the trade union in respect of employees falling under that industry.
- **Partnership agreements** defining the terms of partnership in a business venture including the rights and responsibilities of each partner, profit-sharing arrangements, decision-making processes, provisions for any silent or *commanditarian* partners, and provisions for dissolution of or withdrawal from the partnership.
- **Shareholder agreements** specifying the specific rights and obligations between shareholders such as shareholder voting rights and procedures, dividends and profit distribution, transfer of shares, deadlock resolution mechanisms and dispute resolution mechanisms. Such agreements cannot have provisions that override the terms of the MoI and/or are contrary to the Companies Act.
- **Construction contracts** defining the scope of work, payment terms, timelines, quality standards, and dispute resolution mechanisms. Most construction contracts in South Africa will be international standards like NEC (New Engineering Contracts) and FIDIC (Fédération Internationale des Ingénieurs-Conseils, which translates to The International Federation of Consulting Engineers), or South African specific ones like JBCC (Joint Building Contracts Committee), or construction contracts adopted by a particular industry, or even bespoke construction contracts adopted by the larger companies who have their own templates.
- **Licencing agreements** governing the terms between a licensor and the licensee in which the licensor grants the licensee the right to use the licensor's intellectual property, such as a patent, trademark, copyright, or know-how. In exchange, the licensee pays the licensor a royalty or fee. Licensing agreements are a common way for businesses to monetise their intellectual property and for other businesses to gain access to valuable intellectual property that they may not have the resources to develop themselves.
- **Franchise agreements** governing the relationship between a franchisor and a franchisee setting out the terms for use of the business model, intellectual property, support services, and financial arrangements.
- **Agency agreements** defining the terms 'a principal' and 'an agent', authorising the agent to act on behalf of the principal. It will detail the agent's authority, responsibilities, the duration of the mandate and any fees or commissions payable.

- **Merger and acquisition agreements** detailing the terms and conditions for the merger of two or more legal entities or the acquisition of the one by the other, the purchase price and modality of payment (shares or cash or a combination of these, or other), representations and warranties, transfer of employees (if applicable), regulatory approvals from, for example, the Competition Commission, and so on.
- **Confidentiality agreements/non-disclosure agreements (NDAs)** protecting sensitive and proprietary information from disclosure to third parties, what is protected, what is the intended use for the confidential information being exchanged, duration of the confidentiality, etc.

Each type of contract has its unique features and considerations and needs careful legal advice to ensure they accurately reflect the intentions of the parties.

Boilerplate conditions

Contracts are essential for business, but legal jargon can be confusing. We provide a breakdown of common boilerplate (standard) clauses you will encounter in most South African contracts:

- **Entire agreement.** This clause states that the written contract is the final, complete agreement, superseding any prior discussions or agreements. The purpose of this is to prevent prior documents and discussions from binding the parties.
- **Severability.** If a part of the contract is found invalid, the remaining parts will still be enforceable. This prevents the entire contract from collapsing due to one problematic clause.
- **Amendments.** Any changes to the contract must be made in writing and signed by authorised representatives of both parties.
- **Non-waiver.** If one party overlooks a breach of contract by the other party, it does not mean they waive their right to enforce that clause in the future.
- **No assignment.** Neither party can assign their rights or obligations under the contract to another party without written consent from the other party.
- **Governing law.** This clause specifies the legal system that will apply if there is a dispute about the contract, eg South African law.
- **Dispute resolution.** This clause outlines how disagreements will be resolved. Options include escalation within the two parties' senior management, ADR (mediation), court action, or binding arbitration.
- **Force majeure.** This clause excuses a party from fulfilling their obligations if unforeseen events beyond their control prevent them from doing so (eg natural disasters, wars). The clause should specify the types of events covered and the notification process in such situations.
- **Limitation of liability.** This clause limits the amount of damages one party can recover from the other for a breach of contract. It often excludes consequential or indirect damages.
- **Notices.** This clause specifies how and where legal notices should be sent under the contract. Consider including both physical and electronic communication options.

- **Counterparts.** This clause allows the contract to be signed in multiple counterparts, each considered an original document. This avoids the need for all parties to be present for a single signing.
- ***Contra proferentem* rule exclusion.** The general legal rule interprets ambiguities in contracts against the party who drafted the contract. This clause excludes that rule, meaning ambiguities will not be interpreted against the drafter.
- **Effective date.** This clause specifies the date the contract takes effect, which may be different from the signing date.

Understanding these boilerplate clauses is essential for businesses entering into contracts in South Africa. By familiarising yourself with these terms, you can ensure your contracts are clear, protect your interests, and avoid misunderstandings.

Breach of contract and remedies

When a party does not fulfil its contractual obligations, it is a breach of the contract entitling the innocent party to certain remedies.

What can the innocent party do?

The law provides the innocent party with the following remedies:
- **Specific performance.** Force the breaching party to fulfil their obligations (eg deliver on a promised service or payment as per the contract).
- **Damages.** Seek financial compensation for the losses caused by the breach.
- **Cancellation.** Terminate the contract and claim damages.

Important considerations

- **Follow contractual procedures.** Adhere to any notice requirements outlined in the contract (written notices, timeframes).
- **Paper trail is key.** Document the breach to demonstrate you acted reasonably.
- **Limitation of liability clauses.** Parties can agree to limit their liability towards one another, and courts (or arbitrators) will uphold such clauses unless there is gross negligence, fraud, or a conflict with public policy.

Understanding your rights and remedies in case of a breach is crucial for making informed decisions and protecting yourself in business agreements.

Electronic signatures

The Electronic Communications and Transactions Act of 2002 legalises the use of electronic signatures for both commercial and non-commercial contracts. These electronic signatures hold the same legal weight as if the contract had been hand-signed. However, there are specific exceptions, as mandated by other laws, which require physical signatures. These exceptions include land sale agreements and immovable property transfer agreements, long-term lease agreements, a testator's signature on a will (although, strictly speaking, wills are not contracts), and promissory notes. *See Chapter 55* for further details.

Delictual law and unjustified enrichment

Outside of contract law, discussed above, your business operations can be impacted by two other important legal areas – delictual law and unjustified enrichment.

Delictual law (known in other countries as tort law)

Delictual law deals with harm caused to others (persons or property) that cannot be dealt with under contracts. For example, if a neighbouring business causes damage to your business, there is no contract that will be in place to deal with this but the law of delict will help to recover any damages you suffered.

Businesses can be held liable for:
- **Negligence.** Employees or agents causing harm through carelessness.
- **Intentional acts.** Assault, defamation, etc.

To claim delictual liability, the harmed party (plaintiff) must prove:
- **Unlawful act.** Defendant's action or omission broke the law or reasonable standards.
- **Causation.** The unlawful act caused the harm.
- **Damages.** The plaintiff suffered actual, quantifiable losses (financial, physical, emotional).
- **Fault.** The defendant was negligent or intentional (with some exceptions).

Unjustified enrichment

Unjustified enrichment deals with situations where one party is enriched at another's expense without legal justification.

Examples in a business context:
- **Mistaken payment.** Recovering funds mistakenly paid to someone else.
- **Unauthorised services.** A business benefiting from unauthorised services rendered (eg your neighbouring business took steps to put out a fire at your factory).

How understanding these laws benefits your business

- **Reduces liability.** Identify and address potential delictual or enrichment situations.
- **Protects assets.** Minimise legal exposure and financial losses.
- **Recovers assets.** Reclaim funds or property gained unjustly by others.
- **Protects reputation.** Deal with delictual claims promptly and effectively.

By understanding these legal concepts, you can take proactive steps to safeguard your business in South Africa.

Arbitration

Commercial disagreements are inevitable. The primary options to resolve disputes are litigation by referring the matter to courts or to arbitration or referring the matter to mediation.

Referral of dispute to court (litigation)

- **Standard option.** This is the traditional method for dispute resolution.
- **Public record.** Court proceedings and filings are open to the public.
- **Judge selection.** No control over the judge assigned to your case.
- **Potentially lengthy.** Court cases can take a long time to conclude.
- **Rigid procedures.** Court rules dictate the process, offering less flexibility.

Arbitration (alternative dispute resolution)

- **Private and confidential.** Protects sensitive business information.
- **Neutral decision-maker(s).** Parties choose experienced arbitrators for a fair resolution.
- **Faster resolution.** Arbitration is often quicker than litigation but this is not always the case.
- **Flexible procedures.** Rules can be adapted to the specific dispute.
- **Internationally recognised.** Enforceable under the New York Convention on the Recognition and Enforcement of Foreign Arbitral Awards.

When is arbitration a good choice?

- **International disputes.** Ideal for cross-border disagreements.
- **Complex matters.** Well-suited for intricate legal or technical issues.
- **Long-term relationships.** Maintains confidentiality and preserves business ties.
- **Specialised knowledge.** Arbitrators can have expertise relevant to the dispute while judges who get assigned a case in court may not necessarily have the required experience or knowledge.

What to include in an arbitration clause

- **Binding arbitration.** Clearly state that the arbitration award is final.
- **Appeals process (optional).** Specify if appeals are allowed and to whom.
- **Timeline.** Set a time limit for initiating arbitration.
- **Location and language.** Decide on the venue and language for the hearing.
- **Number and selection of arbitrators.** Determine how many arbitrators there will be and how they will be chosen.
- **Arbitration body.** Choose an arbitration institution such as the Arbitration Foundation of Southern Africa (AFSA), International Chamber of Commerce ICC), etc.
- **Cost allocation.** Outline how arbitration costs will be divided.
- **Interim relief.** Specify the right to seek temporary solutions from a court.

Remember:
- A silent contract defaults to court proceedings unless both parties agree to arbitration.
- Courts enforce arbitration awards, overturning them only in rare cases.

Alternative Dispute Resolution

Alternative dispute resolution (ADR) offers an alternative method of resolving disputes between commercial parties instead of referring the matter to court or arbitration.

What is ADR?

ADR stands for Alternative Dispute Resolution. Examples include negotiation and mediation.

Benefits of ADR

- **Confidentiality.** Protects sensitive business information.
- **Flexibility.** Tailored to your specific needs and preferences.
- **Cost and efficiency.** Saves time and cost compared to litigation through court or arbitration.
- **Control.** You have more control over the process.
- **Relationship preservation.** Fosters collaboration and lessens hostility.

Drawbacks of ADR

- **Enforceability.** Agreements might not be self-enforcing, requiring court intervention.
- **Limited scope.** May not be suitable for complex legal issues or high-value claims.
- **Expertise cost.** Skilled mediators can add to the overall cost.

ADR options

- **Court-referred mediation.** Courts can suggest mediation in some cases (family law, commercial disputes with prior mediation agreement).
- **Arbitration institutions.** AFSA can assist with appointing a mediator.
- **Legal associations.** Law Society of South Africa offers ADR training and resources.
- **Commercial organisations.** Chambers of commerce promote ADR use among members.
- **Government agencies.** CCMA (Commission for Conciliation, Mediation and Arbitration) helps with labour disputes.
- **DiSAC.** South African Dispute Settlement Accreditation Council, a professional body for mediators and arbitrators.

Summary

Contract law in South Africa is both sophisticated and intricate, stemming from its rich common law heritage dating back centuries and interwoven with modern statutory laws that govern or influence various aspects of contract agreements, as well as the law of delict and unjustified enrichment. It is important to remember:

- While you do not need to be a lawyer to grasp the intricacies of contract law, it is essential to understand the contracts you sign or draft for your business.
- Implement standardised contract templates to streamline interactions with your customers and suppliers.
- Familiarise yourself with the fundamental principles of contract law, such as the requirements of the Consumer Protection Act and other important pieces of legislation that are most critical to your line of business.
- Maintain a registry and copies of all finalised contracts.
- Do not sign any contract without understanding at least the fundamental terms.
- Having a good grasp of the basic principles of contracting, knowing what you sign, and maintaining good record-keeping of contracts signed are all critical to managing the risk to your business and avoiding (or at the minimum, mitigating the risk of) disputes or litigation with customers and suppliers.
- Consider referring matters to arbitration in cases of complexity or cross-border disputes.
- ADR can be a better alternative to resolving disputes.
- Litigation (whether in court or arbitration) is costly and time consuming. You should provide adequate resources to the dispute and appoint qualified legal advisors to represent you. Inform your insurers in case of any claims that could result in liability for you and for which the insurer has an obligation to indemnify you – failure to notify the insurer could result in your insurance claim being rejected.
- Seek legal guidance on any of these aspects if you have any questions or concerns.

Chapter 48: Consumer Protection Act

The Consumer Protection Act of 2008 (CPA) is a landmark piece of legislation that safeguards consumer rights and promotes fair business practices. The primary goal of the CPA is to establish consumer rights and supply free, effective, and efficient enforcement of those rights through the establishment of the National Consumer Commission (NCC), the National Consumer Tribunal (NCT), and various industry ombuds. If your business is engaged in the provision of goods and services to consumers in the country, then you should ensure you act in accordance with this law.

Key aims of the CPA

The CPA imposes a range of obligations on businesses to ensure fair and ethical treatment of consumers. Some of the key requirements include:
- Create consumer rights and enforcement of consumer rights.
- Protection of vulnerable consumers.
- Promote fair business practices.
- Improve standards of consumer information, prohibit unfair marketing and business practices.
- Promote a fair, accessible and sustainable marketplace for consumer products and services.
- Promote responsible consumer behaviour.
- Create a consistent legislative and enforcement framework for consumer protection rights.

What are the consumer's rights?

Consumer rights under the Act can be summarised as follows:
- **Right to equality** in the consumer market and protection against discriminatory marketing practices, ie not to be subject to any form of unfair discrimination based on gender, race, disability and other categories.
- **Right to privacy** of their information and not to receive unsolicited advertising and to opt out of direct marketing at any time.
- **Right to choose** a supplier or service provider of their choice, to cancel or renew a fixed-term agreement and to request pre-authorisation for repairs and maintenance services.
- **Right to return goods** that could not be examined prior to delivery and to seek refund for defective or unsafe goods provided it is done within a reasonable time.
- **Right to disclosure of information** of the products and services, including relevant agreements that must be in plain and simple language, documents and other information related to the transactions (such as invoices, suppliers' details, description of the goods, pricing information, etc).
- **Right to fair and responsible marketing practices** including protection against or full disclosure related to bait marketing, negative option marketing,

catalogue marketing, trade coupons and promotions, customer loyalty programmes, etc.

- **Right to fair and honest dealings** including against unconscionable conduct (eg harassment or taking advantage of those who are vulnerable), false or misleading or deceptive representations, fraudulent or pyramid schemes, etc.
- **Right to fair, just, and reasonable terms and conditions** that is written in plain and understandable language including accessibility to contracts; suppliers cannot create transactions that are prohibited by other laws or are illegal in any way, etc.
- **Right to fair value, good quality and safety** including goods free of defects, high quality service, timely performance and completion of the services, an implied warranty of quality or repaired goods, warnings of any risks, to claim damages for injuries, etc.
- **Additional rights** as detailed in the Act.

Who does the CPA apply to?

The CPA applies to all businesses that supply goods and services to consumers in South Africa. This includes both domestic and foreign businesses. The CPA also applies to transactions that occur online or through other electronic means.

Who does the CPA not apply to?

The CPA is primarily aimed at protecting individual consumers and small businesses to shield them from unfair terms and conditions by suppliers. Juristic entities with an annual turnover of R2 million or more at the time of the transaction are not entitled to the same protection, except for certain provisions such as Section 61, which deals with liability for damages caused by defective or unsafe goods. Note that due to the exemption of juristic entities from the Act, sole proprietors (being individuals) are entitled to all the protections under the CPA. Partnerships are expressly defined as being of the same status as companies so if the partnership's turnover is less than R2 million the Act will apply to them.

The CPA has certain other exemptions to which the Act does not apply, such as goods or services supplied to the Government, credit agreements under the National Credit Act of 2005, or employment or collective bargaining agreement arrangements and other exemptions.

Regulatory bodies

The National Consumer Commission (NCC) is the primary regulator responsible for enforcing the CPA. The NCC has a range of powers, including the ability to investigate complaints, issue compliance orders, and impose penalties on businesses that contravene the CPA.

Other relevant regulatory bodies include:

- **The Competition Commission of South Africa (CCSA).** The CCSA is responsible for enforcing competition law, which includes provisions that protect consumers from anti-competitive practices.
- **The Advertising Standards Authority of South Africa (ASA).** The ASA regulates advertising and marketing practices and can act against businesses that engage in misleading or deceptive advertising.
- **The Financial Sector Conduct Authority (FSCA).** The FSCA regulates the financial services industry and has powers to protect consumers from unfair or deceptive practices.
- **Other regulatory bodies** will have authority based on the specific industry in which you operate.

Retention period of records

Under the CPA, the general retention period is three years for all records.

We recommend that you seek legal advice for specific queries related to your record-keeping and retention periods. See also *Chapter 59* on record-keeping and specifically the section on *Record retention periods*.

Summary

The CPA is an essential tool for safeguarding consumer rights and promoting fair business practices in South Africa. Businesses have a responsibility to comply with the CPA and ensure that they treat their customers fairly and ethically. Consumers should be aware of their rights under the CPA and should not hesitate to act if they believe they have been unfairly treated. Juristic entities with an annual turnover of R2 million or more, at the time of the transaction, are not entitled to protection under the CPA (except for certain provisions like Section 61). If you are supplying goods and services to individuals and small businesses, you should ensure your terms and conditions of supply and your actions follow the provisions of the CPA. Seek the aid of legal advisors to help draft compliant terms and conditions, and in the case of any disputes arising.

Chapter 49: National Credit Act

The National Credit Act of 2005 (NCA) regulates consumer credit and promotes fair and responsible lending practices. It aims to protect consumers from unfair and unethical credit practices (predatory practices), promote financial literacy, and ensure a sustainable and responsible credit market. If you provide any form of credit falling within the ambit of the Act, it is critical you understand the requirements of and follow this Act.

Purpose of the NCA

The NCA serves several important purposes in the South African credit market:

- Protects consumers from unfair and unethical credit practices, ensuring that they are treated fairly and responsibly throughout the credit process.
- Promotes financial literacy by requiring credit providers to a) provide consumers with clear and concise information about credit products, and b) enable them to make informed decisions.
- Promotes a sustainable and responsible credit market by encouraging responsible lending practices and reducing the risk of over-indebtedness among consumers.

Key requirements of the NCA

The NCA imposes a range of obligations on credit providers to ensure transparent and responsible credit practices. These requirements include:

- Credit providers must provide consumers with clear and concise information about the terms and conditions of credit agreements, including interest rates, fees, and repayment obligations.
- Credit providers must conduct thorough affordability assessments to ensure that consumers can afford the credit they are applying for without experiencing financial hardship.
- Credit providers must avoid misleading or deceptive marketing practices and ensure that their advertising is targeted responsibly.
- Credit providers must provide access to debt counselling and repayment assistance programmes for consumers who are struggling with debt.
- Credit providers must have effective mechanisms for handling consumer complaints and resolving disputes promptly and fairly.
- Regulation of maximum interest rates and maximum fees for agreements falling under the Act.

It applies to any party supplying credit, as defined under the Act, such as credit facilities, credit transactions, credit guarantees and any combination of a credit facility or credit transaction. The Act is not limited to just parties ordinarily supplying credit such as banks and retail stores – it is broader than this.

In addition, the Act regulates debt counsellors including their applications, registration and provision of services to consumers.

Consumer protection rights under the NCA

The consumer protection rights under the Act can briefly be described as follows:

- **To apply for credit.** Every individual has the right to apply for credit, regardless of their background or circumstances. Credit providers cannot arbitrarily deny someone the opportunity to apply.
- **Protection against discrimination.** The Act prohibits credit providers from discriminating against consumers based on race, gender, religion, disability, or any other protected characteristic. The credit application should be assessed solely on the financial standing and creditworthiness of the applicant.
- **Right to be informed about rejection.** The applicant has the right to ask for a clear explanation in writing of any rejection of their application for credit. The credit provider must state the specific reasons for rejection, allowing the applicant to address any concerns or potential errors.
- **Free copy of credit agreements.** Creditors are entitled to receive a free copy of their credit agreement once approved and agreed. This document must outline the terms and conditions of the loan, including interest rates, fees, repayment schedule, and their rights and responsibilities.
- **Plain and simple language.** Credit agreements should be written in clear and concise language that can be easily understood by the creditor. Avoidance of jargon and technical terms that might confuse or mislead the consumers is important.
- **Confidentiality of personal information.** Credit providers must treat the creditor's personal and financial information with strict confidentiality. They can only share this information with authorised third parties, such as credit bureaus, and only for legitimate purposes.
- **Understanding of fees and costs.** Before agreeing to any credit agreement, the applicant has the right to understand all associated fees, costs, interest rates, the total repayment amount and any other relevant details. Transparency is critical to making informed financial decisions by consumers.
- **Control of marketing communications.** Consumers have the right to choose whether they want to receive marketing communications from the credit provider via phone, SMS, mail, or e-mail. They have the right to opt out of such campaigns and control how their information is used for marketing purposes.
- **Debt counselling access.** Consumers that find themselves in financial distress have the right to assistance from a registered debt counsellor. The Act supports access to debt counselling services to help individuals manage their finances and overcome financial difficulties.

Regulatory bodies

The implementation and enforcement of the NCA are overseen by several regulatory bodies:

- **National Credit Regulator (NCR)** is the primary regulator responsible for enforcing the NCA. It has a range of powers, including investigating complaints, issuing compliance orders, and imposing penalties on credit providers who violate the Act.
- **Financial Sector Conduct Authority (FSCA)** oversees the financial sector, including credit providers. It works closely with the NCR to ensure that credit providers follow the NCA and other relevant regulations. Such collaboration is needed as per the Financial Sector Regulation Act of 2017, which is the governing law of the FSCA.
- **National Consumer Commission (NCC)** promotes consumer rights and protects consumers from unfair business practices. It works with the NCR to educate consumers about their credit rights and supply support for those facing credit problems. The NCC is the regulatory body set up under the Consumer Protection Act.

Who does the Act apply to?

The Act applies to any person entering into a credit agreement, from individuals using credit cards and taking out loans to businesses accessing finance. It protects consumers from unfair lending practices, regulates credit providers, and promotes responsible credit granting and use. Any person or company providing such credit to consumers must therefore comply with the Act.

Who does the Act not apply to?

The purpose of the Act is to protect consumers against unfair credit practices. It does not apply to juristic entities with an annual turnover or assets that exceed R1 million at the time the agreement is entered into by the parties. Accordingly, sole proprietors and companies with turnover and assets less than R1 million will be afforded protection under the Act. Partnerships are regarded as legal entities for purposes of the Act but may have some protections depending on the circumstances.

Retention period of records

Under the NCA, there are retention periods ranging from one year up to five years depending on the type of record.

We recommend that you seek legal advice for specific queries related to your record-keeping and retention periods. See also *Chapter 59* on record-keeping and specifically the section on *Record retention periods*.

Summary

The NCA plays a vital role in ensuring fair and responsible credit practices in South Africa. It protects consumers from exploitation, promotes financial literacy, and contributes to a sustainable credit market. It is complementary to the Consumer Protection Act in that they both intend to protect ordinary consumers (vs juristic persons). By understanding and following the NCA, credit providers can help to foster a responsible and inclusive financial system in South Africa. If you are providing credit as envisaged by the NCA, you should ensure you have a thorough understanding of its requirements and take appropriate steps to follow the Act. Seek legal advice in case of any queries and for the drafting of any credit agreements.

Chapter 50: Broad-Based Black Economic Empowerment

The Broad-Based Black Economic Empowerment (BBBEE) legislation is a transformative policy in South Africa. It aims to address historical economic imbalances arising from the apartheid era, where Black people, who make up most of the population, were systematically marginalised and excluded from participating in the economy. This policy seeks to rectify these disparities by dismantling barriers to the participation of Black people in the economy. Through various empowerment initiatives, BBBEE strives to create a more inclusive and fair business environment.

Understanding the historical context and goals of BBBEE is essential to navigating the business arena. This section explores the requirements of BBBEE, its status, calculation methods, and additional information. By unpacking these elements, we gain a deeper appreciation for BBBEE's significance in promoting economic inclusivity in South Africa.

Objectives of BBBEE

Due to the historical context and to redress the economic imbalances faced by Black people, the Broad-Based Black Economic Empowerment Act of 2013 was passed into law.

The term 'Black people' or 'Black' is a generic term that means Africans, Coloureds, and Indians:
a) who are citizens of the Republic of South Africa by birth or descent, or
b) who became citizens of the Republic of South Africa by naturalisation:
   i. before 27 April 1994, or
   ii. on or after 27 April 1994 and who would have been entitled to acquire citizenship by naturalisation prior to that date.

The principal beneficiaries of BBBEE are Black people, women, and people with disabilities, all of whom are regarded as having been disadvantaged during apartheid.

The primary goals of BBBEE are to:
- **Promote economic inclusion.** Create opportunities for historically disadvantaged individuals to actively take part in the mainstream economy.
- **Address inequality.** Redistribute wealth and economic opportunities to rectify historical imbalances.
- **Foster skills development.** Encourage the development of skills and expertise within Black communities.

- **Promote ownership.** Increase Black ownership and control of businesses in South Africa.

The importance of BBBEE in business engagement and transformation

While BBBEE is not mandatory for all businesses, it is often a requirement for companies that wish to engage with government entities to secure public contracts. Certain private industries (such as mining) that are dependent on government permits will require their suppliers to be BBBEE compliant. Many other businesses voluntarily adopt BBBEE principles to show their commitment to transformation, inclusivity, and good corporate citizenship and to enhance their public image. By creating the demand-side for BBBEE compliance in certain industries and for large companies, it has a trickle-down effect of transforming the value chain and including Black people in the economy.

Elements of BBBEE

BBBEE in South Africa is founded on five main pillars, which are designed to promote economic participation and equitable wealth distribution among previously disadvantaged groups. These pillars are:

- **Ownership.** This pillar focuses on increasing the ownership of enterprises by Black people, particularly in significant and influential sectors. It encourages the transfer of ownership and control of South Africa's economic resources to Black people.
- **Management control.** This aspect is about the participation of Black people in the decision-making processes of businesses. It aims to ensure that Black people are adequately represented in executive and senior management positions.
- **Skills development.** This pillar emphasises the importance of training and developing skills among Black people. The goal is to increase the number of black professionals and skilled workers in the economy to ensure a more equitable representation in the workforce.
- **Enterprise and supplier development.** This component focuses on supporting and nurturing Black-owned businesses, including small, medium, and micro enterprises (SMMEs), to ensure their sustainable growth and participation in the mainstream economy. It involves preferential procurement from Black-owned suppliers and investing in the development of these enterprises.
- **Socio-economic development.** This final pillar concentrates on contributing to the society in which a business operates. It involves initiatives that contribute to the socio-economic development of Black communities, such as educational programmes, healthcare initiatives, and infrastructure development.

These pillars are integral to the BBBEE framework, aiming to reduce inequalities and promote economic growth and social development in a manner that includes all segments of the South African society.

Each of the above five elements has several points that contribute to the overall scorecard for the company. The number of points for each element is complicated as there several sub-sets, bonus points, principles and exceptions that are applicable. The total number of points for each element is as follows:

- Ownership: 25
- Management control: 19
- Skills development: 20 (+5 possible bonus points)
- Enterprise and skills development: 40 (+4 possible bonus points)
- Socio-economic development: 5
- Total possible points: 118

The scorecard (based on total points scored) gives rise to a BBBEE level, which in turn results in a particular spend recognition.

Points	BBBEE level	Spend recognition %
100+	1	135
95 to 99	2	125
90 to 94	3	110
80 to 89	4	100
75 to 80	5	80
70 to 74	6	60
55 to 69	7	50
40 to 54	8	10
0 to 39	Non-compliant	0

A company that scores 97 points therefore qualifies as a BBBEE level 2 and its customers can recognise the spend they have with the company to the value of 125% (in other words, 25% more than the total spend qualifies as a bonus recognition for the customer). On the other hand, a company that scores 78 points qualifies as a bonus recognition of only 80% because their BBBEE scorecard is a level 5. There is therefore a clear incentive for companies to score higher levels. The customers can then use the totality of their BBBEE recognition points from their suppliers to help improve their own BBBEE scorecards.

Understanding the difference between enterprise and supplier development

The number of points assigned to enterprise and supplier development is considerable and proves how companies can help Black economic transformation through supporting smaller Black-owned businesses.

Enterprise development pertains to support provided to new and emerging businesses that are Black-owned or contribute to Black economic empowerment. The focus is on fostering the growth and development of these enterprises, often through financial and non-financial aid, mentorship, training, and other forms of support.

Supplier development, on the other hand, involves initiatives aimed at improving and empowering existing suppliers, particularly those that may be small or historically disadvantaged. Supplier development programmes may include capacity-building, skills transfer, and other interventions to enhance the capabilities of existing suppliers, enabling them to become more competitive and sustainable.

While both enterprise development and supplier development are paramount components of BBBEE strategies, they address various stages of a business' life cycle and focus on distinct aspects of economic empowerment within the broader context of the BBBEE framework.

BBBEE certificates

Companies seeking a BBBEE certificate must undergo a verification process conducted by verification agencies accredited by the South African National Accreditation System (SANAS). The verification agency appoints its own SANAS approved verification agent that assesses the company's compliance with BBBEE principles and determines their BBBEE score. Higher scores indicate greater compliance. The verification is performed annually, and the BBBEE certificate is valid for the following year. All relevant information must be provided to the verification agency so that it can perform its review under the BBBEE Act.

Certain companies are exempt from the verification process, including exempt micro enterprises (EMEs) with a turnover below R10 million and startup enterprises in their first year. EMEs can obtain a certificate through the CIPC BizPortal at no cost while larger companies not meeting the exemptions must undergo the full verification process.

It is important to follow relevant sector codes and provide accurate information during the verification process or to CIPC. Deliberate misrepresentation is a criminal offence, so honesty and accuracy are essential when providing information to the relevant agencies.

Retention period of records

Under the Broad-Based Black Economic Empowerment Act, there are no specified record retention periods.

We recommend that you seek legal advice for specific queries related to your record-keeping and retention periods. See also *Chapter 59* on record-keeping and specifically the section on *Record retention periods*.

Summary

BBBEE continues to be a vital component of South Africa's transformation agenda, promoting economic inclusivity and equal opportunity. While not universally mandatory, its impact extends across various sectors, shaping business practices and fostering a commitment to social and economic justice. Understanding and embracing the principles of BBBEE is not only a legal requirement for many businesses but also a strategic imperative to contribute to a more equitable, inclusive, and prosperous South Africa.

It is important to note that while the information provided is based on a general or generic scorecard, there are also sector-specific BBBEE scorecards. It is critical to carefully determine whether to apply the generic scorecard or the sector-specific one based on the industry your business falls into. For companies operating in multiple sectors, this introduces added complexity as they may need to comply with more than one industry scorecard or decide on an appropriate approach.

BBBEE is a complex and challenging subject, especially for foreign companies seeking to establish a business in South Africa. Selling a portion of the business to third parties can pose specific challenges, which may require the company to maximise scoring on other elements to achieve a better level of compliance.

It is worth noting that the summary provided in this chapter serves as a simplistic illustration of the elements, scoring process, and certification related to BBBEE. For any queries or assistance regarding BBBEE, it is advisable to consult BBBEE advisors or attorneys who specialise in this area. They can provide comprehensive guidance tailored to your specific business needs and circumstances.

Chapter 51: Access to information and data privacy

South African laws require companies to follow certain requirements in respect of information held or processed by it that pertains to individuals, and in some cases, even other companies. The relevant laws are the Promotion of Access to Information Act of 2000 (PAIA) and the Protection of Personal Information Act of 2013 (POPIA). Although the two acts both involve information, they have different goals and apply to distinct types of information.

The PAIA is based on the constitutional right of citizens to access information to enforce or protect their rights. PAIA therefore aims to promote transparency, accountability, and effective governance of all institutions (both public and private).

POPIA, on the other hand, enshrines the protection of the personal information of individuals and legal entities. It provides various rights to these individuals and legal entities to protect their right to personal information, and places significant obligations on companies and government bodies to protect such information.

POPIA and PAIA are enforced by the Information Regulator.

Below we provide a summary of both Acts and what companies must do to meet their obligations.

Promotion of access to information (PAIA)

PAIA was enacted by Parliament to follow the requirements of Section 32 of the Constitution. Section 32 provides citizens with a general right of access to information held by any public or private body for the protection or enforcement of any other right. This enhances transparency, accountability, and democracy. Persons requiring the information must complete a prescribed form, set out the information or documents they are seeking, and set out the basis of the right to such information. The information must then be provided by the relevant public or private body within a prescribed period unless they have grounds to refuse to supply such information in which case the body must give reasons to the requestor.

The grounds for refusing to supply the information are:
- In the case of a public body, the protection of the public interest or national security concerns.
- The protection of the confidential or proprietary information of the body.
- By disclosing the information, it will contravene the personal information of another person.
- The requestor does not have a right to such information.

Every public and private body must:

- Appoint an information officer who will handle receiving requests under PAIA and ensure compliance with the law,
- Put in place a PAIA manual accessible to the public (eg on their website) and at the company's principal place of business, which details the following:
  - The kind of information it keeps.
  - Name and contact information of the information officer.
  - The procedure for requesting information.
  - The fees to be charged for supplying access to the information (the fees are prescribed amounts under the Act and cannot be exceeded).
  - The company's procedures for refusing access to information.
  - The company's complaints procedure.

Prior to POPIA coming into law, the requirement was to register the information officer with the South African Human Rights Commission. POPIA now regulates the PAIA manual requirements and registration of the information officer. There is no requirement to register the PAIA manual with the Information Regulator.

Protection of personal information (POPIA)

POPIA is specifically aimed at the protection of any person's personal information (such person is referred to as a 'data subject'). This extends to legal entities although it is not clear what a company's personal information means; the Information Regulator may at the proper time supply the necessary clarification. It is possible that, for example, a private company's financial statements should be treated as personal information and that any other company (eg a customer or supplier that demands the statements as part of its onboarding and risk review policy) that processes such statements must do so in accordance with the Act. In respect of individuals, personal data relates to an identifiable, living, natural person and includes two types of information – personal information and special personal information.

- **Personal information** under POPIA includes names, contact details (such as address, telephone, and email information), identity and passport numbers, employment history, financial information.
- **Special personal information** is a sub-category of personal information but afforded more protection under the Act. It includes details about the person's race, ethnic origin, trade union membership, political opinions, religious or philosophical beliefs, health or sex life, biometric information, and criminal history. Special personal information is regarded as more personal and therefore afforded greater protection to avoid harm, discrimination, or violation of the individual's rights. Anyone processing special personal information must take greater precautionary measures when handling special personal information.

POPIA establishes a framework for the lawful and responsible processing of personal information (including special personal information) by any other person and this can be an individual, a company or public body (called a 'responsible party'). The fundamental requirements include:

- **Lawful processing of personal information.** The information must be processed in a lawful and transparent manner based on one of the lawful grounds specified in POPIA:
    - Informed consent provided by the data subject.
    - Necessity of processing the information for the performance of a contract.
    - Compliance with a legal obligation.
    - Protection of legitimate interests.
    - Performance of a public law duty.
- **Purpose limitation.** Personal information must be collected for a specific, explicitly defined, and legitimate purpose and should not be used for any other purpose.
- **Data minimisation.** The collection of the personal information must be limited to what is necessary for the specific purpose for which it is being collected – unnecessary or excessive personal information gathering is not allowed.
- **Quality of information.** The entity processing the data (the responsible party) must ensure the personal information is correct and complete, and that errors are corrected.
- **Accountability.** The responsible party is accountable for following POPIA, which includes implementing measures to secure the integrity and confidentiality of the information, and to take steps to prevent loss, damage, unauthorised access, or unlawful processing of the information.
- **Openness and transparency.** Data subjects must be informed whenever there is processing of their personal information, including the lawful purpose, the identity of the party responsible for such processing, and the data subject's rights in respect of their information.
- **Security safeguards.** The responsible party must secure the integrity and confidentiality of personal information through proper technical and organisational safeguards, including protection against loss, unauthorised access or disclosure, alteration, or destruction.
- **Data subject rights.** Includes the right of the individual to access the personal information held by the responsible party, the right to correction of the information, the right to object to the processing of the information, and the right to be forgotten.
- **Cross-border transfer** of personal information to another country is only allowed if the recipient of the information is subject to a law or a binding agreement that supplies adequate levels of data protection similar to what is required under POPIA.
- **Special personal information** may only be processed under specific circumstances and with enhanced levels of safeguards.

If a responsible party is using third parties to process personal information, it should ensure such third parties comply fully with the requirements of POPIA and that adequate agreements between the responsible party and the third party are put in place to ensure adherence to the law.

POPIA requires a privacy policy to be put in place to show compliance with the Act.

Similar to PAIA, POPIA requires a company to appoint an information officer and such officer must be registered with the Information Regulator. The Regulator will provide a document confirming the appointment. The Regulator must be informed of any changes to the information officer. In addition, POPIA requires a company to keep a privacy policy setting out the obligations of the responsible parties in accordance with the Act.

POPIA and PAIA manuals, policy

Since both POPIA and PAIA mandate organisations to keep a manual or policy on information (albeit for different aims and purposes), and the appointment of an information officer, it is possible to have a combined manual if there is a clear indication of the different types of information, goals, rights, and obligations under each Act. The manual should be made publicly available and at the registered office of the company. Some companies choose to have a separate PAIA manual and privacy policy.

Retention period of records

Under the Promotion of Access to Information Act and the Protection of Personal Information Act, there are no specified record retention periods. However, it should be noted that under the Protection of Personal Information Act, anyone processing personal information is required to retain such records only for such periods as is necessary. See also *Chapter 55* regarding *the Electronic Communications and Transactions Act.*

We recommend that you seek legal advice for specific queries related to your record-keeping and retention periods. See also *Chapter 59* on record-keeping and specifically the section on *Record retention periods.*

Summary

Although both PAIA and POPIA govern legal rights and obligations in respect of information, PAIA covers information necessary for the protection and enforcement of any right whereas POPIA covers personal information protection.

Ensure you put in place a PAIA and POPIA manual, or a PAIA manual and privacy policy specific to your company and register the information officer with the relevant regulators. Requests for information should be treated seriously and follow the relevant laws. Ensure personal information is protected and treated in accordance with POPIA.

Fines and penalties can be imposed for non-compliance or data breaches, including fines up to R10 million and/or ten years imprisonment.

Chapter 52: Occupational Health and Safety Act

The Occupational Health and Safety Act of 1993 (OHS Act) is the primary legislation governing occupational health and safety in South Africa. The OHS Act aims to protect the health and safety of workers at work and to prevent occupational injuries and diseases.

Roles and responsibilities

The OHS Act outlines the roles and responsibilities of various stakeholders in ensuring a safe and healthy work environment:

- **Employers** have a primary responsibility to provide a safe and healthy work environment for their employees and others (such as visitors, customers, suppliers, etc). The primary responsibility falls on the chief executive officer or managing officer, or person of equivalent status within the company to ensure the OHS Act is adhered to. This includes identifying and assessing hazards, implementing proper controls, supplying training and instruction, and supporting a safe working environment.
- **Employees** also have a duty to take reasonable care of their own health and safety, and for others, and to cooperate with their employer to ensure a safe working environment.
- **Health and safety representatives (HSRs)** are elected by employees to represent their interests in OHS matters. HSRs have the right to inspect the workplace, investigate incidents, and make recommendations to the employer.
- **OHS committees** are set up at workplaces with more than 20 employees to promote OHS and aid consultation between employers and employees.
- **The Chief inspector of OHS** and their team of inspectors, who are officers of the Department of Employment and Labour, handle enforcing the OHS Act and investigating workplace accidents and diseases. They have extensive powers particularly in cases of serious incidents, including the power to shut down a facility until their investigation is completed and they are satisfied the workplace is safe.

Delegation of powers

Employers can delegate their OHS responsibilities to competent persons, such as supervisors, managers, or external consultants. However, employers are still ultimately accountable for ensuring compliance with the OHS Act. The chief executive officer (or equivalent officer), or Section 16(1) appointment, is the person primarily responsible for ensuring adherence to the OHS Act. A Section 16(1) appointee (ie the chief executive officer) can appoint several Section 16(2) officers for assigning specific OHS responsibilities to competent persons under their control. This delegation of authority, known as Section 16(2) appointments, allows employers to effectively distribute OHS responsibilities based on the ability and experience of their personnel but does not take away from the overall responsibility of the employer and its chief executive officer, or equivalent officer. Section 37(2) agreements deal with the specific arrangements between employers and contractors or sub-contractors who perform work on-site. This provision requires employers to enter into written agreements with contractors or sub-contractors, outlining the contractor or sub-contractor's respective responsibilities for ensuring OHS compliance during the work process.

The OHS Act is based on the following key principles:

- **Prevention.** The primary focus is on preventing accidents and diseases rather than relying on reactive measures.
- **Hierarchy of controls** should be applied, starting with eliminating hazards at the source, followed by engineering controls, administrative controls, and personal protective equipment (PPE).
- **Worker participation.** Workers should be involved in identifying hazards, assessing risks, and developing and implementing OHS controls.
- **Continuous improvement.** OHS management systems should be continuously reviewed and improved to ensure ongoing effectiveness.

Post-COVID and remote working

The COVID pandemic and the rise of remote work have brought about new challenges and considerations for occupational health and safety globally, and South Africa is not immune from this (pardon the expression). Employers and employees alike must adapt their OHS practices to ensure a safe and healthy work environment in both traditional office settings and remote work arrangements.

Employers continue to have the primary responsibility for providing a safe and healthy work environment for their employees, regardless of where the work is performed. This includes conducting risk assessments, implementing proper controls, and supplying training and instruction on OHS hazards and risks. In the context of remote work, employers may need to provide other support, such as ergonomic assessments, training on home office safety, and guidance on managing work-life balance. What is required by employers is based on the risk assessment and what is reasonable to expect of a responsible employer.

Employees also have a duty to take reasonable care of their own health and safety and cooperate with their employer to ensure a safe working environment. This includes reporting hazards, taking part in training, and following safety procedures. In the context of remote work, employees should take steps to create a safe and healthy workspace at home, follow ergonomic guidelines, and manage their work hours to avoid excessive workloads and fatigue.

The OHS Act is still applicable to remote work arrangements, and employers must take proactive steps to ensure compliance. This may involve:
- Extending workplace inspections to cover home offices.

- Providing resources for employees to conduct their own risk assessments.
- Offering training on remote work safety.
- Establishing clear communication channels to report hazards and incidents.
- Promoting a culture of OHS awareness and prevention.

By adapting OHS practices to address the unique challenges of remote work, employers and employees can work together to support a safe and healthy work environment for all.

Retention period of records

Under the Occupational Health and Safety Act, there are various record retention periods depending on the type of record. This can vary from three years (for reports on incidents and recommendations by the health and safety committee to the employer) to 30 years (eg for hazardous biological agent matters and medical surveillance records) and even up to a minimum of 40 years (eg for asbestos related issues).

We recommend that you seek legal advice for specific queries related to your record-keeping and retention periods. See also *Chapter 59* on record-keeping and specifically the section on *Record retention periods*.

Summary

The OHS Act plays a fundamental role in safeguarding the health and safety of workers in South Africa. By understanding and following the Act's provisions, employers can create a safer and healthier work environment for their employees, including considering remote working. All companies, and their employees, have a responsibility to ensure compliance with the OHS Act regardless of size or complexity. Clearly, companies with more complex structures, such as factories or dealing with various hazards, will have higher duties of awareness and care. You should consult with expert OHS professionals on your specific needs and requirements to create a safe workplace and follow the Act.

Chapter 53: Environmental laws

South Africa is renowned for its rich biodiversity, picturesque landscapes, and diverse ecosystems. Section 24 of the Constitution enshrines the principle of environmental protection including that people are entitled to an environment that is not harmful to their health and well-being. Preserving the country's natural heritage is essential for the country's economic, social, and environmental well-being. To safeguard the environment, South Africa has implemented a comprehensive legal framework that sets forth environmental principles, sets up regulatory standards, and empowers enforcement mechanisms.

Key environmental laws

South Africa's environmental legal framework encompasses a wide range of laws, regulations, and policies. Some of the most prominent environmental laws include:

- **The National Environmental Management Act (NEMA) of 1998** serves as the overarching framework for environmental management in South Africa. It sets up principles for sustainable development, environmental impact assessments, and integrated environmental management.
- **The National Environmental Management: Protected Areas Act (NEMPAA) of 2003** provides for the protection and conservation of ecologically viable areas, including national parks, nature reserves, and world heritage sites. It outlines the management and expansion of these protected areas.
- **The National Environmental Management: Waste Act (NEMWA) of 2008** regulates the management of waste from cradle to grave, addressing waste generation, storage, treatment, disposal, and recycling. It promotes waste reduction, reuse, and recovery.
- **The National Environmental Management: Air Quality Act (NEM:AQA) of 2004** safeguards air quality by setting emission standards, controlling air pollution sources, and promoting air quality monitoring and management.
- **The National Environmental Management: Biodiversity Act (NEMBA) of 2004**, protects the country's rich biodiversity by regulating the use, exploitation, development, conservation, and management of living organisms and their genetic resources.
- **The World Heritage Convention Act of 1999** provides for the cultural and environmental protection and sustainable development and related activities of South Africa's world heritage sites. South Africa's world heritage sites include uKhahlamba-Drakensberg Park, Vredefort Dome, Mapungubwe Cultural Landscape, Richtersveld Cultural and Botanical Landscape, Fossil Hominid Sites of South Africa (found at Sterkfontein, Swartkrans and Kromdraai), iSimangaliso Wetland Park, Maloti-Drakensberg Transboundary Park, Cape Floral Region Protected Areas, Khomani Cultural Landscape, and the Barberton Makhonjwa Mountains.

Enforcement agencies

The administration and enforcement of environmental laws in South Africa are overseen by several regulatory bodies:

- **The Department of Forestry, Fisheries and the Environment (DFFE)** is the lead government agency responsible for environmental policy, legislation, and enforcement. It oversees the implementation of environmental laws and coordinates with other government departments.
- **The Environmental Management Inspectorate (EMI)** or the Green Scorpions, as they are known to the public, are government officials from national, provincial, and local government, including the parks authorities, who handle compliance and enforcement activities related to environmental laws.
- **The South African National Parks (SANParks)** is a state-owned agency responsible for managing national parks in South Africa. It protects and conserves the parks' biodiversity and promotes eco-tourism.

There are also several civil society organisations, registered as NPCs and PBOs that actively promote environmental protection.

Compliance requirements

Businesses and individuals in South Africa must follow the environmental laws and regulations. Key compliance requirements include:

- **Obtaining environmental permits.** Businesses that engage in activities with potential environmental impacts may require environmental permits from relevant authorities.
- **Conducting environmental impact assessments (EIAs).** Projects that could significantly affect the environment may require environmental impact assessments to evaluate their potential impacts and develop mitigation measures.
- **Implementing environmental management plans.** Businesses should develop and implement environmental management plans to manage waste, control pollution, and minimise their environmental footprint.
- **Reporting environmental incidents.** Businesses must report environmental incidents, such as spills or pollution, to the local, provincial, and national government authorities.

Retention period of records

Under the various environmental laws mentioned in this chapter, there are either no specified record retention periods or retention periods depending on record types or indefinite retention periods.

We recommend that you seek legal advice for specific queries related to your record-keeping and retention periods. See also *Chapter 59* on record-keeping and specifically the section on *Record retention periods*.

Summary

South Africa's environmental laws play a critical role in protecting the country's natural heritage and in promoting sustainable development. By understanding and following these laws, businesses and individuals can contribute to a healthier environment for present and future generations. Contravention of environmental laws can result in significant fines and penalties, and reputational damage to the company. There are many environmental experts, including specialised environmental lawyers, who can help you navigate the relevant laws and regulations, advise and conduct EIAs and help with the relevant environmental management plans.

Chapter 54: Competition law and intellectual property

Competition law

The Competition Act of 1998 is the cornerstone of competition law in South Africa, promoting fair and competitive markets for the benefit of consumers, businesses, and the overall economy. The Act adopts the same principles of fair competition as most other countries. The Act prohibits anti-competitive practices such as price-fixing, cartels, and abuse of dominance, ensuring that businesses compete on their merits, do not collude with one another, and that consumers have access to a wide range of goods and services at competitive prices.

Main requirements of companies

The Act imposes several obligations on companies to ensure that their business practices follow competition law. These obligations include:

- **Refraining from anti-competitive agreements** (whether in writing, verbal or tacit). Companies must not enter into agreements with competitors that restrict competition, such as agreements to fix prices, divide markets or customers or suppliers, blacklist particular customers or suppliers, prevent the entry of new competitors, or limit production. The key part is the collusion of competitors as this results in a reduction of competition, which is harmful to consumers.
- **Avoiding abuse of dominance.** Companies with a dominant market position must not abuse their power to harm competitors or consumers, or others. This includes acts such as predatory pricing, exclusive dealing arrangements, and refusals to deal. There is no prohibition from companies having a dominant position – only that they must not act in an abusive way that results in harm to competitors, customers, suppliers, and consumers.
- **Merger control.** Companies must notify the Competition Commission of mergers and acquisitions that meet certain turnover thresholds to ensure that these transactions do not result in a substantial lessening of competition.
- **Compliance with Competition Commission decisions.** Companies must follow the decisions and orders issued by the Competition Commission, including orders to cease anti-competitive practices and pay penalties.

Regulatory bodies and courts

The Competition Act sets up key authorities responsible for enforcing competition law:

- **The Competition Commission** is an independent body responsible for investigating suspected anti-competitive practices, conducting merger reviews, and issuing decisions and orders to enforce the Act.
- **The Competition Tribunal** is an independent tribunal that reviews appeals against decisions of the Competition Commission.

- **The Competition Appeal Court** is responsible for hearing any appeals involving competition matters.

Additional provisions of the Act

The Competition Act also includes provisions on a range of other competition-related issues:

- **Price discrimination.** Companies are prohibited from charging different prices for the same product or service to different customers without justification.
- **Collective buying power.** The Act recognises the potential for collective buying power to harm competition and provides for measures to address this issue.
- **Horizontal and vertical restraints.** The Act distinguishes between horizontal restraints (agreements between competitors) and vertical restraints (agreements between companies at various levels of the supply chain) and applies different rules to each.
- **Competition remedies.** The Act provides for a range of remedies to address anti-competitive conduct, including orders to cease practices, divest assets, pay penalties and fines that can be up to 10% of the company's annual turnover in the country for the preceding year (inclusive of exports from the country by the company), and criminal offences with imprisonment of up to ten years (depending on the severity of each offence). There is also provision for leniency for any company that first reports and cooperates fully on anti-competitive behaviour.

Summary

The Competition Act of 1998 plays an essential role in promoting competition and protecting consumers in South Africa. By understanding and following the Act's provisions, companies can avoid potential penalties and reputational damage, while also contributing to a more dynamic and competitive economy.

Intellectual property

As with most modern economies, the protection of intellectual property (IP) provides the bedrock of a sophisticated society that rewards innovation and creativity. IP encompasses a range of intangible assets, including inventions, trademarks, copyrights, and industrial designs, which represent the creative and innovative output of individuals and businesses. In South Africa, a comprehensive legal framework safeguards IP rights, enabling businesses to use their intellectual assets for competitive advantage and economic growth.

Applicable laws

- **Patents Act of 1977** provides for the protection of inventions – new products, processes, or methods that are novel, useful, and non-obvious.
- **Trade Marks Act of 1993** protects trademarks such as words, symbols, or logos that distinguish the goods or services of one trader from those of another.
- **Copyright Act of 1978** protects original literary, musical, artistic, and other works, including books, music, paintings, and films.

- **Designs Act of 1996** protects the features of shape, configuration, pattern, or ornament of an article.
- Other legislation-protecting industries, eg plant species and places of origin.

Regulatory bodies

The administration and enforcement of IP rights in South Africa is overseen by the CIPC who administers the registration of patents, trademarks, designs, and plant varieties. The Department of Trade, Industry and Competition (DTIC) is also responsible for ensuring the overall competitiveness of the country, which would include IP rights protection. CIPC is an agency of the DTIC.

Benefits of IP protection

- **Commercial advantage.** IP rights enable businesses to differentiate their products and services, attract investment, and generate revenue from licencing or franchising.
- **Economic growth.** IP protection fosters innovation and creativity, leading to new products, services, and industries, driving economic growth and job creation.
- **Consumer confidence.** IP protection ensures that consumers have access to genuine products and services, promoting consumer confidence and fair market practices.
- **Technology transfer.** IP protection helps technology transfer and collaboration among businesses, promoting the adoption of innovative technologies and advancements.
- **Global competitiveness.** Strong IP protection enhances a country's global competitiveness, attracting foreign investment and enabling businesses to compete effectively in international markets.

Retention period of records

Under the Competition Act and the various intellectual property laws mentioned above, there are no specified record retention periods. Given the importance of IP, it is advisable to retain all related records for the duration that the IP is valid plus at least three to five years thereafter. Note that the regulatory bodies may retain such IP records as required by the relevant laws.

We recommend that you seek legal advice for specific queries related to your record-keeping and retention periods. See also *Chapter 59* on record-keeping and specifically the section on *Record retention periods*.

Summary

IP plays a vital role in South Africa's economic and technological development. The country's comprehensive IP legal framework and dedicated regulatory bodies provide a robust environment for protecting the creativity and innovation of individuals and businesses. By using IP effectively, South Africa can continue to foster a culture of innovation, drive economic growth, and enhance its global competitiveness.

Speak to an IP attorney for any queries about or to register your IP rights. You will need to register your IP in each country in which you want your IP rights protected so this adds to the complexity, duration, and costs. However, if you have a significant invention or other IP right you wish to protect, you should take the necessary steps to protect your interests. This should form part of your business plan and your risk management strategy.

Chapter 55: Electronic Communications and Transactions Act

The Electronic Communications and Transactions Act (ECTA) of 2002 regulates electronic communications and transactions and promotes the use of electronic signatures. It provides a legal framework for the validity and enforceability of electronic contracts, the admissibility of electronic records as evidence, and the protection of electronic transactions.

Key provisions of the ECTA

- **Legal recognition of electronic contracts.** Electronic contracts are as legally binding and enforceable as if physically signed, ensuring that agreements formed online carry the same weight as traditional paper-based contracts.
- **Admissibility of electronic records.** Electronic records can be used as evidence in legal proceedings, eliminating the need for paper-based originals. This provision enhances the admissibility and reliability of electronic documents.
- **Recognition of electronic signatures.** Electronic signatures are equivalent to handwritten signatures, helping secure and convenient electronic transactions. It sets up distinct levels of electronic signature security, ensuring that signatures used for high-value transactions meet strict security requirements.
- **Protection of electronic transactions.** Provides safeguards against unauthorised access, data interception, and tampering in electronic transactions, protecting the integrity and confidentiality of electronic communications.
- Where specific laws require physical signatures, the ECTA will not apply. For example, the sale of land, long-lease agreements, signing of wills, etc.

The ECTA plays a pivotal role in helping the growth and adoption of e-commerce in South Africa and ensures the country stays in-step with international norms and best practices. By providing a legal framework for electronic communications and transactions, the ECTA has instilled confidence in online transactions, encouraged businesses to adopt digital technologies, and promoted the development of a digital economy.

Retention period of records

Under the Electronic Communication and Transactions Act, any personal information processed by a data controller must be retained for as long as such information is used plus one year thereafter. See also *Chapter 51* regarding the Protection of Personal Information Act.

We recommend that you seek legal advice for specific queries related to your record-keeping and retention periods. See also *Chapter 59* on record-keeping and specifically the section on *Record retention periods*.

Chapter 56: Economic crime laws

Crime should be the last thing one considers when setting up a business. However, it is necessary to consider, at a high level, the most important economic crime laws in South Africa so you and your company remain compliant. Economic crime poses a significant threat to business, economy, and the well-being of society worldwide, and more so for a country like South Africa, which has high crime rates including economic crime. In South Africa, economic crime encompasses a range of offences aimed at gaining illicit financial benefits through fraudulent or deceptive means. These offences undermine fair competition, erode public trust, and hinder economic growth at the cost of the economy and the people, exasperating unemployment and inequality. To combat economic crime, South Africa has implemented a comprehensive legal framework and set up dedicated enforcement agencies.

Key economic crime laws

South Africa's economic crime landscape is governed by an intricate legal framework that prohibits and penalises various forms of economic misconduct. The primary laws include:

- **The Prevention and Combating of Corrupt Activities Act (PRECCA) of 2004** is the cornerstone of South Africa's anti-corruption legislation. It criminalises bribery, corruption, fraud, and abuse of power in both the public and private sectors. This includes both the receiving and giving of bribes and prohibits facilitation or grease/expediting payments.
- **The Prevention of Organised Crime Act (POCA) of 1998** targets organised crime syndicates involved in money laundering, racketeering, and the proceeds of crime. It supports asset forfeiture, witness protection, and specialised investigative powers.
- **The Financial Intelligence Centre Act (FICA) of 2011** aims to prevent and detect financial crime by setting up reporting obligations for financial institutions and designated entities. It requires reporting of suspicious transactions and cross-border financial flows.
- **Protected Disclosures Act (PDA) of 2000** is a law that protects employees who make disclosures of wrongdoing in the workplace. The PDA defines wrongdoing as any conduct that is illegal, irregular, or contrary to law or good business practice. This can include violation of economic crime laws. The PDA also protects employees who make disclosures to external parties, such as the media or the police.
- **The Companies Act: The Companies Act, No. 71 of 2008** contains provisions addressing corporate fraud, insider trading, and market abuse. It imposes duties on company directors and prescribes measures to safeguard shareholder interests.

It is important to note that there are many other laws that create criminal liability, and it is not the intention of this chapter or this book to elaborate on all these sanctions.

Enforcement agencies

South Africa has set up general and specific bodies to investigate and prosecute economic crimes:

- **The Special Investigating Unit (SIU)** is an independent statutory body tasked with investigating corruption, maladministration, and fraud in the public sector. It has the power to subpoena witnesses, seize assets, and prosecute offenders.
- **The Financial Intelligence Centre (FIC)** handles receiving, analysing, and issuing financial intelligence to relevant authorities for investigation and prosecution. It helps information sharing between financial institutions and law enforcement agencies.
- **The Directorate for Priority Crimes Investigation (DPCI)**, otherwise known as the Hawks are the South African Police Service's specialised unit for investigating organised crime, cybercrime, and economic offences. They have the ability and resources to tackle complex economic crime cases.
- **The South African Police Service (SAPS)** has overall responsibility for the investigation of all crimes.
- **The National Prosecuting Authority (NPA)** handles prosecuting those accused of committing economic crimes and presenting the cases before the courts.
- **The Department of Justice and Constitutional Development** has overall government responsibility for the administration of justice.

Enforcement mechanisms

South Africa's economic crime enforcement mechanisms include:

- **Investigations.** Law enforcement agencies conduct investigations to gather evidence and identify suspects. They use various techniques, including financial analysis, undercover operations, and electronic surveillance.
- **Prosecutions.** Upon gathering sufficient evidence, prosecutors start criminal proceedings against suspected economic offenders. The prosecution process involves presenting evidence in court, seeking convictions, and obtaining proper penalties.
- **Courts.** The judiciary hears cases brought by the NPA and decides whether the accused is guilty beyond a reasonable doubt, or innocent. Specialised criminal courts are also set up to hear specific types of cases including economic crimes.
- **The Department of Correctional Services.** Where an accused has been found guilty by the courts and imprisonment is found warranted, the Department handles the incarceration.
- **Asset forfeiture.** Economic crime proceeds can be forfeited to the State, depriving offenders of their ill-gotten gains. Asset forfeiture orders are issued by courts based on evidence linking the assets to criminal activities.

- **Prevention measures.** Economic crime prevention strategies include promoting ethical business practices (such as organisations adopting codes of conduct), raising awareness (by way of training programmes), and implementing internal controls within organisations to prevent violation of laws.
- **Self-reporting and whistle-blowing mechanisms.** Detection of crimes through self-reporting by organisations (as discussed below). Creating whistleblowing mechanisms within organisations to report unethical or illegal conduct and ensuring a zero-tolerance culture of retaliation for people making good faith reports of actual or potential violations.

Reporting obligations

In terms of Section 34 of PRECCA, any director, secretary or manager of a company, or partner in a partnership, or member of a CC, or a sole proprietor, or equivalent positions in other types of entities, has an obligation to report any actual or reasonably suspected economic crimes such as bribery and corruption, fraud, embezzlement, forgery or uttering of a forged document where the amount is more than R100 000. The Section 34 report must be made to the SAPS who will issue a case number. The matter will be investigated by the authorities. The company, partnership, CC, or sole proprietor (as is the case) must cooperate in the investigation and supply any documents requested by the investigators. Failure to report such matters is a criminal offence.

Retention period of records

Under the Acts, there are generally no specified record retention periods. Note, however, that under the Financial Intelligence Centre Act, reportable transactions and related documents must be retained for a period of five years. Given the nature of these laws, if you have any records related to them, we recommend a retention period of at least the duration of any actual or potential investigations, and subsequent appeals, plus three years thereafter.

We recommend that you seek legal advice for specific queries related to your record-keeping and retention periods. See also *Chapter 59* on record-keeping and specifically the section on *Record retention periods*.

Summary

Economic crime remains a persistent challenge, but South Africa's robust legal framework and dedicated enforcement agencies prove a strong commitment to combating these offences. Businesses and individuals can play a vital role in preventing economic crime by adhering to ethical standards, reporting suspicious activities, and supporting initiatives that promote transparency and accountability. All companies, and particularly directors, should take measures to prevent, identify and report any criminal activities. Consult with an attorney in case of any concerns or queries, and for assistance with any reporting obligations when needed.

Chapter 57: Promotion of Administrative Justice Act

The Promotion of Administrative Justice Act of 2000 (PAJA) is a key piece of legislation in South Africa that guarantees fair administrative action by the Government (it does not apply between private bodies). The purpose of the law is to give effect to the constitutional right to lawful, reasonable, and procedurally fair administrative action, as well as the right to written reasons for such action by government bodies.

Key features

- **Right to lawful, reasonable, and procedurally fair administrative action.** This right ensures that decisions made by government bodies are based on the law, are not arbitrary or capricious, and are made following a fair process.
- **Right to written reasons.** This right allows individuals to understand the reasoning behind administrative decisions and to challenge them if necessary.
- **Internal remedies.** PAJA supplies a framework for internal appeals within the relevant government body before seeking external remedies through the courts. An example of this would be the Tax Board and Tax Courts for tax disputes before referring the matter to the relevant high court.
- **Judicial review.** Individuals can apply to the courts to review administrative decisions on various grounds, including illegality, irrationality, and procedural unfairness.
- **Standing.** PAJA grants individuals and organisations the right to challenge administrative decisions that affect them directly and materially.
- **Costs.** The courts have discretion to award costs against the relevant government bodies in certain cases where the administrative action was found to be unlawful or unreasonable.

PAJA applies to a wide range of administrative actions, including decisions made by:
- Government officials and departments.
- Regulatory bodies, eg CIPC, SARS.
- Local authorities such as municipalities.
- Other public bodies exercising public power.

Benefits of PAJA

- **Promotes good governance.** PAJA encourages government bodies to be more accountable and transparent in their decision-making processes.
- **Protects individual rights.** PAJA ensures that individuals are treated fairly when dealing with the State.

- **Provides access to justice.** PAJA allows individuals to challenge unfair administrative decisions through accessible internal and external remedies.

PAJA is a complex piece of legislation, but it is essential for ensuring fair and just administrative action in South Africa. It acts as an important way for individuals and companies to hold government officials and government bodies accountable for their actions and decisions.

Retention period of records

Under the Promotion of Administrative Justice Act, there are no specified record retention periods,

We recommend that you seek legal advice for specific queries related to your record-keeping and retention periods. See also *Chapter 59* on record-keeping and specifically the section on *Record retention periods*.

Chapter 58: Other laws and regulations

It is not possible to describe all laws and regulations in South Africa. It is important, however, that you consider all applicable laws and regulations that are relevant to your specific business depending on the industry you operate in. To gain a proper understanding of what specific laws and regulations apply, you should consider the following resources:

- Certain industries will be regulated by specific laws like mining, financial services, energy, electronic communication, real estate, food processing, healthcare, construction, and professions, to name a few.
- Consult legal advisors to gain a thorough understanding of the exact laws and regulations applicable to your business.
- Consult industry bodies and associations to understand applicable industry requirements.
- Speak to industry experts and peers.
- Research government websites such as individual department sites most relevant to your business.
- Research acts and regulations: *https://www.gov.za/documents/acts* and *https://www.justice.gov.za/legislation/notices/notice_list.html*
- Do your own research by visiting relevant government ministry websites, industry association sites, etc.
- Do not utilise a sole source of information – if the information from multiple sources corresponds with one another then you can assume it is correct but if it does not, consult with an attorney or industry experts.
- Remember laws and regulations are constantly changing so be sure to remain current to stay compliant.
- Record retention periods for specific laws and regulations – please seek the advice of a legal advisor for any queries on retention periods. See also the section *Record retention periods* in *Chapter 59* for some general guidance.

Chapter 59: Record-keeping

Records are the backbone of a well-managed business, supplying a historical account of transactions and serving as a crucial resource for decision-making, evidencing compliance to applicable laws and regulations, and for dispute resolution. Record-keeping is like an insurance policy – you never know its true value until you need it. Remember when you needed to claim on a warranty for a defective product but could not locate the proof of payment, or needed a critical email to prove something but could not find it? Implementing good record-keeping practices is vital for maintaining a structured, organised, and well-maintained business.

Advantages of good record-keeping

- **Adherence to corporate governance principles.** Transparent and correct records prove a commitment to ethical business practices and corporate governance.
- **Compliance with applicable laws.** Keeping comprehensive records ensures compliance with various laws and regulations governing businesses, including companies' laws, tax laws, employment laws, other applicable laws relevant to your industry as well as any industry-specific regulations.
- **Risk mitigation.** Well-maintained records help identify and mitigate potential risks by providing a clear picture of the company's financial health, transactions, and contractual obligations.
- **Facilitation of financial reporting.** Detailed records serve as the foundation for preparing correct and complete financial statements, aiding in budgeting, forecasting, and financial analysis.
- **Readiness for regulatory enquiries.** In case of regulatory audits or enquiries (eg by SARS), having organised records ensures that necessary documents can be promptly presented, proving compliance and transparency.
- **Support in dispute resolution.** Records act as critical evidence in the resolution of disputes, whether with customers, suppliers, or other stakeholders. They provide a documented trail of transactions and agreements.

Guidelines for effective record-keeping

Records should adhere to the following:

- **Organised and easily accessible.** Implement a systematic filing system that allows for quick retrieval of documents when needed.
- **Maintaining a consistent naming convention** for documents (a nomenclature) will help in finding documents easily, eg [Customer name] inv xx, [date of invoice].
- **Digital storage solutions** can enhance accessibility and ensure effective back up of documentation.

- **Hard copies** should be scanned and electronically stored, and the originals kept in reputable off-site storage companies or other safe areas.
- **The ECT Act** makes digital storage and signatures easier to do business vs manually doing so. See *Chapter 55* for more information on this Act.
- **Unaltered and transparent.** Records should remain unaltered and presented in a way that accurately reflects the information held – see also the ECT Act mentioned above. Any amendments or changes should be transparent and well-documented.
- **Record retention.** See the separate section below.

Types of records to keep

- **Company records**
  - Certificate of incorporation.
  - MoI.
  - Share register.
  - Board and board committee documentation (such as board packs) including minutes.
  - Register of board members, company secretary and public officer.
  - Board resolutions.
  - Shareholder meeting documentation including minutes.
  - AGM documentation including minutes.
  - Annual returns sent to CIPC.
  - Licences and permits required by the business and provided to the company by the relevant regulators.
  - All filings and communications with regulators.

- **Sales records**
  - Customer invoices.
  - Service orders.
  - Purchase orders.
  - Warranty documentation.
  - Proof of payments.
  - Numerically ordered invoices, following VAT requirements if applicable.
  - Sales and marketing reports.
  - Brochures and marketing materials.

- **Purchase records (from suppliers and service providers)**
  - Supplier invoices.
  - Service orders.
  - Purchase orders.
  - Warranty documentation.
  - Proof of payments.

- **Contracts**
  - Customer and supplier contracts.
  - General terms and conditions.

- Loan/credit agreements.
- Lease agreements.

Financial records
- Monthly bank statements, carefully checked and reconciled to all financial transactions.
- Critical documentation supporting monthly bookkeeping.
- Investment and interest income documents.
- Accounts receivable and accounts payable ageing reports.
- Inventory ageing reports.
- Income statements and balance sheets for relevant periods.
- Annual financial statements, including audited financial statements where applicable, with all supporting documentation.

Tax records
- Income tax returns.
- Provisional tax returns.
- PAYE.
- VAT invoices for both inputs and outputs.
- Reconciliation statements.
- Detailed records supporting all other tax-related transactions and filings.

Intellectual property – Patents
- Conception records, documenting the initial idea and its development process, including sketches, drawings, prototypes, and lab notebooks.
- Disclosure records, maintaining logs of who has knowledge of the invention and when, including meeting minutes and signed confidentiality agreements.
- Filing documents – copies of patent applications, filing receipts, and communication with the CIPC.

Intellectual property – Trademarks
- Trademark usage records – proof of commercial use of the trademark in South Africa, including invoices, marketing materials, and sales brochures.
- Logo design files, maintaining the original vector files and design history of the trademark.
- Registration documents – copies of trademark registration applications, certificates, and renewal documents.

- **Intellectual property – Copyrights**
  - Creation records – dates and evidence of creation, like timestamps on files, project records, and witness statements.
  - Copyright registration documents – copies of copyright applications and registration certificates.

- **Intellectual property – Trade secrets**
  - Identification and classification – defining and listing your valuable trade secrets, categorising them by level of sensitivity.
  - Controlled access and restrictions – documenting who has access to the trade secrets and implementing secure storage and access protocols.

- **Intellectual property – Additionally**
  - Licence agreements – documentation of any licencing or assignment of IP rights to third parties.
  - NDAs – ensuring employees and collaborators sign NDAs to protect trade secrets.
  - Maintain accurate employee records – documenting inventions and contributions to IP development, including inventor statements and assignment agreements.

- **Employment records**
  - Employment contracts.
  - Salary payments/slips.
  - Time sheets.
  - Payroll registers.
  - UIF, SDL and PAYE records and payments.
  - Leave records.
  - IRP5/IT3a tax documents provided to employees.
  - Disciplinary code.
  - Code of conduct.
  - Bargaining council agreements.
  - Disciplinary hearing records and records of other disciplinary measures (eg written warnings).
  - Employment equity reports and plans.
  - Training records.

- **Occupational health and safety records**
  - Section 16(1), 16(2) and 37(2) appointments.
  - Minutes of safety committee meetings.
  - Records related to any workplace incidents or accidents.
  - Health and safety policy and plans.
  - Training records.
  - Emergency procedures.
  - Personal protective equipment records.
  - Health reports.

- **General**
  - All records required by laws relevant to your industry.
  - All records required to be kept in accordance with industry standards or professional association bodies.

Remember, while this list supplies a foundation, businesses should tailor their record-keeping practices to their specific industry requirements and applicable laws. Regularly reviewing and updating record-keeping procedures ensures continued compliance and readiness for business growth.

Record retention periods

There are many laws and regulations with differing retention periods that need to be adhered to before it is permissible to destroy the records. Even within the laws and regulations, there are differing retention periods depending on the type of record. We have supplied the retention periods of some records under the various chapters but it is not possible to supply detailed guidance on individual retention periods for records under all laws and regulations. You should speak to a legal advisor if you require specific information on retention periods per relevant laws and regulations.

We provide the following general guidance to assist you in good record retention practices:

- Adopt a common naming convention for all records across your business and communicate this to employees. This will assist in identifying and retrieving documents easily and destroying them when they are no longer legally and commercially required.
- Retain records for the duration that they are required plus a period of at least three years unless the law specifically requires a longer retention period.
- A record is regarded as 'required' because it is commercially valuable or relevant (eg a contract currently being executed) and necessary to the business, and/or legally required.
- Records should be kept in their original form and not be altered in any way.
- Under the Electronic Communications and Transactions Act, except for certain types of records that are required to be maintained in hardcopy format (see *Chapter 55*), a record can be kept in electronic format. We recommend hardcopy original documents to be scanned and filed electronically in your secure storage platform and the hardcopy to be filed offsite in a secure location. Electronically generated documents should be filed in your secure storage platform.
- Records related to personal information under the Protection of Personal Information Act should only be retained for the duration that they are required plus one year thereafter. See also the Electronic Communications and Transactions Act, and *Chapters 51 and 55*.

- In case of any regulatory investigation or litigation (whether begun or probable), you should not destroy any records related to such investigation or litigation even if you know the retention period has expired as this will amount to obstruction of justice. Maintain such records until the investigation or litigation, and any appeals, have been resolved and after consulting with your legal advisor.
- Once a record has passed its retention period and is not subject to any regulatory investigation or litigation, nor commercially valuable, it should be safely destroyed from digital platforms and hardcopies should be physically destroyed. A record of what has been destroyed should be kept for good governance purposes (eg a register setting out the type of record destroyed, date of destruction, the name of the person authorising it and the name of the person who destroyed the record).

MARKETING AND OPERATIONAL CONSIDERATIONS

"Continuous improvement is better than delayed perfection."
~ Mark Twain

"Don't find customers for your products, find products for your customers."
~ Seth Godin

In the upcoming chapters, we will provide a general overview of important marketing and operational considerations that are relevant to businesses. It's important to note that this list is not exhaustive, and the specific measures and strategies you need to implement will depend on the size and type of business you operate.

Operational considerations are important for the smooth functioning of your business. Topics we will cover include efficient resource allocation, supply chain management, implementing quality control measures, streamlining processes, optimising productivity, payroll, and financial management, and ensuring compliance with relevant regulations and standards. These operational measures are essential for achieving operational excellence, maximising efficiency, delivering value to customers, and ensuring the profitability of your business.

Marketing considerations play a paramount role in ensuring the success of your business. We will explore key aspects such as market research, understanding your target audience, developing a compelling brand identity, positioning your products or services, and implementing effective marketing channels and strategies. These considerations will help you reach and engage your customers, differentiate yourself from competitors, and build brand awareness and loyalty.

It is important to emphasise that the suitability and relevance of these marketing and operational considerations will vary depending on the unique characteristics of your business, such as its size, industry, target market, and available resources. Our goal is to provide you with a broad understanding of these considerations, enabling you to assess their applicability and tailor them to your specific business context.

Chapter 60: Key operational considerations

Establishing a successful business in South Africa extends beyond comprehending setting up your company, considering the legal and regulatory framework, the employment of personnel and considering a myriad of tax issues. It also entails making strategic operational decisions that will influence the day-to-day functioning and long-term sustainability of your business venture. It is not possible to consider the individual requirements of each business or industry for purposes of this book, but this chapter gives general guidance on key operational considerations that businesses must address. Operational decisions form a critical part of your business plan and should be considered when conducting your risk management overview.

Location of business

Selecting the best location for your business is a critical decision that affects various aspects of operations, including customer accessibility, supplier proximity, and overall business costs. Carefully evaluate potential locations by considering the following factors:

- **The nature of your business.** A company supplying consulting services will have vastly different (and simpler) requirements compared to a manufacturing operation. Consider the exact requirements of your business.
- **Customer proximity.** Prioritise locations that are easily accessible to your target customer base. Factors such as foot traffic, transportation options, and proximity to competing businesses play a significant role in accessing your customer base.
- **Supplier proximity.** If your business relies on physical goods from suppliers, consider the distance to your primary suppliers as this will be material to your costs and how you bill your customers. Minimising transportation costs can improve profit margins, improve your competitiveness, enhance supply chain efficiency, and reduce the risk of supply disruptions.
- **Business costs.** Evaluate the financial implications of various locations, including rent or property rates and taxes, utilities, and local licencing fees. Balance these costs against the potential benefits of the location, such as increased customer traffic or reduced supplier transportation costs.
- **Business environment.** Assess the overall business environment of the chosen location. Consider factors such as crime rates, zoning regulations, the availability of skilled and unskilled labour, and any potential government incentives or economic development initiatives such as special economic zones.

Leasing vs buying premises

The decision to lease or buy premises depends on many factors, including financial considerations, business growth projections, and access to capital.

- **Leasing** offers flexibility and lower upfront costs, as businesses do not need to make a substantial down-payment. However, leasing can limit control over the property and may have restrictions on renovations or alterations. Additionally, long-term leasing agreements may lock businesses into a location that may not align with future growth plans. Long-term leases may also contain triple net lease requirements, which will add to the cost and management of the property by the lessee. A triple net lease means the lessee, in addition to paying rent, is also responsible for the cost of taxes, insurance and maintenance and repairs for the interior of the building.
- **Buying** a property provides greater control and potential long-term cost savings, as businesses avoid ongoing lease payments and may benefit from property appreciation over time. However, buying property requires a significant upfront investment and may limit flexibility in moving or expanding operations. In addition, once you have bought the property, you will need to factor in the cost of maintenance, utilities, levies, and taxes.

Ultimately the decision whether to lease or buy is dependent on your short- or long-term goals and access to funding. For startup and small businesses, long-term commitments through purchasing premises may not be a good starting point. For service businesses that can conduct their venture remotely, it will make sense to run your business from your home to reduce costs but as your business expands and you employ others, separate premises may be required.

Ensure any agreements, whether you choose to lease or buy, are carefully drafted to reflect the intentions of the parties, the agreed price, and other key terms. Seek legal advice for the relevant drafting. Speak to property experts for guidance on the specific market conditions and to help with negotiations between the parties.

Permits and registrations

Depending on the nature of the business, various permits and registrations may be needed to operate legally in South Africa. These may include:

- **Business licences.** Most local municipalities require businesses to obtain a business licence to operate within their jurisdiction. The specific requirements vary by municipality, and businesses should consult with their local municipality to find the necessary steps and documentation.
- **Environmental permits.** Businesses that handle hazardous materials or generate industrial waste may require environmental permits from the Department of Environmental Affairs, or local municipal approvals. These permits ensure that businesses adhere to environmental regulations and minimise their impact on the environment and local communities.
- **Industry-specific permits.** Certain industries, such as mining, financial services, energy, electronic communication, real estate, food processing, healthcare, or

construction, may have other permit requirements specific to their sector. Businesses should research and obtain the necessary permits to ensure compliance with industry regulations.

- **Zone restrictions.** It is essential to consider whether the area where you intend to operate your business conforms to any zoning requirements. Zoning regulations may restrict certain types of activities in specific zones, allowing only certain types of manufacturing while prohibiting more advanced or specialised forms.

Speaking to local chambers of commerce, town council experts, local government officials and local lawyers will help you gain a complete understanding of the exact permit requirements, fees, and timeline for approvals.

Information technology systems

In today's technology-driven world, businesses of all sizes rely on robust and reliable information technology (IT) systems to support their operations, manage data, help communication, and gain a competitive edge. Establishing a strong IT infrastructure is critical for businesses in South Africa to run efficiently, enhance customer service, and adapt to the ever-changing technological landscape.

Consider the following:

- **Needs assessment.** Conduct a thorough needs assessment to identify the specific IT requirements of the business, considering factors such as business size, industry, and operational processes.
- **Hardware and software selection.** Choose proper hardware and software solutions that align with the identified needs and budget. Evaluate factors such as scalability, performance, reliability, security, compatibility with existing systems and the reputation of the manufacturers of the solutions, together with warranty periods and after-sales support.
- **Data management.** Implement effective data management practices to ensure data integrity, security, and accessibility. This includes storage requirements and data backup, disaster recovery plans, and access control measures.
- **Network infrastructure.** Set up a reliable and secure network infrastructure to support data communication, internet access, and employee connectivity. Consider factors such as bandwidth requirements, network security protocols, and remote access capabilities.
- **Cybersecurity.** Implement robust cybersecurity measures to protect against cyberattacks, data breaches, and unauthorised access. This includes firewalls, intrusion detection systems, data encryption, and employee cybersecurity training.
- **IT support.** Set up a reliable IT support system to address technical issues, provide user help, and support IT infrastructure. This may involve in-house IT staff, outsourced managed IT services, or a combination of both.
- **IT budget.** Set up a comprehensive IT budget to allocate resources for hardware, software, maintenance, and support services. Align the IT budget with the overall business strategy and consider future growth projections.

- **Personal data protection.** The protection of personal information is a mandatory legal requirement – see the section on POPIA in *Chapter 51*.

Benefits of effective IT systems

- **Enhanced efficiency.** Streamline business processes, automate tasks, and improve communication through integrated IT systems.
- **Improved customer service.** Provide faster response times, personalised interactions, and online self-service options through e-commerce platforms and customer relationship management (CRM) systems. Many customers also expect suppliers to have advanced and secure IT systems to protect their data that may be stored on suppliers' infrastructure.
- **Supply chain management.** Effectively manage the selection, onboarding and purchase of goods and services from suppliers to support your business operations.
- **Data-driven decision-making.** Leverage data analytics and business intelligence tools to gain insights from customer behaviour, market trends, and operational performance.
- **Competitive advantage.** Stay ahead of the competition by adopting innovative IT solutions, improving operational efficiency, and enhancing customer experience.
- **Business continuity.** Protect against data loss, minimise downtime, and ensure business continuity through disaster recovery plans and robust cybersecurity measures.

By carefully considering IT needs, selecting the right solutions, implementing effective data management practices, and setting up a reliable IT infrastructure, businesses can enhance operational efficiency, improve customer service, and gain a competitive edge in the digital marketplace. Investing in robust IT systems is an investment in the future growth and sustainability of any business.

South Africa has a sophisticated IT industry and you will find easy access to solutions and service providers to meet your business needs.

Insurance

Businesses should consider various insurance policies to protect against potential risks and financial losses. Insurance is a grudge purchase – nobody really wants it. However, the impact to your business when it loses key assets will have far greater ramifications to the sustainability of your business if you don't have critical insurance cover. Key insurance types are described below but not all of them will apply to your business – as part of your business plan and risk management process, you must assess what insurance types are relevant to your business and industry.

- **Property insurance** covers damage or loss to business premises, equipment, and inventory. This insurance provides protection against events such as fire, theft, vandalism, or natural disasters.

- **Liability insurance** protects the business from claims arising from injuries or property damage caused by its operations or products. This insurance can cover legal fees, settlements, and medical expenses resulting from third-party claims.
- **Business interruption insurance** covers losses incurred due to business disruptions, such as fire, natural disasters, or theft. This insurance provides financial compensation for lost revenue, ongoing expenses, and any other costs incurred due to the interruption of business operations.
- **Professional liability or professional indemnity insurance** protects professionals from lawsuits arising from errors or omissions in their work. This is typically taken by persons providing professional services or advice such as accountants, lawyers, engineers, architects, medical practitioners, etc. Directors and officers (D&O) liability insurance is a type of professional liability insurance.
- **Cyber liability insurance** protects businesses from losses arising from cyberattacks, data breaches, ransomware, etc.
- **Marine, cargo, and transport insurance** is essential for businesses involved in the transportation of goods by sea, air, or land. These types of insurance policies provide financial protection against various risks associated with the movement of goods. Depending on the contractual terms of a contract, the customer may be required (or choose) to take out such insurance.
- **Motor vehicle insurance** covers loss to vehicles and for injuries or death arising out of accidents involving vehicles.
- **Key person insurance** is a type of life insurance policy that a company takes out on the life of a key employee. This employee is considered critical to the success of the company, and their death or disability could have a significant negative impact on the business. For example, the chief executive or chief financial officer or the person with knowledge critical to the business (the inventor or innovator), or a partner (in a partnership).
- **Product liability insurance** supplies protection in the event products cause injury or death to third parties.
- **Contractor's liability insurance**, also known as contractor's general liability insurance, is designed to protect contractors from financial losses arising from legal liabilities incurred during their work. It covers injuries to third parties, property damage, and personal and advertising injuries.
- **Construction insurance**, a broad category of insurance policies that provide financial protection for various risks associated with construction projects such as property damage, death or injury, professional liability/indemnity, environmental, or failure to complete the works on time or according to the agreed specifications.
- **Environmental insurance** is taken out specifically to cover a company against environmental damage. This may also form part of the liability insurance or other insurance types mentioned above, depending on the policy wording.
- **Workers' compensation**, which we discussed under COIDA and UIF in *Chapters 27 and 38* provides coverage for employees who sustain injuries or illnesses arising from their employment. This insurance covers medical expenses, lost wages, and vocational rehabilitation costs for work-related injuries or illnesses.

- **SASRIA insurance** is a special insurance provided by the government in case of damage caused to a business due to riot, strike, terrorism, public disorder, or politically motivated damage to property.

In addition to the above business insurance types, there are also personal insurance types such as life insurance, income protection, disability or dreaded disease insurance, health insurance, retirement insurance (such as pension funds, provident funds, and retirement annuities) and home-owners insurance, to name a few.

South Africa has a sophisticated insurance industry, and most insurers will be able to supply the above covers. Ensure you shop around for the best prices and covers, and keep the following in mind:

- Consider the ones most relevant to your business based on your risk profile.
- Use only reputable insurers and brokers.
- Disclose all material facts when applying for insurance.
- All insurance policies will come with exceptions, exclusions, deductibles, limits, sub-limits, waiting periods, etc. Be sure to understand these.
- Understand the basic requirements of your policy cover before signing up and raise any questions with the insurer or your broker.
- Annually re-evaluate your policies to ensure you are adequately covered and not under-insured.
- In case of any claim, notify the insurer timeously and disclose all material facts. Failure to disclose vital information, or not informing the insurance within a specified period or a reasonable period, could result in the claim being rejected.
- Pay your premiums timeously to avoid risk of the policy lapsing.
- Although it may be tempting to forego insurance cover or let policies lapse when economic times are hard, the cost of not having coverage will pose a catastrophic risk to your business. Speak to your insurance broker annually to review your policies, covers, premiums, change in circumstances and options to reduce premiums or coverage, and the consequences to your business.

Risk management

All businesses must consider, as part of their business plan, the factors that pose a risk to the company. Risk management, plans and policies are all part of good governance, and to ensure the sustainability of the business. A robust risk management policy and plan act as a shield for your organisation, protecting it from potential threats and guiding your response when they arise. Political and economic instability can lead to currency fluctuations, policy changes, and social unrest, all capable of disrupting the operations of your company. Crime, a persistent concern, can manifest as theft, fraud, or even physical harm, affecting your operations and reputation. The public infrastructure system provides several challenges in the form of power outages, water shortages, and unreliable transportation, hindering your day-to-day efficiency. Labour markets, with their unique skills gap and potential for strikes, require careful consideration and proactive strategies. Corruption, a pervasive risk, needs ethical vigilance and a commitment to transparent practices. Considering the risks posed to your business will aid your preparedness. By embracing a proactive approach to risk management, you can mitigate the impact.

Here are the key elements you need to include:

Scope and purpose
- Clearly define the scope of the risk policy, outlining which areas and activities it covers.
- State the purpose of the policy, emphasising its commitment to identifying, assessing, and mitigating risks to ensure business continuity and success.

Risk identification
- Establish a process for identifying potential risks, encouraging input from all levels of the organisation.
- Categorise risks based on their likelihood and impact, using a risk matrix or similar tool.
- Consider internal factors (eg operational inefficiencies, financial challenges) and external factors (eg economic downturns, regulatory changes).

Risk assessment
- Analyse each identified risk, assessing its probability of occurrence and potential impact on your organisation (financial, reputational, operational).
- Prioritise risks based on their severity, focusing first on those with high likelihood and high impact.

Risk response
- Document specific response strategies for each prioritised risk.
- These strategies can include avoiding, transferring, mitigating, or accepting the risk based on its nature and severity. For example, taking out insurance policies can help to transfer or mitigate the risks.
- Clearly assign responsibility for implementing each response strategy to personnel within your organisation with the requisite skills to deal with the issue. For owner-managed businesses with no employees, the owner will need to take responsibility or outsource to appropriate advisors to assist.

Communication and training
- Communicate the risk management policy and plan to all employees, ensuring everyone understands their roles and responsibilities.
- Provide training on risk identification, assessment, and response procedures.

Monitoring and review
- Regularly monitor and update your risk register, reflecting changes in your organisation or the external environment.
- Conduct periodic reviews of the risk management policy and plan, ensuring its effectiveness and alignment with your overall business strategy.

Other risk considerations
- **Incident response protocols.** Include procedures for responding to specific types of incidents, such as thefts, cyberattacks or data breaches.
- **Business continuity plans.** Make plans to ensure critical operations continue even during a disruptive event.
- **Compliance.** Ensure your risk management framework adheres to relevant laws and regulations.
- **Reporting.** Depending on the nature of the risk that arises, you may have reporting obligations to regulators (such as the Information Regulator in case of a data breach, the SAPS in case of economic crimes exceeding R100 000, the stock exchange in case of any factor that requires disclosure under the listing requirements, etc) and/or to your insurers. Also consider reporting obligations to the board of directors, your auditors (where applicable) and shareholders.

Remember, a successful risk management policy and plan are living documents, constantly evolving to adapt to your organisation's needs and the changing landscape of threats. By proactively identifying, assessing, and mitigating risks, you can build a resilient organisation that thrives in the face of uncertainty.

See also the section on *Insurance* above.

Payroll and financial management

We have provided detailed information on employment issues and employment tax considerations in *Chapters 22 to 45* and financial management issues in *Chapters 17 to 21*.

Consider what systems and processes you need to meet your payroll requirements, eg PAYE, UIF, SDL, IRP5 certificates, etc. Carefully evaluate your business size and complexity when choosing a payroll software or service provider. Look for features like automated calculations, compliance checks, and employee self-service options. Building a competent payroll team or appointing a reliable external service provider is crucial for accuracy and efficiency. Keep your employees informed about their payslips, tax deductions, and leave policies. Transparency fosters trust and reduces payroll-related enquiries.

Similarly, a financial management system should be tailored to your specific needs. Maintain meticulous records of all income and expenses to follow tax regulations and track your business performance. Utilise digital accounting tools for efficient data management. Create realistic financial plans and projections to guide your business decisions. Regularly review and adjust your budget to adapt to changing circumstances. Monitor your incoming and outgoing cash flow closely to avoid unexpected shortfalls. Invest in strategies like receivables management and inventory optimisation to support a healthy cash position. Generate regular financial reports like income statements and balance sheets to assess your financial health and identify areas for improvement, and for the preparation of annual financial statements.

There are various online solutions that combine both payroll and financial management tools covering (depending on the solution):

- **Bookkeeping.** Tracking of income and expenses, categorising transactions, creation of invoices and bills, managing accounts payable and receivable.
- **Financial reporting.** Generating reports such as income statements, balance sheets, and cash flow statements to gain insights into your financial health.
- **Tax preparation.** Calculating and filing taxes automatically or with guidance and simplifying year-end workflows.
- **Payroll.** Managing payroll, pay employees, track taxes, and generate pay slips.
- **Inventory management.** Tracking inventory levels, set reorder points, and generate purchase orders.
- **Project management.** Tracking project costs, manage budgets, and collaborate with team members.

Some of the online solutions you can investigate include Sage, QuickBooks, Pastel. Xero, Fresh Books, and Zoho Books.

Alternatively, there are many accounting firms for all business sizes that can provide the same services as the online ones. The advantage of finding the right accounting firm partner is that you get to establish a more personal relationship and address queries and concerns with individual professionals. Ultimately, it is about what suits your business, and your budget. Ensure, you consider the payroll and financial management systems as part of your business plan and for budget planning purposes.

Other operational considerations

- **Facilities management.** Develop effective facilities management practices to ensure the upkeep, maintenance, and safety of your business premises. This includes setting up regular maintenance schedules, promptly addressing repair needs, and implementing safety protocols to prevent accidents and injuries.
- **Inventory management.** Implement efficient inventory management systems to optimise stock levels, minimise storage costs, and prevent stockouts. This includes tracking inventory levels, setting reorder points, and implementing forecasting techniques to predict demand.

- **Security measures.** Due to high crime levels, it is critical to implement proper security precautions to protect your business assets. Consider relevant controls as part of the risk management plan and use reputable security companies for managing your security needs. Ensure security service providers have policies, procedures, and personnel to meet your requirements, and they keep suitable insurance policies to cover you in case of a claim due to their negligent acts or deliberate acts by their employees.
- **Supply chain management.** Set up reliable supplier relationships and implement supply chain management strategies to ensure prompt delivery of goods and services. Diversification is always important – while it is always critical to have good relationships with key suppliers, you do not want to be wholly dependent on single-source suppliers. Putting your eggs in different baskets helps catastrophic shocks to your supply chain.
- **Energy supply and resilience.** The current energy crisis means you need to consider alternative energy sources to avoid loadshedding causing disruption to your business. Solar energy is the most common method to ensure constant energy supply but other sources, depending on your location and cost, include wind and biomass. If you are leasing premises, you should consider whether such alternative sources are already available, and if not, who will pay for it (the landlord or lessee), and any permissions that may be needed from the landlord or authorities. These considerations should form part of your business plan and risk management policy.

Summary

The operations of a business form the core foundation for its success. Understanding and addressing your specific operational requirements, incorporating them into your business plan, and effectively managing resources and costs are essential for achieving operational excellence and driving overall business growth.

Chapter 61: Marketing and sales

The success of any business is dependent on you being able to effectively promote your goods and services to your customers. In this chapter, we will explore marketing and sales strategies tailored to the South African market, to help you grow and support a sustainable business.

Remember, even if you are not an expert at marketing, you should consider employing appropriately qualified professionals or outsourcing to a marketing company. The below is merely a guide on what to consider.

Understanding the South African market

It is essential to understand the unique characteristics of the South African market:

- **Diverse demographics.** South Africa has a diverse population with diverse cultures, languages, and economic backgrounds. This diversity translates into a wide range of consumer preferences and needs.
- **Tech-savvy consumers.** Smartphone penetration and internet usage are high in South Africa, making digital marketing channels essential for reaching your target audience.
- **Competitive landscape.** The South African business landscape is generally competitive with consumers having a wide array of choice. This requires innovative and effective marketing strategies to stand out.
- **Income inequality and unemployment.** As mentioned elsewhere in this book, South Africa has high-income inequality with a large segment of the population being poor, a growing middle class and a smaller but high net-worth income group. Understanding this disparity will help you to tailor your goods and services to the demographic you are targeting. South Africa has high unemployment and considering this factor is critical to understanding the local market conditions.
- **Legal and regulatory framework.** Understanding and following relevant marketing and advertising laws and following laws that govern your specific products or services is essential to adverse legal consequences. Examples would be the Consumer Protection Act and the National Credit Act.

Creating a professional public presence

In today's digital age, creating a professional image is vital for any business, be it a budding startup or an established corporation. This professional demeanour not only attracts customers but also instils confidence in various stakeholders such as investors, lenders, and suppliers. The cost associated with creating and maintaining your website should be considered as an essential investment in your business. These expenses should be included in your business plan, as well as incorporated into your financial and budgeting processes.

Professional website

A website acts as the digital face of your business. It should effectively communicate what your organisation offers, its values, and how clients can engage with your services. Key elements of a good business website include:

- **Clear description of products and services.** What your business does should be clear to visitors.
- **About us section.** Introduce your team and company ethos to establish trust.
- **Contact information.** Make it easy for clients and partners to reach you.
- **Other information.** As discussed elsewhere in this book, essential information such as the PAIA manual, data privacy policy, company code of conduct, etc should also be available on the website.

Domain registration and email

A custom domain name (eg www.yourcompany.co.za) not only reinforces your brand but also lends credibility. Coupled with a professional email address (eg name@yourcompany.co.za), it sets a professional tone in all communications. When choosing a domain registrar and hosting service, consider the following:

- **Local registrars.** A registrar, in the context of domain names and the internet, is an organisation accredited by a domain name registry to manage the registration of domain names. It acts as an intermediary between the registry and the domain name holder (ie your business), handling tasks such as domain registration, renewal, and management. Besides these primary services, many registrars also offer web hosting, where your website's files are stored and served, and other services such as SSL certificates for website security, professional email hosting, and website building tools. Essentially, registrars are key facilitators for individuals or organisations looking to obtain, renew, and manage a domain name, ensuring its continued registration and functionality. The following registrars can be considered and compared – Afrihost, Google, GoDaddy, Axxess and xneelo.
- **Features and pricing.** Compare what each provider offers in their package, such as email hosting, SSL certificates for website security, and customer support. Local providers may offer better localised support and pricing in Rands.
- **Scalability.** Ensure that the provider can scale with your business, offering more resources as your online presence grows.

Website development and hosting

Developing a website need not be a costly affair. Several user-friendly platforms offer cost-effective solutions:

- **DIY website builders.** Tools such as Wix, Squarespace and Shopify are great for those with limited technical skills, offering drag-and-drop interfaces to build websites.
- **WordPress.** For more control and scalability, WordPress is a popular option. While it has a steeper learning curve, it offers greater customisation.
- **Web development services.** If your budget allows, consider hiring a professional web developer for a bespoke website.

Hosting

The hosting of your website is another critical factor. Hosting is a service that stores and serves website content on a server, making it accessible on the internet for users to visit and interact with. Many domain registrars offer hosting services, but you can also opt for dedicated hosting providers for potentially better performance and support. Opting for dedicated hosting providers, as opposed to shared hosting or hosting services offered by domain registrars, can potentially offer better performance and support for your website. Dedicated hosting involves leasing an entire server solely for your use, which can lead to faster loading times and improved handling of web traffic due to not sharing resources such as CPU and RAM with other websites. It also provides enhanced security and greater control over server settings and software installations, making it suitable for websites with specific needs or high traffic volumes.

While dedicated hosting typically comes with more comprehensive and faster support services, it is important to consider that it is generally more expensive than shared hosting options, requiring a balance between the benefits and the higher costs to determine its suitability for your business needs.

Social media presence

Although detailed later in this chapter, establishing a presence on relevant social media platforms is integral to your public image. These platforms offer direct ways to engage with your audience, understand their needs, and promote your products or services.

Brand identity

A strong brand identity is the foundation of successful marketing. Consider these elements:

- **Unique selling proposition (USP).** Clearly define what makes your business different and valuable to potential customers. In a competitive environment, most companies are manufacturing goods or supplying services that others are also capable of providing. If you have an innovative solution with no competitors, then this gives you a competitive advantage ('your moat' as they say). But if you do not and you are competing against others for customers' business, then focus on what gives you an upper hand, such as the quality of your offering, better pricing, superior service, customer focus, timeous communication, on-time delivery, availability of spare parts, longer warranty periods, and so on.
- **Brand voice and personality.** Develop a consistent tone and style that resonates with your target audience.
- **Visual identity.** Design a memorable logo, colour scheme, and brand assets to create a visually impactful representation of your business. This will help with your identity with customers and other stakeholders. Use the visual identity assets consistently on your products and in your letterheads, terms and conditions, brochures, website, social media, and marketing materials.

Marketing mix

The marketing mix encompasses the seven key elements that drive customer acquisition:

- **Product.** Ensure your product or service meets the needs and preferences of your target audience. Offer compelling features and benefits that differentiate you from competitors, such as the quality of your offering, a customer focus sales team, communication skills, availability of parts, account management for key customers or geographies, loyalty programmes, etc.

- **Price.** Set competitive prices that consider your production costs, market conditions, and customer value perception. Investigate public sources to decide your competitors' pricing – remember not to infringe competition laws by speaking to competitors about their pricing (nor obtain your competitor's confidential pricing information from customers or other third parties). If needed, engage a third-party marketing company to help (that must similarly adhere to competition law principles).

- **Place.** Make your product or service readily available to your target audience through proper channels, including online platforms, physical stores, or partnerships with distributors, resellers, agents, etc.

- **Promotion.** Implement effective promotional strategies to reach your target audience and increase brand awareness.

- **People.** This element refers to everyone directly or indirectly involved in the consumption of a service or product, including the company's staff and target audience. The interaction between customers and employees plays a crucial role in customer satisfaction and perception of service quality. Training, motivation, and rewarding systems for employees can significantly impact the delivery and quality of the service or product, thereby influencing customer acquisition and retention.

- **Processes.** The delivery and execution of your service are pivotal. Processes refer to the methods and procedures companies use to deliver their products and services to customers. This includes the sales transactions, customer support, and after-sales services. Efficient processes improve customer experience, enhance service quality, and can streamline the path to purchase, making it easier and more appealing for customers.

- **Physical evidence.** This component pertains to the physical environment where the service is delivered and where the company and customer interact. It also involves any tangible components that facilitate the performance or communication of the service. For product-based businesses, this could relate to packaging. For service-based businesses, physical evidence could include the layout of a retail store, the design of a website, or the appearance of staff members. This evidence helps customers form perceptions and expectations about the quality of the product or service before they make a purchase.

Digital marketing strategies

Harnessing the power of the internet and social media is essential for success. Consider these strategies:

- **Website.** As detailed above, get a professional website consistent with your brand that can act as your primary place where customers can learn about your business and offering.
- **Domain registration and email.** Paying to get a domain registration with your company name along with company email addresses is an essential part of a professional image. A Gmail address, or similar, is not professional. Obtaining a website, domain registration and professional email addresses is very affordable. There are many service providers to choose from both locally and internationally.
- **Social media marketing.** Engage your target audience on relevant social media platforms, create valuable content, and run targeted advertising campaigns. The number of social media platforms to market on is vast so consider your budget and the target audience when deciding which platforms are best suited for your purpose. The most common social media platforms to advertise on are:
  - Facebook
  - Instagram
  - YouTube
  - TikTok
  - LinkedIn
  - Twitter
  - Pinterest
  - Reddit
- Advertising on all these platforms is not possible especially if you are working on a budget, so consider which ones will have the best outreach to potential customers.
- **Content marketing.** Create informative and engaging content, such as blog posts, infographics, and videos on your website to drive traffic to your platform and thereby increase your profile.
- **Search engine optimisation (SEO).** Optimise your website and online content to rank higher in search engine results pages, making it easier for potential customers to find you.
- **Email marketing.** Build an email list and send targeted campaigns to nurture leads, promote new products, and drive sales. Remember to ensure that email lists comply with the Consumer Protection Act and Protection of Personal Information Act as detailed in *Chapters 48 and 51,* respectively.

Traditional marketing strategies

While digital marketing holds immense potential, traditional channels still have a role to play, more so given your target audience:

- **Print advertising.** Consider placing advertisements in relevant publications or local newspapers to reach a specific audience.

- **Public relations.** Build positive relationships with industry experts, journalists, and media outlets to generate positive publicity and brand awareness.
- **Events and sponsorships.** Take part in industry events or local community activities to connect with potential customers and build relationships. This increases your visibility and brand reputation.

Summary

Marketing and sales are essential drivers of business growth. By understanding the unique characteristics of the South African market, developing a strong brand identity, implementing effective digital and traditional marketing strategies, you can attract customers, drive sales, and set up a thriving business in South Africa. Remember to stay informed about evolving trends and adapt your approach as needed to ensure long-term success.

CONCLUSION

This book is not just about knowledge; it is a launchpad for entrepreneurs, existing businesses and foreign investors alike. Packed with insights into business and company structures, legalities, taxes, personnel management, operational considerations and marketing strategies, it has prepared you to dive into the vibrant South African market. Do not let the information overwhelm you – use it as your guiding light. Embrace the unique rhythm of South Africa where resilience and adaptation are key.

As you absorb the information and contemplate where to begin, it is natural to feel a mix of excitement and trepidation. If you are an existing business owner, many of the issues we have discussed may already be familiar to you and be part of your organisation. For entrepreneurs and small businesses looking to transform their organisation into a company, or foreign companies looking to establish a local presence, the journey ahead promises not just success, but inevitable bumps along the way. Keep in mind that achieving success is not a linear journey; it is a dynamic process that involves continuous learning, determination and adaptation. Along the way, you will encounter various challenges, opportunities, setbacks, and achievements, all of which contribute to your overall growth and accomplishments.

For those setting out on an entrepreneurial journey (be it as a sole proprietor, part of a partnership or forming a small owner-managed company), when the inevitable troughs, setbacks or drops in enthusiasm overcome you, remember what your motivations are, think of how far you have come (even if you still have far to go), focus on the attributes that drove you to start your own business venture. Accept that setbacks are inevitable – it is what you do next that will decide your fate. For existing businesses and foreign companies, you will undoubtedly have much experience in navigating the nuances, challenges and opportunities of operating your business and it is just a matter of honing your skills and knowledge to the topics addressed in this book to transform and build a successful business in South Africa.

In the opening chapters, we spoke about the attributes that entrepreneurs, and in fact all businesspeople will need – patience, perseverance, a positive disposition, a constantly learning mindset, accepting failure as par for the course and building on the lessons learnt, seeking expert help and so on. One step at a time, one brick at a time, pouring the concrete – these are all necessary building blocks for your business. Remember the Baobab started from a seed!

Embrace the inherent unique qualities of the South African market. This land of challenges and opportunities, and unwavering resilience, thrives on nimble adaptation. Stay on your toes and do not hesitate to pivot when opportunity beckons or when a business idea is no longer feasible. Remember, agility is your friend in this ever-evolving landscape.

Nurture your team. They are the beating heart of your venture. Foster a culture of collaboration, open communication, and continuous learning. Celebrate their successes, empower their initiatives, and invest in their growth. A happy and motivated team is an unstoppable force.

Surround yourself with people that will help you achieve your goals – appoint expert advisors to guide you through complexities that are not your area of expertise; speak to peers and industry experts. Engage with people who will challenge you and make you think things through – but not those who will bring you down and crush your dreams and enthusiasm.

Learn about your customers and their needs. Be agile in how you respond to them – a client-driven mindset, setting competitive pricing and value propositions, staying true to your word, and communicating often and effectively with them. Understand your product and service offering and constantly evolve to remain relevant to your customers' needs.

Understand your supply chain – your suppliers are as essential as your customers. Remember they too are businesses looking to create value and the relationships you build with suppliers must be mutually beneficial.

Although this book is at an end, your journey is just beginning. And what an exciting journey it will be. There will be challenges, there will be opportunities, there will be success. In the opening sections of this book, we spoke about the learning mindset necessary for all businesspeople and quoted Lao Tzu "A *journey of a thousand miles begins with a single step*". If you have read thus far, you have already covered a great many miles in terms of increasing your level of knowledge. It is what comes next that counts. Feeling overwhelmed is normal but as we have said – daunting, but undaunted. Remember, thousands of South African businesses began with a single step, each paving the way for the one you might take tomorrow, or today. So, step boldly, dream big, and remember, your thousand-mile journey starts right now, with the flicker of an idea and the courage to take those next steps. Embrace the journey – head up, smile, focus, be positive, show grit and determination, and enjoy your new adventure.

Glossary of terms

ADR	*Alternative Dispute Resolution*
AGM	*Annual General Meeting*
AR	*Annual Return*
BBBEE	*Broad-Based Black Economic Empowerment*
BRICS	*Brazil, Russia, India, China and South Africa*
CAC	*Competition Appeal Court*
CC	*Close Corporation*
CCS	*Competition Commission of South Africa*
CGT	*Capital Gains Tax*
CIPC	*Companies and Intellectual Property Commission*
COMESA	*Common Market for Eastern and Southern Africa*
CSIR	*Council for Scientific and Industrial Research*
D&O	*Directors and Officers*
DBSA	*Development Bank of Southern Africa*
EME	*Exempt Micro Enterprise*
EMI	*Environmental Management Inspectorate*
ERN	*Employer Registration Number*
ETI	*Employer Tax Incentive*
FBT	*Fringe Benefit Tax*
FIC	*Financial Intelligence Centre*
FIDIC	*International Federation of Consulting Engineers*
FSCA	*Financial Sector Conduct Authority*
IDC	*Industrial Development Corporation*
IMF	*International Monetary Fund*
LAC	*Labour Court of Appeal*
LRA	*Labour Relations Act of 1995*
MoI	*Memorandum of Incorporation*
NCC	*National Consumer Commission*
NCOP	*National Council of Provinces*

NCT	*National Consumer Tribunal*
NDA	*Non-Disclosure Agreement*
NEF	*National Empowerment Fund*
NPC	*Non-Profit Company*
PAYE	*Pay As You Earn*
PBO	*Public Benefit Organisation*
PIS	*Public Interest Score*
ROE	*Return of Earnings*
SARS	*South African Revenue Service*
SBC	*Small Business Corporation*
SCA	*Supreme Court of Appeal*
SDL	*Skills Development Levy*
SEZ	*Special Economic Zone*
SME	*Small and Medium Enterprise*
SMME	*Small, Medium and Micro Enterprise*
SOC	*State-Owned Company*
STT	*Securities Transfer Tax*
TCS	*Tax Compliance Status*
UIF	*Unemployment Insurance Fund*
VAT	*Value-Added Tax*

Legislation and regulatory bodies

Acts

Alienation of Land Act of 1981
Arbitration Act of 1965
Auditing Professions Act of 2005
Basic Conditions of Employment Act of 1997 (BCEA)
Broad-Based Black Economic Empowerment Act of 2013
Close Corporations Act of 1984
Companies Act of 1973 (repealed)
Companies Act of 2008
Competition Act of 1998
Compensation for Occupational Injuries and Diseases Act of 1993 (COIDA)
Consumer Protection Act of 2008
Copyright Act of 1978
Customs and Excise Act of 1964
Designs Act of 1996
Electronic Communications and Transactions Act of 2002 (ECTA)
Employment Equity Act of 1998 (EEA)
Employment Tax Incentive Act of 2013
Financial Intelligence Centre Act of 2011 (FICA)
General Laws (Anti-Money Laundering and Combating Terrorism Financing)
Amendment Act of 2022 Income Tax Act of 1962
Labour Relations Act of 1995
Legal Practice Act of 2014
National Credit Act of 2005
National Environmental Management Act of 1998 (NEMA)
National Environmental Management: Air Quality Act of 2004
National Environmental Management: Biodiversity Act of 2004
National Environmental Management: Protected Areas Act 2003
National Environmental Management: Waste Act of 2008
Occupational Health and Safety Act of 1993
Patents Act of 1977
Pension Funds Act of 1956
Prescription Act of 1969
Prevention and Combating of Corrupt Activities Act of 2004
Prevention of Organised Crime Act of 1998
Promotion of Access to Information Act of 2000
Promotion of Administrative Justice Act of 2000
Protected Disclosures Act of 2000
Protection of Personal Information Act of 2013
Public Finance Management Act of 1999

Securities Transfer Tax Act of 2007
Skills Development Levies Act of 1999
Special Economic Zones Act of 2014
Tax Administration Act of 2011
Trade Marks Act of 1993
Transfer Duty Act of 1949
Unemployment Insurance Act of 2001
Unemployment Insurance Contributions Act of 2002
Value-added Tax Act of 1991
World Heritage Convention Act of 1999

Government departments and regulatory bodies

Advertising Standards Authority of South Africa (ASA)
Arbitration Foundation of South Africa (AFSA)
Companies and Intellectual Property Commission (CIPC)
Compensation Fund
Competition Commission of South Africa (CCSA)
Competition Tribunal
Council for Conciliation, Mediation, and Arbitration (CCMA)
Department of Employment and Labour
Department of Finance
Department of Justice and Constitutional Development
Department of Trade, Industry and Competition
Development Bank of Southern Africa (DBSA)
Directorate for Priority Crimes Investigation (DPCI)
Financial Intelligence Centre (FIC)
Financial Sector Conduct Authority (FSCA)
Independent Regulatory Body for Auditors (IRBA)
Information Regulator
Legal Practice Council (LPC)
National Credit Regulator (NCR)
National Consumer Commission (NCC)
National Consumer Tribunal (NCT)
National Prosecuting Authority (NPA)
National Treasury
South African Human Rights Commission (SAHRC)
South African National Accreditation System (SANAS)
South African Police Service (SAPS)
South African Reserve Bank (SARB)
South African Revenue Service (SARS)
Special Investigating Unit (SIU)
Unemployment Insurance Fund (UIF)